The
Glaze
Book

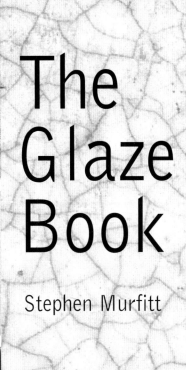

The Glaze Book

Stephen Murfitt

krause
publications

First published in the United States of America in 2002 by

 **krause
publications**

700 E. State Street • Iola, WI 54990-0001
Please call or write for our free catalog of publications. Our
toll-free number to place an order or obtain a catalog is 1-800-
258-0929.

ISBN 0-87349-276-5

Library of Congress Catalog Card No. 2001095628

This book was conceived, designed, and produced by
Quarto Publishing plc
The Old Brewery
6 Blundell Street
London N7 9BH

Senior Project Editor Tracie Lee Davis
Senior Art Editor Sally Bond
Assistant Art Director Penny Cobb
Designer Karin Skånberg
Editor Mary Senechal
Picture Researcher Sandra Assersohn
Art Director Moira Clinch
Publisher Piers Spence

Note to the reader
Many ceramic materials are toxic and hazardous if not handled
carefully. Please study carefully the health and safety information
on pages 16-17 and adhere to good practice at all times. The author,
publisher, and copyright holder cannot be held liable if this advice is
disregarded. While every care has been taken with the color
reproduction in this book, the limitations of the printing process
mean we cannot guarantee total color accuracy in every instance.

Manufactured by Universal Graphics Pte Ltd., Singapore
Printed by Midas Printing Ltd., China

QUAR.BGLZ

9 8 7 6 5 4 3 2 1

Contents

Introduction

Contemporary potters are constantly developing ways of enhancing the surfaces of their work. The approaches they use are as varied as the potters themselves. This book contains recipes for glazes with fired results over the entire temperature range—from earthenware through stoneware and porcelain. The results provide the starting points for students and potters to explore and achieve a vast array of surface effects. Glazes from low-fired through high-fired offer a limitless palette of color, and the variables within this range permit an infinite number of effects. Many of these are demonstrated throughout this book.

ORIGINS OF GLAZE

The earliest known use of glaze dates back to at least 5000 B.C. Glass and the related substances we know as glaze were made in many parts of the ancient world using naturally occurring raw materials and simple processes. The Egyptians discovered glass where sand and sandstone, impregnated with salt, had been fused by fire. By 3000 B.C., the Egyptians were using glazes on some of their pottery. These were alkaline copper glazes, which were used as decorative coatings. Some time later in southwest Asia, glazes were used to add strength and durability to wall tiles, bricks, and pottery. By 1500 B.C., glazes were used as practical and hygienic waterproof layers on pottery.

Some of the earliest glazed objects are now known as Egyptian paste. Soluble sodium compounds were mixed into the clay and used to produce ornaments, beads, and sculptures. During the drying process, the soluble salts migrated with the water to the surface of the object. A scum was formed and melted to form a glass during the firing. The Egyptians then discovered that the addition of copper bearing minerals to the mixture resulted in bright blue and turquoise glazes. The practice of applying the

Above *Vases decorated with the name of Ramses II, 19th Dynasty, 1279–1213 B.C. These early Egyptian vases have a blue and turquoise finish, which evolved from Egyptian paste.*

glaze materials to the surface of the ware, enabling greater control over the thickness and color, followed.

LEAD GLAZES

The discovery of lead was an important step in the early development of glazes. It is believed to have taken place in ancient Syria or Babylonia. There, potters began to make various colored lead glazes with the addition of metal oxides such as copper, iron, and manganese. This advance was clearly demonstrated on the large architectural tiles and reliefs produced in the region (*see right*).

The knowledge of lead glazes spread to China, where some of the earliest glazes—dating from about 500 B.C.— were made with lead. The Chinese also made improvements to the pottery kiln, enabling regular firings of at least 2192°F (1200°C) from perhaps as early as the sixth century B.C. Much later, in medieval Europe, potters dusted galena powder (lead ore) onto the surface of damp pots, creating a sufficient coating of lead to form a glaze on the fired piece.

Above *A glazed brick relief of a lion, one of a series of sacred animals lining the Processional Way, Babylon. Built during the reign of Nebuchadnezzar II, 604–562 B.C.*

Advances in the use of lead made possible the creation of glazes that melted at higher temperatures. There was no awareness of lead poisoning until the nineteenth century!

ASH

Another early glaze was produced by ash, which was blown through the kiln by the draft of the fire and formed a coating on the surface of the ware. Ancient Chinese and Japanese pots have

Left *Storage jar with sgraffito decoration and galena glaze, by Michael Cardew.*

Left *Japanese Tamba pottery, which is wood fired and often glazed with an ash deposit forming a glass in the firing.*

a glaze on one side only, or on the shoulder, which was created in this way. Many of these early glazes were probably discovered by chance rather than by design. The process of glazing was—and remains—a matter of mixing a few ceramic materials and subjecting them to a suitable atmosphere and degree of heat.

Above *Three vases by Victor Knibbs, dipped in white glaze, then splashed with colored glaze.*

TEXTURE AND FINISH

Glazes can be shiny, satin, matte, transparent, opaque, and white or colored. For utilitarian pottery, the surface has a special significance. For example, a smooth finish is easy to clean and therefore more hygienic than a textured surface. Special effects such as crackles, lusters, and pinholing are more suitable for decorative and sculptural pieces.

Left *Stoneware dish by Tony Pugh, decorated with multiple poured glazes.*

Technical Terms Used In The Book

OXIDIZED AND REDUCED FIRING An oxidizing atmosphere is produced in an electric kiln and can be achieved in all types of kilns. The circulation of air through the kiln during the firing is unrestricted.

Reduction firing takes place in fuel-burning kilns such as gas, oil, wood, or other solid fuels. This is achieved by the restriction of secondary air (containing oxygen) from passing through the kiln during firing. During this "reduction of oxygen" phase in the kiln atmosphere, certain chemical reactions take place in the ware. This will allow a number of reduction effects to take place: e.g. lusters will be created, copper reds will be produced, and iron spot crystals will be drawn to the surface of the glaze.

Throughout this book, oxidized glazes refer to electric kilns and reduced glazes to a gas kiln (flame burning).

Above *A small electric kiln, used for oxidized firings. A gas, wood, or oil (flame) kiln is generally used for reduction firing.*

BISCUIT FIRING (OR SINGLE FIRING)
After drying, the work is biscuit fired to 1796–2012°F (980–1100°C). This makes the ware porous and strengthens it for decoration and glazing. When the temperature goes higher, the clay becomes less porous.

If glazed work is first fired to a low temperature, such as raku (see page 10), the higher biscuit firing produces a more vitrified (and durable) clay body. "Raw glazing" omits the biscuit firing. The work is put through a single glaze firing. This is obviously more hazardous, because it involves the handling and glazing of unfired work. It does, however, cut out additional firing costs and handling time.

GLAZE TEMPERATURE RANGES
Earthenware: 1742–2102°F (950–1150°C).
Stoneware and porcelain: 2192–2372°F (1200–1300°C).

GLAZE FIRING The final temperature for a glaze firing depends on the type of glaze and clay body used. As the temperature increases, the glaze begins to melt and fuse with the clay body. The materials in the glaze interact with materials in the clay body. This reaction is known as "interface." The amount of time a firing takes to reach the required temperature affects the "interface" reaction.

Above *Different bodies and glazes require different firing methods. Earthenware tends to be oxidized, while stoneware and porcelain can be either oxidized or reduced.*

Some potters "soak" the kiln at the end of a firing—that is, they sustain the optimum temperature to allow the combined body and glaze to mature.

RAKU After biscuit firing, the work is glaze fired. This is usually done in a specially made kiln. Once the required temperature is reached, or it can be seen that the glaze is melted, the pots are removed from the kiln and placed into bins of combustible materials, such as sawdust or wood shavings. This provides a post-firing "reduction" atmosphere, creating a number of effects, including metallic lusters, crackle glazes, and smoked surfaces. See page 102.

SALT AND SODA FIRING This process involves the introduction of salt into the kiln atmosphere at around 2264°F (1240°C). The salt fuses with the silica in the clay body or slip to produce the characteristic orange-peel effect associated with salt and soda glazing. See page 194.

WOOD FIRING With a flame-burning atmosphere in the kiln, wood firing creates rich, warm surfaces, with flashing. The ash deposits interact with the clay and slip surfaces to form glazed areas. A constant vigil, with regular stoking, is necessary to achieve a steady temperature rise.

SAWDUST FIRING Brick kilns or metal containers are filled with sawdust into which the ware is placed. The sawdust is lit at the top and smolders slowly through to the base of the kiln. After cooling, the pots are removed and cleaned to reveal a black carbon effect.

SAGGAR FIRING A saggar is a lidded refractory box containing combustible material. The ware within the saggar is protected from the kiln's atmosphere and can be "reduced" in an oxidized environment. Glazed work can be smoke-fumed in this way. The kiln and immediate area must be well ventilated to take away fumes produced during this process.

Above *A pot being brought out of the kiln. The tongs are being inserted into the "neck" of the pot, ready to lift it out. It will be given two to three hours post-firing reduction before being allowed to cool. The pot will then be scrubbed clean to reveal the characteristic raku luster.*

Below *On the left is a saggar with pots carefully arranged with combustible material such as sawdust and wood shavings added. On the right, after the firing, the sawdust is burned to ash. The area of the pots covered by the sawdust will be matte velvet.*

How To Use This Book

Oxidized or Reduced *"Oxidized" means that the tile was fired in clean air in an electric kiln. "Reduced" means that the tile was fired in a gas kiln with clean air (oxygen) restricted in the latter stages of firing.*

Description *Information about the finish and texture as well as the color of the glaze.*

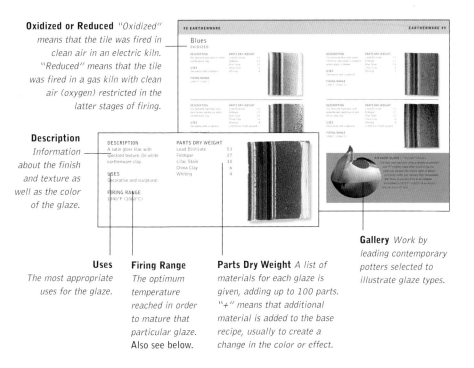

Gallery *Work by leading contemporary potters selected to illustrate glaze types.*

Uses *The most appropriate uses for the glaze.*

Firing Range *The optimum temperature reached in order to mature that particular glaze. Also see below.*

Parts Dry Weight *A list of materials for each glaze is given, adding up to 100 parts. "+" means that additional material is added to the base recipe, usually to create a change in the color or effect.*

NOTES ON FIRING RANGES

Soak time—30 minutes Once the optimum temperature is reached, the kiln is kept at that temperature for the given "soak time."

2336–2372°F (1280–1300°C) with reduction starting at 1580°F (860°C) The temperature at which the reduction process starts depends on whether light or heavy reduction is required. To start the process, "secondary air" (drawn from outside the kiln) is restricted by closing down bungs and air vents on the kiln in stages.

Firing has a 12-hour cycle Variable on firing type. 12 hours is typical for a reduction firing cycle for stoneware.

Post-firing reduction—1 hour A practice associated with raku firing. After the glaze firing, the piece is put into an atmosphere with oxygen restricted. This can be achieved by placing the ware in a lidded bin/container and covering it with combustible material, or by introducing combustible material into the kiln once the temperature has been allowed to drop below red heat.

CHAPTER 1

Materials and Techniques

When choosing a glaze it is useful to know how its ingredients affect color and finish. The tools used, mixing the glaze correctly, and the application method chosen will all contribute to the final outcome.

Glaze Raw Materials

Glaze is made of three basic elements: silica, alumina, and a flux. Silica forms the glass. Alumina gives the clay some "body" and stability, helping to create an effective surface coating. Flux controls the melting temperature of the glaze. The combination of materials will affect the appearance of the glaze and control the temperature at which it needs to be fired to reach its maturation point. The following is a list of materials commonly used in glaze formulation with various firing conditions and in different mixtures.

Left *Details of different glaze finishes. Above is a raku pot revealing luster; below is a crackle glaze.*

GLAZE MATERIALS

Alkaline frit is a combination of sodium, potassium, and silica. Alkaline frits are used for crackle glazes.

Alumina acts as a stabilizer and increases the viscosity of a glaze.

Ball clay contains both alumina and silica.

Barium carbonate is used as a secondary flux at stoneware temperature and produces matte or semi-matte surfaces at earthenware temperatures.

Bentonite helps to suspend the particles of glaze powder solution when added in quantities of up to 3 percent.

Borax frit is a powerful flux at earthenware temperatures. Borax is a good alternative for lead, when a leadless glaze is required. Small amounts of borax can be added to stoneware glazes to lower their melting point.

China clay contains alumina and silica. It can be used to make a shiny glaze matte. It is highly refractory and can also be used to raise the maturation point of a glaze.

China clay

Colemenite (calcium borate or borocalcite) is a strong flux at earthenware temperatures. It can also be used as a flux in stoneware glazes. It intensifies colors produced by oxides.

Dolomite is a source of calcium and magnesium, and promotes matteness in stoneware glazes. It is also an opacifier, which by itself has a distinctly oatmeal appearance.

Feldspar always contains silica, alumina, and fluxes. It is commonly used in stoneware glazes. When a recipe states "feldspar," feldspar-potash should be used. Feldspar-soda contains more soda than potash and has a lower melting point. Nepheline syenite is a form of feldspar that contains more soda and potash than silica. It is used where a low maturation point is required. Cornish stone is a feldspar with a higher silica content causing it to melt at a higher temperature than other feldspars.

Ilmenite is used in small amounts with rutile to give textured glazes. It can also be used as a coloring pigment in stoneware glazes.

Lead is used in its fritted form of lead bisilicate or lead sesquisilicate. It is a powerful flux. Lead glazes produce rich colors when used with coloring oxides. Do not use copper colorants in lead glazes on pottery intended for food and drink. It increases the amount of lead released from the glaze.

Copper carbonate

Red iron oxide

Magnesium carbonate is a high-temperature flux. When used in amounts of up to 10 percent, it aids production of satin matte glaze surfaces.
Silica (flint and quartz) is the essential glass-forming ingredient in all glazes. It is found naturally in clays and wood ash and is also available in the forms of flint and quartz. Both are used to introduce silica into glazes, helping to raise the melting point and inhibit crazing.
Talc (French chalk) is high in magnesium content and helps to make a matte surface in stoneware glazes.
Whiting (limestone) is used as a flux when introduced in small quantities. In amounts over 25 percent, it promotes matteness in the glaze.
Zinc oxide is used as a secondary flux in quantities of up to 5 percent. When used in amounts of over 10 percent, it produces a frosty, matte surface and is a useful opacifier.

Left *A rich surface has been achieved by the application of stains and oxides. By Kate Malone.*

THE OXIDE COLORANTS

Cobalt oxide is a powerful coloring oxide, producing blues in reduction and oxidation at up to 1½ percent. Cobalt carbonate is a similar, though milder, colorant.
Copper oxide produces a range of greens in oxidation firings. In alkaline glazes it gives turquoise blues, and in lead-based glazes a range of bottle greens. In reduction firings, small amounts (3–5 percent) permit the formation of copper-red glazes known as ox blood or "sang de boeuf."
Chrome oxide produces a range of greens. In the presence of tin, chrome can create a strong pink/red and affect other glazed work.
Iron oxide is the most frequently used colorant in ceramics. It is known as ferrous oxide, ferric oxide, magnetite, ocher, hematite, or crocus martis.

Right
Porcelain bowl with copper-red glaze by Gareth Mason.

According to its strength, it colors glazes from pale honey to near black in oxidation firings. In reduction, it helps to make a *celadon* glaze (gray-green stoneware or porcelain glaze) green, gray, or blue. Up to 12 percent gives rich brown reds to black tenmokus (stoneware glazes).
Manganese dioxide produces browns in oxidation firings and lead glazes. In alkaline bases, it yields plum/purple colors. Blended with cobalt oxide in reduction firings, it gives shades of violet.
Nickel oxide produces brown through gray-green. In reduction firings, gray tends to result. In oxidation firings, pale creams and light browns occur when magnesium is present.
Rutile is a titanium ore that contains some iron. It provides a color range from cream through tan in oxidation firings. In reduction, it can produce blue-white.
Tin oxide in amounts from 5 to 10 percent produces a soft, blue-white opacity. It does not melt completely in the glaze, so it fills the glaze with white particles, making it opaque.
Vanadium and uranium oxide help to produce yellows, especially in lead glazes. Uranium oxide is rarely available nowadays.

GLAZE STAINS

Prepared ceramic stains are oxide-based blends mixed with stabilizing materials, fired and then ground for use in powder form. The stains permit a predictable range of colors as an alternative to the coloring oxides. Stains can be mixed with oxides—either for painting or as an addition to glaze or slip—giving the more textural quality of oxides more stability and color.

'Lime Green' glaze stain

Tools and Equipment

Many of the items necessary for glazing can be obtained for a relatively small outlay, and normal household items can be used; for instance, screw-top jars are useful for storing small amounts of materials such as oxides and glaze stains. A good range of sieves is essential.

More important than expensive equipment is an understanding of the dangers inherent in mixing and applying glaze, and a rigid adherence to safe practice.

For mixing a glaze, you will need:

- Accurate scales, for small and large quantities of materials.
- Sieves with various mesh sizes. Typical mesh sizes are 60, 80, 100, 120: the highest being the finest mesh. It is possible to go up to a 200 mesh but a 60–80 size is suitable for general purposes; for spraying, a finer size (100 to 120) is necessary in order to allow the mixture to pass through the small nozzle of a spray gun.

Below Accurate scales, a sieve, and brushes are necessary for mixing a glaze.

- Large brush for pushing materials through sieve.
- Bucket, and various kinds of plastic ware for safe, airtight storage of materials.
- Slats to support sieves over a bucket.
- Measuring cup for the required amount of water.

HEALTH AND SAFETY: IMPORTANT PRECAUTIONS

Many ceramic materials are toxic and must be handled with extreme care. Take precautions, especially when preparing dry materials, to prevent the inhalation of dust particles. Wearing and using the correct equipment will protect you from hazardous substances. Ask for individual health and safety data sheets when purchasing ceramic materials. These will enable you to assess any risk and apply any control measures needed.

TOXIC ELEMENTS OF PARTICULAR CONCERN:

Element	Sources
Silica	Quartz, flint, frits, feldspars, clays, and glazes.
Vanadium	Vanadium pentoxide and ceramic colors.
Cadmium and selenium	Ceramic colors and glazes.
Lead	Lead oxide, frits, and glazes.
Chromium	Chrome oxide and some ceramic colors.
Copper	Copper oxide, carbonate, and some ceramic colors.
Zinc	Zinc oxide, some ceramic colors.
Borax	Borax frits.

Safety Tips

- Avoid creating dust at all times when preparing work or when cleaning up.

- Vacuum floors and wet-clean work surfaces.

- Never inhale or ingest powders.

- Wear a safety mask (face respirator) and protective gloves when preparing glaze from soluble materials. Wear gloves when using wet glaze. This prevents toxins from being absorbed through the skin.

- Wear a safety mask (face respirator) when spraying glaze and color. Use proper extraction equipment when using a spray gun or airbrush.

- Wear protective clothing and wash it regularly. Wear sensible footwear, never sandals.

- Store materials in carefully labeled, lidded containers, and always check the instructions on raw materials carefully.

- Keep all ceramic materials away from children and pets.

- Never eat in your work area.

- Tie back long hair.

Below *Clockwise from left: goggles, safety mask, heatproof gloves.*

Mixing a Glaze

It is vital to follow the advice given in the Safety Tips on page 17. Mix all materials in powder form into water as quickly and carefully as possible. Dust is the number one health hazard. Develop a system for organizing your materials in clearly labeled containers with airtight lids.

1 Weigh the dry ingredients and gently add them to a larger quantity of water than is eventually required. This gives a thin mixture that reduces dust and helps to avoid lumps.

2 Allow the mixture to stand for a few hours and "slake down." Then blend the liquid—either by hand or with an electric mixer—to break up any remaining lumps.

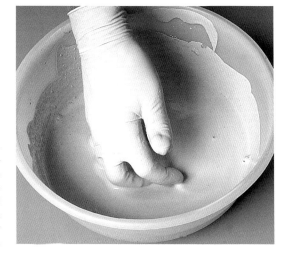

4 The thickness of the glaze depends upon the chosen method of application: dipping, pouring, or spraying, for example. As an approximate guide, glaze intended for dipping should have the consistency of cream. A glaze for spraying should be sieved through a 120 mesh and is slightly thinner in consistency. Test glaze thickness by dipping a finger, or a piece of biscuited pot, into the well-stirred mixture. If the glaze runs off, it is too thin. Allow the glaze to settle, so that the ingredients sink to the bottom. This can take from one to 24 hours, depending on the materials in the glaze. High-clay glazes are slower to settle, whereas non-plastic ingredients, such as frits, settle quickly.

3 Put the mixture twice through a sieve of suitably sized mesh using a glaze brush or a domestic dishwashing brush. Use a 60 mesh to begin with if the mixture is particularly lumpy, then progress to a 100. This process will result in a homogeneous, evenly mixed glaze.

5 Excess water can be removed from the top of the glaze by carefully ladling it out. Always stir the glaze thoroughly before use to ensure an even mix of all the materials. When frits are used, constant stirring is necessary to prevent them from settling to the bottom of the bucket.

Left *Commercially produced glazes can be bought from most pottery suppliers. They come in powder or liquid (ready-mixed) form. A huge range of glazes and glaze colors come, ready to paint on, in small screw-top jars.*

Methods of Application

Experimentation is the key to developing original and personal ways of working with glazes. An infinite variety of surfaces is possible, and there are countless techniques for achieving them. The following are some of the most frequently used. Resists such as wax, latex, and masking tape can be applied prior to glazing to mark out areas to be left unglazed.

Left *Dish by Rob Bibby. Glaze is painted on over a tin glaze.*
Right *Thrown bowl by Sutton Taylor, with multicolored lusters derived from gold, silver, and copper.*

Dipping is a quick and efficient method. The pot is immersed in the glaze for a few seconds, and can be dipped again for another couple of seconds. This is known as "double dipping," which can produce an additional range of decorative results.

Pouring Glaze can easily be poured onto small pots held over a bowl or bucket to catch the excess liquid. Larger pots can be stood on wooden slats over a suitable container. The glaze is then poured evenly around the pot.

Brushing and painting (including splashing, sponging, and stippling): Any brush can be used for brushing on glaze— from specialist Japanese *hakes* to regular housepainting brushes. One of the main advantages of painting is the smaller quantity of glaze required. There are many possibilities for building up layers of different colors and surface textures. Using brushes, or a simple ladle or slip trailer, glaze can be splashed, trailed, or squirted onto the surface. This can create dramatic areas of "surface incident," where one glaze overlaps another with dynamic splash patterns. Glaze can also be stippled on, using a brush or sponge. Additional decoration can be achieved by sponging glazes on top of one another. The sponge can also be cut and shaped to create particular motifs.

Spraying glaze has some advantages in particular situations. Spray can be applied to a vitrified surface and used for gradations of color. Only small amounts of glaze are necessary. Suitable equipment is essential: a spray gun, compressor, spray booth, and an extractor fan with an outside exhaust. The fine airborne glaze spray must not be breathed in, and a suitable dust mask must always be worn. Glaze to be sprayed needs to be sieved through a 120-mesh sieve so that the spray nozzle does not become blocked.

CHAPTER 2

Glaze Recipes

Accompanying the recipes in the following section is a gallery of pieces by individual potters, many of whom have outlined the methods involved in producing their own work. Hopefully, this will enable the reader to dip in, secure a foothold, and begin their own journey of investigation and experimentation.

Earthenware

The tiles in this section were all made from either Potclays LT25 white earthenware or Valentines red terra cotta clays. The tiles were all biscuit fired to 1859°F (1015°C).

Earthenware is usually fired to temperatures below 2174°F (1190°C) and within the range of 1742–2102°F (950–1150°C). The fired clay remains somewhat porous and open in structure. Most of the world's pottery is earthenware. This is due to the abundance of earthenware clay (i.e. clay firing to hard ceramic within the earthenware temperature range) and the relative ease of reaching the temperatures necessary to fire it in the kiln. Earthenware is softer and more fragile than stoneware or porcelain but less brittle. The color range of earthenware clays encompasses a rich and varied palette. These body colors, combined with the brilliant range of colors possible from low-fired glazes, make

SUSAN BRUCE | TALL FORMS Hand built using white earthenware mixed with colored clays. After bisque firing, colors are added using underglaze stains. Transparent glaze is applied to selected areas. The pots were then fired to 2048°F (1120°C) in an electric kiln.

KATE MALONE | TUTTI FRUITY BLACKBERRY Hand-built form bisque fired to 2156°F (1180°C). Layers of an industrial base glaze are brushed on. The borax contained in the glaze helps provide the strong colors. Each piece has two glaze firings, sometimes more, to achieve the desired effects.

STEPHEN MURFITT |
HAND-BUILT FORM

A copper loaded glaze was first brushed into the textured areas of the bisque-fired form. Then layers of alkaline frit based glaze containing iron were sprayed over before raku firing.

KATE MALONE |
"CARNIVAL WARE"

Thrown and hand-formed mugs and jugs, made in "T" material clay body and bisque fired to 2156°F (1180°C). Several layers of colored base glaze are thickly applied with brushes. Each layer is fired to 1940°F (1060°C).

earthenware an exciting medium for color expression.

Generally, the brilliant and varied color range possible in ceramics is mainly associated with lower firing techniques. At these lower temperatures the ingredients in the glaze that contain the color-giving properties remain stable. They are more likely to "burn out" at the higher stoneware and porcelain temperatures. However, there are now available commercial glaze stains and colors that remain stable up to those higher temperatures. This all helps to make possible a more varied color palette within a wider firing range.

Earthenware fired in the middle range of temperature, from about 2048–2156°F (1120–1180°C), will have the strength, density, and durability of glaze normally associated with stoneware, yet it retains a greater potential for more varied and brilliant colors, typical of lower firing.

The following are earthenware clays:
Raku: Porous body; soft glaze.
Slipware: Mostly porous body with little integration of body, slip, and glaze; soft glaze.
Creamware: Porous body in spite of possible high biscuit-firing temperature; soft glaze.
Majolica and faience: Porous body; soft glaze.

Naturals and Browns
OXIDIZED

DESCRIPTION
Dry/matte very fine light
oatmeal on white earthenware
clay.

USES
Mainly sculptural.

FIRING RANGE
1976°F (1080°C)
Soak time—30 minutes

PARTS DRY WEIGHT

Lead Bisilicate	47
Potash Feldspar	25
China Clay	16
Whiting	12
+ Manganese Dioxide	3
Rutile Oxide	3

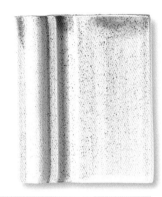

DESCRIPTION
Semi-gloss transparent cream
with very fine dark speckled
surface on white earthenware
clay. Use a finer mesh sieve
(120) if speckle not required.

USES
Decorative and sculptural.

FIRING RANGE
1940°F (1060°C)

PARTS DRY WEIGHT

Lead Bisilicate	53
Feldspar	27
Yellow Stain	10
China Clay	6
Whiting	4

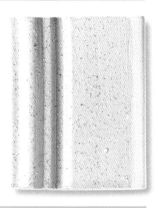

DESCRIPTION
A glossy mid-brown with dark
speckled texture on white
earthenware clay.

USES
Domestic and decorative.

FIRING RANGE
2012°F (1100°C)

PARTS DRY WEIGHT

Lead Bisilicate	60
Cornish Stone	30
China Clay	5
Whiting	5
+ Manganese Dioxide	3
Rutile Oxide	3

DESCRIPTION
Satin/gloss red/brown speckled
and mottled on light yellow/
cream surface on white
earthenware clay.

USES
Decorative and sculptural.

FIRING RANGE
1940°F (1060°C)

PARTS DRY WEIGHT
Lead Bisilicate	50
Feldspar	20
China Clay	10
Whiting	10
Yellow Stain	10
+ Red Iron Oxide sprayed	

DESCRIPTION
Matte dark red/brown blending
to speckled dark brown on
white earthenware clay.

USES
Decorative and sculptural.

FIRING RANGE
1940°F (1060°C)

PARTS DRY WEIGHT
Lead Bisilicate	53
Feldspar	27
Tin Oxide	10
China Clay	6
Whiting	4
+ Manganese Dioxide sprayed	

DESCRIPTION
Matte, dark red/brown blending
to dark speckle on pale
yellow/cream on white
earthenware clay.

USES
Decorative and sculptural.

FIRING RANGE
1940°F (1060°C)

PARTS DRY WEIGHT
Lead Bisilicate	53
Feldspar	27
Yellow Stain	10
China Clay	6
Whiting	4
+ Manganese Dioxide sprayed	

Naturals and Browns
OXIDIZED

DESCRIPTION
A glossy "warm" yellow tan on red terra cotta clay (with a hint of green).

USES
Domestic and decorative.

FIRING RANGE
1976°F (1080°C)

PARTS DRY WEIGHT
Lead Bisilicate	60
Cornish Stone	30
China Clay	5
Whiting	5
+ Yellow Ocher	3
Rutile Oxide	3

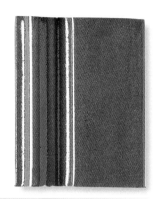

DESCRIPTION
Satin/gloss brown with fine dark speckles (of manganese) on red terra cotta clay.

USES
Domestic and decorative.

FIRING RANGE
1976°F (1080°C)

PARTS DRY WEIGHT
Lead Bisilicate	62
Cornish Stone	30
Whiting	5
China Clay	3
+ Rutile Oxide	3
Manganese Dioxide	1

DESCRIPTION
Glossy even brown on red terra cotta clay.

USES
Domestic and decorative (with colored slips).

FIRING RANGE
1976°F (1080°C)

PARTS DRY WEIGHT
Lead Bisilicate	60
Cornish Stone	30
China Clay	5
Whiting	5
+ Manganese Dioxide	3
Rutile Oxide	3

DESCRIPTION
Semi-gloss dark brown
on red terra cotta clay.

USES
Domestic and decorative.

FIRING RANGE
1976°F (1080°C)

PARTS DRY WEIGHT

Lead Bisilicate	60
Cornish Stone	30
China Clay	5
Whiting	5
+ Rutile Oxide	3
Manganese Dioxide	1
Cobalt Carbonate	0.5

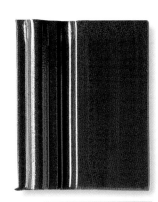

DESCRIPTION
Glossy dark brown on red
terra cotta clay.

USES
Domestic and decorative.

FIRING RANGE
1976°F (1080°C)

PARTS DRY WEIGHT

Lead Bisilicate	62
Cornish Stone	30
China Clay	3
Whiting	5
+ Red Iron Oxide	1
Cobalt Carbonate	0.5

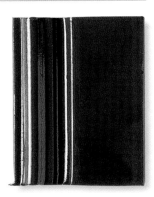

BRYAN TRUEMAN I LIDDED JAR

This lidded jar is made with a terra cotta clay body. It was coated
with a ball-clay based slip with further colored slips and glazes to
achieve this multi-layered effect. The base glaze Bryan Truman uses is
a transparent earthenware glaze consisting of the following: Lead
Bisilicate 74, China Clay 10, Silica 10, Potash Feldspar 5, Bentonite
1, plus various oxides and commercial stains.
Fired to 2057°F (1125°C) in an electric kiln. Height 13 in (33 cm).

Yellows and Oranges
OXIDIZED

DESCRIPTION
Glossy light yellow on white earthenware clay.

USES
Domestic and decorative.

FIRING RANGE
1868–2120°F
(1020–1160°C)

PARTS DRY WEIGHT

B 276 Leadless Transparent Glaze	100
+ B 100 Yellow Glaze Stain	5

DESCRIPTION
Glossy bright yellow on white earthenware clay.

USES
Domestic and decorative.

FIRING RANGE
2012°F (1100°C)

PARTS DRY WEIGHT

Lead Bisilicate	62
Cornish Stone	30
Whiting	5
China Clay	3
+ Yellow "Body" Stain	5

DESCRIPTION
Glossy golden yellow on white earthenware clay.

USES
Mainly decorative.

FIRING RANGE
2012°F (1100°C)

PARTS DRY WEIGHT

Lead Bisilicate	62
Cornish Stone	30
Whiting	5
China Clay	3
+ Yellow "Body" Stain	5
Yellow Iron Oxide	5

DESCRIPTION
Light opaque glossy
orange/beige on white
earthenware clay.

USES
Domestic and decorative.

FIRING RANGE
1868–2120°F
(1020–1160°C)

PARTS DRY WEIGHT
B 277 Leadless White
   Opaque Zirlon Glaze 100
+ B 100 Yellow
   Glaze Stain   2.5
B 122 Orange
   Glaze Stain   2.5
Blythe Strong Red
   Glaze Stain   2.5

DESCRIPTION
Glossy, opaque orange/peach
on white earthenware clay.

USES
Domestic and decorative.

FIRING RANGE
1868–2120°F
(1020–1160°C)

PARTS DRY WEIGHT
B 277 Leadless White
   Opaque Zirlon Glaze 100
+ B 122 Orange
   Glaze Stain   5
Blythe Strong Red
   Glaze Stain   5

DESCRIPTION
Glossy light yellow/orange on
white earthenware clay.

USES
Domestic and decorative.

FIRING RANGE
1868–2120°F
(1020–1160°C)

PARTS DRY WEIGHT
B 276 Leadless
   Transparent Glaze   100
+ B186 Mandarin Yellow
   Glaze Stain   5

Yellows and Oranges
OXIDIZED

DESCRIPTION
Glossy light maize yellow on white earthenware clay.

USES
Domestic and decorative.

FIRING RANGE
1868–2120°F
(1020–1160°C)

PARTS DRY WEIGHT
B 276 Leadless
   Transparent Glaze   100
+ B 101 Maize Yellow
   Glaze Stain   5

DESCRIPTION
Glossy yellow on white earthenware clay.

USES
Domestic and decorative.

FIRING RANGE
1868–2120°F
(1020–1160°C)

PARTS DRY WEIGHT
B 276 Leadless
   Transparent Glaze   100
+ B 100 Yellow
   Glaze Stain   10

DESCRIPTION
Glossy yellow with red terra cotta clay color breaking through.

USES
Domestic and decorative.

FIRING RANGE
1976°F (1080°C)

PARTS DRY WEIGHT
Lead Bisilicate   62
Cornish Stone   30
Whiting   5
China Clay   3
+ Yellow "Body" Stain   5

DESCRIPTION
Glossy orange on white
earthenware clay.

USES
Domestic and decorative.

FIRING RANGE
1868–2120°F
(1020–1160°C)

PARTS DRY WEIGHT
B 276 Leadless
   Transparent Glaze   100
+ B 186 Mandarin
   Glaze Stain   10

DESCRIPTION
Opaque, glossy orange on
white earthenware clay.

USES
Domestic and decorative.

FIRING RANGE
1868–2120°F
(1020–1160°C)

PARTS DRY WEIGHT
B 277 Leadless White
   Opaque Zirlon Glaze 100
+ B 122 Orange
   Glaze Stain   10

DESCRIPTION
Matte yellow/brown, darker
where thicker on white
earthenware clay.

USES
Mainly decorative.

FIRING RANGE
2012°F (1100°C)

PARTS DRY WEIGHT
Lead Bisilicate   58
Cornish Stone   32
China Clay   5
Whiting   5
+ Rutile Oxide   2
   Yellow "Body" Stain 1

Yellows and Oranges
OXIDIZED

DESCRIPTION
Glossy, pale orange, darker where thicker on white earthenware clay.

USES
Domestic and decorative.

FIRING RANGE
1868–2120°F
(1020–1160°C)

PARTS DRY WEIGHT
B 276 Leadless
    Transparent Glaze   100
+ Blythe Strong Red
    Glaze Stain   6
  B 100 Yellow
    Glaze Stain   4

DESCRIPTION
Satin/matte dark oatmeal, with speckles of manganese (unsieved) on white earthenware clay.

USES
Domestic and decorative.

FIRING RANGE
2012°F (1100°C)

PARTS DRY WEIGHT
Lead Bisilicate   62
Cornish Stone   30
Whiting   5
China Clay   3
+ Rutile Oxide   3
  Manganese Dioxide   1

DESCRIPTION
Glossy even yellow/orange on white earthenware clay.

USES
Domestic and decorative.

FIRING RANGE
1868–2120°F
(1020–1160°C)

PARTS DRY WEIGHT
B 276 Leadless
    Transparent Glaze   100
+ B 122 Orange
    Glaze Stain   5

DESCRIPTION
Matte "mustard" yellow, paler where thinly applied on white earthenware clay.

USES
Mainly decorative.

FIRING RANGE
2012°F (1100°C)

PARTS DRY WEIGHT
Lead Bisilicate	58
Cornish Stone	32
China Clay	5
Whiting	5
+ Rutile Oxide	2
Yellow "Body" Stain	1
Yellow Iron Oxide	0.5

DESCRIPTION
Glossy peachy orange on white earthenware clay.

USES
Domestic and decorative.

FIRING RANGE
1868–2120°F
(1020–1160°C)

PARTS DRY WEIGHT
B 276 Leadless Transparent Glaze	100
+ B 101 Maize Yellow Glaze Stain	5
Blythe Strong Red Glaze Stain	5

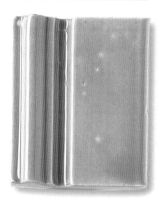

KATE MALONE I GIANT SLICED FRUIT OF YOUR DREAMS

Hand-built and bisque-fired form in "T" material clay body, which provides a suitable base for the brilliant colors. An "industrial" base glaze with added stains and oxides is applied. Further firings with more layers of color are followed by a fourth firing with a mixture of "pebble" applied (a white special-effect liquid base from Ceramatech) over a black slip on the outside and a base glaze on the inside. This gives strong textural effects.

Yellows and Oranges
OXIDIZED

DESCRIPTION
Glossy smooth orange on white earthenware clay.

USES
Domestic and decorative.

FIRING RANGE
1868–2120°F
(1020–1160°C)

PARTS DRY WEIGHT
B 276 Leadless
Transparent Glaze   100
+ B 122 Orange
Glaze Stain   10

DESCRIPTION
A glossy yellow/brown "tan." Darker where glaze is applied more thickly on white earthenware clay.

USES
Domestic and decorative.

FIRING RANGE
2012°F (1100°C)

PARTS DRY WEIGHT
Lead Bisilicate   60
Cornish Stone   30
China Clay   5
Whiting   5
+ Yellow Ocher   3
Rutile Oxide   3

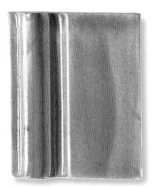

DESCRIPTION
Glossy pinkish orange on white earthenware clay.

USES
Domestic and decorative.

FIRING RANGE
1868–2120°F
(1020–1160°C)

PARTS DRY WEIGHT
B 276 Leadless
Transparent Glaze   100
+ B 100 Yellow
Glaze Stain   5
B 187 Rosso Red
Glaze Stain   5

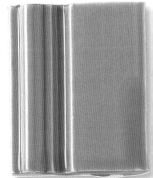

DESCRIPTION
Glossy "blushed" orange on white earthenware clay.

USES
Domestic and decorative.

FIRING RANGE
1868–2120°F
(1020–1160°C)

PARTS DRY WEIGHT
B 276 Leadless
   Transparent Glaze   100
+ B 100 Yellow
   Glaze Stain   5
  B 185 Coral
   Glaze Stain   5

DESCRIPTION
Glossy orange with undercurrents of brown on white earthenware clay.

USES
Domestic and decorative.

FIRING RANGE
1868–2120°F
(1020–1160°C)

PARTS DRY WEIGHT
B 276 Leadless
   Transparent Glaze   100
+ B 101 Maize Yellow
   Glaze Stain   5
  B 187 Rosso Red
   Glaze Stain   5

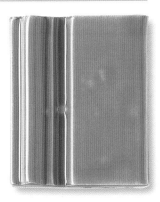

DESCRIPTION
Glossy orange/brown on white earthenware clay.

USES
Domestic and decorative.

FIRING RANGE
1868–2120°F
(1020–1160°C)

PARTS DRY WEIGHT
B 276 Leadless
   Transparent Glaze   100
+ B 100 Yellow
   Glaze Stain   5
  B 108 Chrome Tin
   Pink Glaze Stain   5

Yellows and Oranges
OXIDIZED

DESCRIPTION
Glossy yellow with red
terra cotta clay color breaking
through where glaze is thinly
applied.

USES
Mainly decorative.

FIRING RANGE
1976°F (1080°C)

PARTS DRY WEIGHT
Lead Bisilicate	62
Cornish Stone	30
Whiting	5
China Clay	3
+ Yellow "Body" Stain	5
Yellow Iron Oxide	0.5

DESCRIPTION
Semi-gloss "mustard" yellow
on red terra cotta clay.

USES
Mainly decorative.

FIRING RANGE
1976°F (1080°C)

PARTS DRY WEIGHT
Lead Bisilicate	58
Cornish Stone	32
China Clay	5
Whiting	5
+ Rutile Oxide	2
Yellow "Body" Stain	1
Yellow Iron Oxide	0.5

DESCRIPTION
Matte yellow blending to brown
where thinly applied on red
terra cotta clay.

USES
Mainly decorative.

FIRING RANGE
1976°F (1080°C)

PARTS DRY WEIGHT
Lead Bisilicate	58
Cornish Stone	32
China Clay	5
Whiting	5
+ Rutile Oxide	2
Yellow "Body" Stain	1

DESCRIPTION
Very thin coat of matte vellum white on red terra cotta clay. Would work well over colored stain.

USES
Decorative and sculptural.

FIRING RANGE
1976°F (1080°C)
Soak time—30 minutes

PARTS DRY WEIGHT
Lead Bisilicate	47
Potash Feldspar	25
China Clay	16
Whiting	12

DESCRIPTION
Matte red/brown with unsieved yellow stain providing a "starred" speckle effect on red terra cotta clay.

USES
Decorative and sculptural.

FIRING RANGE
1976°F (1080°C)
Soak time—30 minutes

PARTS DRY WEIGHT
Lead Bisilicate	47
Potash Feldspar	25
China Clay	16
Whiting	12
+ Yellow Stain	3
Rutile Oxide	3

DESCRIPTION
Glossy orange brown on white earthenware clay.

USES
Domestic and decorative.

FIRING RANGE
1868–2120°F
(1020–1160°C)

PARTS DRY WEIGHT
B 276 Leadless Transparent Glaze	100
+ B 100 Maize Yellow Glaze Stain	5
B 108 Chrome Tin Pink Glaze Stain	5

Reds and Purples
OXIDIZED

DESCRIPTION
Glossy, opaque light purple/
pink glaze on white
earthenware clay.

USES
Domestic and decorative.

FIRING RANGE
1868–2120°F
(1020–1160°C)

PARTS DRY WEIGHT
B 277 Leadless White
    Opaque Zirlon Glaze 100
+ B 108 Plum/Pink
    Glaze Stain   5

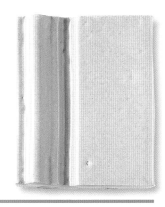

DESCRIPTION
Glossy, opaque /pink glaze on
white earthenware clay.

USES
Domestic and decorative.

FIRING RANGE
1868–2120°F
(1020–1160°C)

PARTS DRY WEIGHT
B 277 Leadless White
    Opaque Zirlon Glaze 100
+ Blythe Strong Red
    Glaze Stain   5

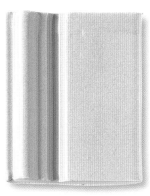

DESCRIPTION
Glossy pale pink on white
earthenware clay.

USES
Domestic and decorative.

FIRING RANGE
1868–2120°F
(1020–1160°C)

PARTS DRY WEIGHT
B 276 Leadless
Transparent Glaze   100
+ Blythe Strong Red
    Glaze Stain   5

DESCRIPTION
Dry/matte pink/white on white earthenware clay.

USES
Decorative and sculptural.

FIRING RANGE
1976°F (1080°C)
Soak time—30 minutes

PARTS DRY WEIGHT

Lead Bisilicate	47
Potash Feldspar	25
China Clay	16
Whiting	12
+ "Clover Red" Stain	2

DESCRIPTION
Glossy pink on white earthenware clay.

USES
Domestic and decorative.

FIRING RANGE
1868–2120°F
(1020–1160°C)

PARTS DRY WEIGHT

B 276 Leadless Transparent Glaze	100
+ B 185 Coral Glaze Stain	5

LINDSAY TOOP I ORNAMENTAL FORM

This form was hand built using white St. Thomas clay body. Color was applied through spraying with layers of matter and shiny glazes enhanced by homemade glaze stains. After a bisque firing the piece was glazed and then fired to 2012°F (1100°C) in an electric kiln (oxidation). Diameter approx. 12 in (32 cm).

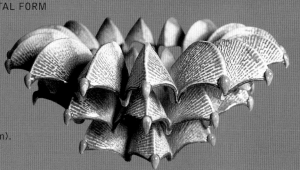

Reds and Purples
OXIDIZED

DESCRIPTION
Glossy orange/red on white
earthenware clay.

USES
Domestic and decorative.

FIRING RANGE
1868–2120°F
(1020°C–1160°C)

PARTS DRY WEIGHT
B 276 Leadless
   Transparent Glaze   100
+ B 187 Rosso Red
     Glaze Stain   10

DESCRIPTION
Glossy pink/red, darker where
more thickly applied on white
earthenware clay.

USES
Domestic and decorative.

FIRING RANGE
2012°F (1100°C)

PARTS DRY WEIGHT
Lead Bisilicate   60
Cornish Stone   30
China Clay   5
Whiting   5
+ Red Stain   5

DESCRIPTION
Glossy orange/pink on white
earthenware clay.

USES
Domestic and decorative.

FIRING RANGE
1868–2120°F
(1020–1160°C)

PARTS DRY WEIGHT
B 276 Leadless
   Transparent Glaze   100
+ B 187 Rosso Red
     Glaze Stain   5

DESCRIPTION
Glossy coral pink/red on white earthenware clay.

USES
Domestic and decorative.

FIRING RANGE
1868–2120°F
(1020–1160°C)

PARTS DRY WEIGHT
B 276 Leadless
    Transparent Glaze   100
+ B 185 Coral
    Glaze Stain   10

DESCRIPTION
Glossy pink/mauve on white earthenware clay.

USES
Domestic and decorative.

FIRING RANGE
1868–2120°F
(1020–1160°C)

PARTS DRY WEIGHT
B 276 Leadless
    Transparent Glaze   100
+ B 108 Chrome Tin
    Pink Glaze Stain   5

DESCRIPTION
Glossy light purple on white earthenware clay.

USES
Domestic and decorative.

FIRING RANGE
1868–2120°F
(1020–1160°C)

PARTS DRY WEIGHT
B 276 Leadless
    Transparent Glaze   100
+ B 119 Purple
    Glaze Stain   5

Reds and Purples
OXIDIZED

DESCRIPTION
Satin/matte yellow/cream
with rusty red/brown
mottled surface on white
earthenware clay.

USES
Decorative and sculptural.

FIRING RANGE
1940°F (1060°C)

PARTS DRY WEIGHT
Lead Bisilicate	57
Feldspar	31
China Clay	7
Whiting	5
+ Red Iron Oxide sprayed	

DESCRIPTION
Matte warm "toasted" red
brown with pink tinge on red
terra cotta clay.

USES
Mainly sculptural.

FIRING RANGE
1976°F (1080°C)
Soak time—30 minutes

PARTS DRY WEIGHT
Lead Bisilicate	47
Potash Feldspar	25
China Clay	16
Whiting	12
+ "Clover Red" Stain	2

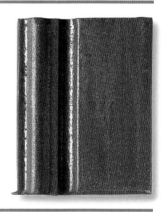

DESCRIPTION
Glossy clear glaze, red
terra cotta on red
earthenware clay.

USES
Decorative and domestic.

FIRING RANGE
1976°F (1080°C)

PARTS DRY WEIGHT
Lead Bisilicate	62
Cornish Stone	30
Whiting	5
China Clay	3

DESCRIPTION
A glossy "perfect red" on
white earthenware clay.

USES
Not food safe! Only suitable for
decorative purposes.

FIRING RANGE
1796–1868°F
(980–1020°C)
(Color burns out if fired above
1868°F/1020°C)

PARTS DRY WEIGHT
P0158 "Pottery Crafts"
    Perfect Red
    Brush-on Glaze   100

DESCRIPTION
Glossy light crimson on white
earthenware clay.

USES
Domestic and decorative.

FIRING RANGE
1868–2120°F
(1020–1160°C)

PARTS DRY WEIGHT
B 276 Leadless
    Transparent Glaze   100
+ B 120 Crimson
    Glaze Stain   5

DESCRIPTION
Glossy mauve/pink on white
earthenware clay.

USES
Domestic and decorative.

FIRING RANGE
1868–2120°F
(1020–1160°C)

PARTS DRY WEIGHT
B 276 Leadless
    Transparent Glaze   100
+ B 108 Chrome Tin Pink
    Glaze Stain   10

Reds and Purples
OXIDIZED

DESCRIPTION
Satin/gloss mottled and speckled red/brown on pink/lilac on red terra cotta clay.

USES
Decorative and sculptural.

FIRING RANGE
1940°F (1060°C)

PARTS DRY WEIGHT
Lead Bisilicate	50
Feldspar	30
Tin Oxide	10
China Clay	6
Whiting	4
+ Red Iron Oxide sprayed	

DESCRIPTION
Semi-gloss red/brown mottled on pale yellow/white surface. Glaze has "crawled" revealing red terra cotta clay body beneath!

USES
Decorative and sculptural.

FIRING RANGE
1940°F (1060°C)

PARTS DRY WEIGHT
Lead Bisilicate	50
Feldspar	20
China Clay	10
Whiting	10
Yellow Stain	10
+ Red Iron Oxide sprayed	

DESCRIPTION
A satin/gloss transparent with mottled red/brown areas, on red terra cotta clay.

USES
Decorative and sculptural.

FIRING RANGE
1940°F (1060°C)

PARTS DRY WEIGHT
Lead Bisilicate	57
Feldspar	31
China Clay	7
Whiting	5
+ Red Iron Oxide sprayed	

DESCRIPTION
Glossy crimson/mauve on white earthenware clay.

USES
Domestic and decorative.

FIRING RANGE
1868°F–2120°F
(1020°C–1160°C)

PARTS DRY WEIGHT
B 276 Leadless Transparent Glaze	100
+ B 120 Crimson Glaze Stain	10

DESCRIPTION
Glossy red/brown on red terra cotta clay.

USES
Mainly decorative.

FIRING RANGE
1976°F (1080°C)

PARTS DRY WEIGHT
Lead Bisilicate	60
Cornish Stone	30
China Clay	5
Whiting	5
+ Red Stain	5

DESCRIPTION
Glossy deep purple on white earthenware clay.

USES
Domestic and decorative.

FIRING RANGE
1868–2120°F
(1020–1160°C)

PARTS DRY WEIGHT
B 276 Leadless Transparent Glaze	100
+ B 119 Purple Glaze Stain	10

Blues
OXIDIZED

DESCRIPTION
Dry textured pale blue on white earthenware clay.

USES
Decorative and sculptural.

FIRING RANGE
1940°F (1060°C)

PARTS DRY WEIGHT

Lead Bisilicate	53
Feldspar	27
Blue Stain	10
China Clay	6
Whiting	4

DESCRIPTION
Dry textured light blue with dark brown speckle on white earthenware clay.

USES
Decorative and sculptural.

FIRING RANGE
1940°F (1060°C)

PARTS DRY WEIGHT

Lead Bisilicate	53
Feldspar	27
Blue Stain	10
China Clay	6
Whiting	4
+ Red Iron Oxide sprayed	

DESCRIPTION
A satin gloss lilac with speckled texture on white earthenware clay.

USES
Decorative and sculptural.

FIRING RANGE
1940°F (1060°C)

PARTS DRY WEIGHT

Lead Bisilicate	53
Feldspar	27
Lilac Stain	10
China Clay	6
Whiting	4

DESCRIPTION
Dry textured blue with warm red terra cotta body in evidence where glaze is thinner.

USES
Decorative and sculptural.

FIRING RANGE
1940°F (1060°C)

PARTS DRY WEIGHT
Lead Bisilicate	53
Feldspar	27
Blue Stain	10
China Clay	6
Whiting	4

DESCRIPTION
Dry textured light blue with green/brown speckling on red terra cotta clay.

USES
Decorative and sculptural.

FIRING RANGE
1940°F (1060°C)

PARTS DRY WEIGHT
Lead Bisilicate	53
Feldspar	27
Blue Stain	10
China Clay	6
Whiting	4
+ Red Iron Oxide sprayed	

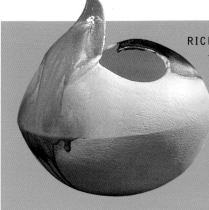

RICHARD SLADE I "PULSE" VESSEL

This form was hand built using a mixture of porcelain and "T" material clays. After bisque firing, the piece was sprayed with several layers of glazes colored by oxides and Potclays High-Temperature Red Stain. It was then fired in an oxidation atmosphere to 2012°F (1100°C) in an electric kiln. Height 11 in (27 cm).

Blues
OXIDIZED

DESCRIPTION
Pale blue gloss surface, pooling to darker blue where glaze is thicker, on white earthenware clay.

USES
Domestic and decorative.

FIRING RANGE
2012°F (1100°C)

PARTS DRY WEIGHT
Lead Bisilicate	62
Cornish Stone	30
Whiting	5
China Clay	3
+ Red Iron Oxide	1
Cobalt Carbonate	0.5

DESCRIPTION
Glossy blue/gray with a hint of turquoise, darker where glaze is thicker, on white earthenware clay.

USES
Domestic.

FIRING RANGE
2012°F (1100°C)

PARTS DRY WEIGHT
Lead Bisilicate	62
Cornish Stone	30
Whiting	5
China Clay	3
+ Copper Oxide	2
Cobalt Oxide	0.5

DESCRIPTION
Matte blue/gray on white earthenware clay. Darker where more thickly applied.

USES
Mainly decorative.

FIRING RANGE
2012°F (1100°C)
Soak time—30 minutes

PARTS DRY WEIGHT
Lead Bisilicate	47
Potash Feldspar	25
China Clay	16
Whiting	12
+ Rutile Oxide	3
Cobalt Oxide	0.5

DESCRIPTION
A glossy blue/gray with
(unsieved) cobalt speckle on
white earthenware clay.

USES
Domestic and decorative.

FIRING RANGE
2012°F (1100°C)

PARTS DRY WEIGHT
Lead Bisilicate	62
Cornish Stone	28
China Clay	6
Whiting	4
+ Rutile Oxide	2
Cobalt Oxide	1

DESCRIPTION
A glossy mid blue, speckled
with red iron, on white
earthenware clay. (If speckling
is not required, the red iron
oxide should be sieved through
a 120 sieve.)

USES
Domestic and decorative.

FIRING RANGE
2012°F (1100°C)

PARTS DRY WEIGHT
Lead Bisilicate	60
Cornish Stone	30
China Clay	5
Whiting	5
+ Red Iron Oxide	1
Cobalt Carbonate	2

DESCRIPTION
Semi-gloss lilac with speckled
texture on red terra cotta clay.

USES
Decorative and sculptural.

FIRING RANGE
1940°F (1060°C)

PARTS DRY WEIGHT
Lead Bisilicate	53
Feldspar	27
Lilac Stain	10
China Clay	6
Whiting	4

Blues
OXIDIZED

DESCRIPTION
A glossy dark blue, darker where more thickly applied on white earthenware clay.

USES
Domestic and decorative.

FIRING RANGE
2012°F (1100°C)

PARTS DRY WEIGHT

Lead Bisilicate	60
Cornish Stone	30
China Clay	5
Whiting	5
+ Cobalt Oxide	2
Red Iron Oxide	1

DESCRIPTION
A glossy dark blue turning to black where glaze was more thickly applied on white earthenware clay.

USES
Domestic and decorative.

FIRING RANGE
2012°F (1100°C)

PARTS DRY WEIGHT

Lead Bisilicate	62
Cornish Stone	28
China Clay	6
Whiting	4
+ Rutile Oxide	2
Cobalt Oxide	2

DESCRIPTION
Matte navy blue, darker where more thickly applied on white earthenware clay.

USES
Decorative and sculptural.

FIRING RANGE
2012°F (1100°C)
Soak time—30 minutes

PARTS DRY WEIGHT

Lead Bisilicate	47
Potash Feldspar	25
China Clay	16
Whiting	12
+ Cobalt Carbonate	2
Rutile Oxide	1

DESCRIPTION
Matte, dark navy blue, lighter where glaze thinner on white earthenware clay.

USES
Mainly sculptural.

FIRING RANGE
1976°F (1080°C)
Soak time—30 minutes

PARTS DRY WEIGHT

Lead Bisilicate	47
Potash Feldspar	25
China Clay	16
Whiting	12
+ Cobalt Oxide	1
Red Iron Oxide	1
Manganese Oxide	0.5

DESCRIPTION
A glossy blue/gray with textured speckled cobalt on surface on white earthenware clay.

USES
Domestic and decorative.

FIRING RANGE
2012°F (1100°C)

PARTS DRY WEIGHT

Lead Bisilicate	62
Cornish Stone	30
Whiting	5
China Clay	3
+ Rutile Oxide	3
Cobalt Oxide	2

ROGER MULLEY I VASE

A dramatically patterned thrown vase, in red marl clay. It has been "raw glazed" using an alkaline frit glaze over colored slips. It was then fired to 1940°F (1060°C) in an electric kiln. Height 18 in (45 cm).

Blues
OXIDIZED

DESCRIPTION
Satin/matte (gloss to dry)
mottled blue/turquoise to
metallic at top of tile on white
earthenware clay.

USES
Decorative and sculptural.

FIRING RANGE
1940°F (1060°C)

PARTS DRY WEIGHT
Lead Bisilicate	57
Feldspar	31
China Clay	7
Whiting	5
+ Cobalt Carbonate sprayed	

DESCRIPTION
Matte speckled blue/white
blending to dry dark
blue/metallic surface on white
earthenware clay.

USES
Decorative and sculptural.

FIRING RANGE
1940°F (1060°C)

PARTS DRY WEIGHT
Lead Bisilicate	50
Feldspar	20
China Clay	10
Whiting	10
Yellow Stain	10
+ Cobalt Carbonate sprayed	

DESCRIPTION
A satin/gloss speckled white on
blue blending to a matte, dark
blue/metallic surface on white
earthenware clay.

USES
Decorative and sculptural.

FIRING RANGE
1940°F (1060°C)

PARTS DRY WEIGHT
Lead Bisilicate	50
Feldspar	30
Tin Oxide	10
China Clay	6
Whiting	4
+ Cobalt Carbonate sprayed	

DESCRIPTION
Satin/gloss lilac/blue, blending
through to mottled green/dark
gray metallic on white
earthenware clay.

USES
Decorative and sculptural.

FIRING RANGE
1940°F (1060°C)

PARTS DRY WEIGHT
Lead Bisilicate	55
Feldspar	25
Lilac Stain	10
China Clay	5
Whiting	5
+ Copper Carbonate sprayed	

DESCRIPTION
Dry textured blue with dark
speckle blending to dark blue
then black on white
earthenware clay.

USES
Decorative and sculptural.

FIRING RANGE
1940°F (1060°C)

PARTS DRY WEIGHT
Lead Bisilicate	53
Feldspar	27
Blue Stain	10
China Clay	6
Whiting	4
+ Cobalt Carbonate sprayed	

DESCRIPTION
Semi-gloss lilac with blue
speckling blending to dark blue
then dry metallic on white
earthenware clay.

USES
Decorative and sculptural.

FIRING RANGE
1940°F (1060°C)

PARTS DRY WEIGHT
Lead Bisilicate	55
Feldspar	25
Lilac Stain	10
China Clay	5
Whiting	5
+ Cobalt Carbonate sprayed	

Blues
OXIDIZED

DESCRIPTION
Dry textured pale blue with black speckling blending to black/metallic on white earthenware clay.

USES
Decorative and sculptural.

FIRING RANGE
1940°F (1060°C)

PARTS DRY WEIGHT
Lead Bisilicate	53
Feldspar	27
Blue Stain	10
China Clay	6
Whiting	4
+ Manganese Dioxide sprayed	

DESCRIPTION
Semi-gloss lilac blending to matte speckled dark brown then metallic on white earthenware clay.

USES
Decorative and sculptural.

FIRING RANGE
1940°F (1060°C)

PARTS DRY WEIGHT
Lead Bisilicate	53
Feldspar	27
Lilac Stain	10
China Clay	6
Whiting	4
+ Manganese Dioxide sprayed	

DESCRIPTION
Dry blue with black speckling blending to black/metallic on red terra cotta clay.

USES
Decorative and sculptural.

FIRING RANGE
1940°F (1060°C)

PARTS DRY WEIGHT
Lead Bisilicate	53
Feldspar	27
Blue Stain	10
China Clay	6
Whiting	4
+ Manganese Dioxide sprayed	

DESCRIPTION
Satin/gloss dark lilac with
black speckling toward edges
of tile on red terra cotta clay.

USES
Decorative and sculptural.

FIRING RANGE
1940°F (1060°C)

PARTS DRY WEIGHT
Lead Bisilicate	53
Feldspar	27
Lilac Stain	10
China Clay	6
Whiting	4
+ Red Iron Oxide sprayed	

DESCRIPTION
Satin/gloss blue/lilac speckle
blending to dark blue then dry
black/metallic at edge on red
terra cotta clay.

USES
Decorative and sculptural.

FIRING RANGE
1940°F (1060°C)

PARTS DRY WEIGHT
Lead Bisilicate	55
Feldspar	25
Lilac Stain	10
China Clay	5
Whiting	5
+ Cobalt Carbonate sprayed	

DESCRIPTION
A glossy mottled blue/white
blending to matte dark
blue/metallic on red terra
cotta clay.

USES
Decorative and sculptural.

FIRING RANGE
1940°F (1060°C)

PARTS DRY WEIGHT
Lead Bisilicate	50
Feldspar	30
Tin Oxide	10
China Clay	6
Whiting	4
+ Cobalt Carbonate sprayed	

Blues
OXIDIZED

DESCRIPTION
Matte gray/blue blending
to black on red terra
cotta clay.

USES
Mainly decorative.

FIRING RANGE
1976°F (1080°C)
Soak time—30 minutes

PARTS DRY WEIGHT
Lead Bisilicate	47
Potash Feldspar	25
China Clay	16
Whiting	12
+ Rutile Oxide	3
Cobalt Oxide	0.5

DESCRIPTION
Satin/matte metallic/tan on
red terra cotta clay.

USES
Mainly sculptural.

FIRING RANGE
1976°F (1080°C)

PARTS DRY WEIGHT
Lead Bisilicate	62
Cornish Stone	30
Whiting	5
China Clay	3
+ Rutile Oxide	3
Copper Carbonate	3

DESCRIPTION
Satin/matte, dark metallic blue,
blending to brown where
thinner on red terra cotta clay.

USES
Mainly sculptural.

FIRING RANGE
1976°F (1080°C)

PARTS DRY WEIGHT
Lead Bisilicate	62
Cornish Stone	30
Whiting	5
China Clay	3
+ Rutile Oxide	3
Copper Carbonate	3
Cobalt Carbonate	1

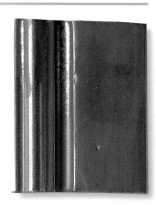

DESCRIPTION
Matte dark blue/black on red terra cotta clay.

USES
Decorative and sculptural.

FIRING RANGE
1976°F (1080°C)
Soak time—30 minutes

PARTS DRY WEIGHT

Lead Bisilicate	47
Potash Feldspar	25
China Clay	16
Whiting	12
+ Cobalt Carbonate	2
Rutile Oxide	1

DESCRIPTION
Satin/matte dark blue with warm red terra cotta revealed where the glaze is thinner.

USES
Decorative and sculptural.

FIRING RANGE
1976°F (1080°C)
Soak time—30 minutes

PARTS DRY WEIGHT

Lead Bisilicate	47
Potash Feldspar	25
China Clay	16
Whiting	12
+ Cobalt Oxide	1
Red Iron Oxide	1
Manganese Oxide	0.5

DESCRIPTION
Gloss, gray/blue, darker where more thickly applied on white earthenware clay.

USES
Decorative and domestic.

FIRING RANGE
2012°F (1100°C)

PARTS DRY WEIGHT

Lead Bisilicate	62
Cornish Stone	30
Whiting	5
China Clay	3
+ Manganese Dioxide	4
Cobalt Carbonate	1

Greens and Turquoises
OXIDIZED

DESCRIPTION
Satin/matte lime green on
white earthenware clay.

USES
Decorative and sculptural.

FIRING RANGE
1940°F (1060°C)

PARTS DRY WEIGHT
Lead Bisilicate	53
Feldspar	27
Lime Green Stain	10
China Clay	6
Whiting	4

DESCRIPTION
Semi-matte textured surface,
red terra cotta warming
surface where glaze application
is thinner.

USES
Decorative and sculptural.

FIRING RANGE
1940°F (1060°C)

PARTS DRY WEIGHT
Lead Bisilicate	53
Feldspar	27
Lime Green Stain	10
China Clay	6
Whiting	4

DESCRIPTION
Satin/matte lime green with
speckled green blending to
matte then dry green on white
earthenware clay.

USES
Decorative and sculptural.

FIRING RANGE
1940°F (1060°C)

PARTS DRY WEIGHT
Lead Bisilicate	55
Feldspar	25
Lime Green Stain	10
China Clay	5
Whiting	5
+ Chromium Oxide sprayed	

DESCRIPTION
Satin/gloss lime green with "red rust" speckle blending to matte mottled rusty red on white earthenware clay.

USES
Decorative and sculptural.

FIRING RANGE
1940°F (1060°C)

PARTS DRY WEIGHT

Lead Bisilicate	60
Feldspar	20
Lime Green Stain	10
China Clay	6
Whiting	4
+ Red Iron Oxide sprayed	

DESCRIPTION
Matte/dry lime green with dark speckle, blending to dark brown/black at base of tile on white earthenware clay.

USES
Decorative and sculptural.

FIRING RANGE
1940°F (1060°C)

PARTS DRY WEIGHT

Lead Bisilicate	53
Feldspar	27
Lime Green Stain	10
China Clay	6
Whiting	4
+ Manganese Dioxide sprayed	

WYNNE WILBUR I LIMES PLATTER

This piece has been made in terracotta clay. It demonstrates the use of a majolica tin glaze, with color brushed on using majolica stain. This is made up of gerstley borate and commercial ceramic stain, 3–4 parts to 1 part cobalt and copper (mix 1 to 1 part). Fired to 1940°F (1060°C) in an electric kiln. Diameter 15 in (38 cm).

Greens and Turquoises
OXIDIZED

DESCRIPTION
Matte to dry mottled/speckled green over green on white earthenware clay.

USES
Decorative and sculptural.

FIRING RANGE
1940°F (1060°C)

PARTS DRY WEIGHT
Lead Bisilicate	50
Feldspar	30
Tin Oxide	10
China Clay	6
Whiting	4
+ Chromium Oxide sprayed	

DESCRIPTION
Dry/matte "mid green," paler where thinly applied on white earthenware clay.

USES
Decorative and sculptural.

FIRING RANGE
2012°F (1100°C)
Soak time—30 minutes

PARTS DRY WEIGHT
Lead Bisilicate	47
Potash Feldspar	25
China Clay	16
Whiting	12
+ Chromium Oxide	3

DESCRIPTION
Dry/matte pale green, darker where more thickly applied on white earthenware clay. Makes a good base for on-glaze colors.

USES
Decorative and sculptural.

FIRING RANGE
2012°F (1100°C)
Soak time—30 minutes

PARTS DRY WEIGHT
Lead Bisilicate	47
Potash Feldspar	25
China Clay	16
Whiting	12
+ Chromium Oxide	3
Rutile Oxide	1

DESCRIPTION
Matte mottled green blending
to a semi-gloss dark speckled
pale yellow/cream on white
earthenware clay.

USES
Decorative and sculptural.

FIRING RANGE
1940°F (1060°C)

PARTS DRY WEIGHT
Lead Bisilicate	53
Feldspar	27
Yellow Stain	10
China Clay	6
Whiting	4
+ Chromium Oxide sprayed	

DESCRIPTION
Mottled and speckled green on
semi gloss. Pale yellow/white
blending through to matte
green and dry metallic surface
on white earthenware clay.

USES
Decorative and sculptural.

FIRING RANGE
1940°F (1060°C)

PARTS DRY WEIGHT
Lead Bisilicate	53
Feldspar	27
Yellow Stain	10
China Clay	6
Whiting	4
+ Copper Carbonate sprayed	

DESCRIPTION
Glossy, mottled green on cream
blending to matte metallic at
base of tile on white
earthenware clay.

USES
Decorative and sculptural.

FIRING RANGE
1940°F (1060°C)

PARTS DRY WEIGHT
Lead Bisilicate	57
Feldspar	31
China Clay	7
Whiting	5
+ Copper Carbonate sprayed	

Greens and Turquoises
OXIDIZED

DESCRIPTION
Satin/matte dark green with
a hint of turquoise on white
earthenware clay. Paler on rims
and edges where glaze is
thinner.

USES
Decorative and sculptural.

FIRING RANGE
2012°F (1100°C)
Soak time — 30 minutes

PARTS DRY WEIGHT
Lead Bisilicate	47
Potash Feldspar	25
China Clay	16
Whiting	12
+ Copper Oxide	2
Cobalt Carbonate	0.5

DESCRIPTION
Dry textured blue blending
to mottled green then gray
metallic, on white
earthenware clay.

USES
Decorative and sculptural.

FIRING RANGE
1940°F (1060°C)

PARTS DRY WEIGHT
Lead Bisilicate	53
Feldspar	27
Blue Stain	10
China Clay	6
Whiting	4
+ Copper Carbonate sprayed	

DESCRIPTION
Dry pale blue speckled with
green and blending through to
solid green on white
earthenware clay.

USES
Decorative and sculptural.

FIRING RANGE
1940°F (1060°C)

PARTS DRY WEIGHT
Lead Bisilicate	53
Feldspar	27
Blue Stain	10
China Clay	6
Whiting	4
+ Chromium Oxide sprayed	

DESCRIPTION
Satin/gloss lilac with speckled green blending to mottled dark green on white earthenware clay.

USES
Decorative and sculptural.

FIRING RANGE
1940°F (1060°C)

PARTS DRY WEIGHT

Lead Bisilicate	55
Feldspar	25
Lilac Stain	10
China Clay	5
Whiting	5
+ Chromium Oxide sprayed	

DESCRIPTION
Satin/gloss lime green with dark speckle (and one stray splodge of dry metallic) blending to mottled then dry gray metallic on white earthenware clay.

USES
Decorative and sculptural.

FIRING RANGE
1940°F (1060°C)

PARTS DRY WEIGHT

Lead Bisilicate	55
Feldspar	25
Lime Green Stain	10
China Clay	5
Whiting	5
+ Copper Carbonate sprayed	

DESCRIPTION
Matte to dry mottled and speckled green on lilac on red terra cotta clay.

USES
Decorative and sculptural.

FIRING RANGE
1940°F (1060°C)

PARTS DRY WEIGHT

Lead Bisilicate	50
Feldspar	30
China Clay	6
Whiting	4
Tin Oxide	10
+ Chromium Oxide sprayed	

Greens and Turquoises
OXIDIZED

DESCRIPTION
Satin/matte gray/green, darker
where more thickly applied on
white earthenware clay.

USES
Mainly sculptural.

FIRING RANGE
2012°F (1100°C)

PARTS DRY WEIGHT
Lead Bisilicate	60
Cornish Stone	30
China Clay	5
Whiting	5
+ Rutile Oxide	3
Manganese Dioxide	1
Cobalt Carbonate	0.5

DESCRIPTION
Matte lime green with dark
speckle blending to dry green
on red terra cotta clay.

USES
Decorative and sculptural.

FIRING RANGE
1940°F (1060°C)

PARTS DRY WEIGHT
Lead Bisilicate	55
Feldspar	25
Lime Green Stain	10
China Clay	5
Whiting	5
+ Chromium Oxide sprayed	

DESCRIPTION
Matte dark green blending to
speckled green on lilac surface
on red terra cotta clay.

USES
Decorative and sculptural.

FIRING RANGE
1940°F (1060°C)

PARTS DRY WEIGHT
Lead Bisilicate	53
Feldspar	27
Yellow Stain	10
China Clay	6
Whiting	4
+ Chromium Oxide sprayed	

DESCRIPTION
Lime green with dark speckling and semi-matte, blending to dark brown/black and dry metallic on red terra cotta clay.

USES
Decorative and sculptural.

FIRING RANGE
1940°F (1060°C)

PARTS DRY WEIGHT

Lead Bisilicate	53
Feldspar	27
Lime Green Stain	10
China Clay	6
Whiting	4
+ Manganese Dioxide sprayed	

DESCRIPTION
Satin/matte mottled honey blending to matte green surface on red terra cotta clay.

USES
Decorative and sculptural.

FIRING RANGE
1940°F (1060°C)

PARTS DRY WEIGHT

Lead Bisilicate	57
Feldspar	31
China Clay	7
Whiting	5
+ Chromium Oxide sprayed	

FENELLA MALLALIEU I TURQUOISE BOWL

A stunning contrast has been achieved on this thrown bowl with earthenware glaze. The orange areas were masked with wax before the piece was dipped in turquoise glaze and then fired to 1940°F (1060°C).

Greens and Turquoises
OXIDIZED

DESCRIPTION
Matte gray metallic blending to lime green with dark speckle on red terra cotta clay.

USES
Decorative and sculptural.

FIRING RANGE
1940°F (1060°C)

PARTS DRY WEIGHT
Lead Bisilicate	55
Feldspar	25
Lime Green Stain	10
China Clay	5
Whiting	5
+ Copper Carbonate sprayed	

DESCRIPTION
Dry blue/green textured surface blending to green toward edge on red terra cotta clay.

USES
Decorative and sculptural.

FIRING RANGE
1940°F (1060°C)

PARTS DRY WEIGHT
Lead Bisilicate	53
Feldspar	27
Blue Stain	10
China Clay	6
Whiting	4
+ Chromium Oxide sprayed	

DESCRIPTION
Semi-gloss lilac with speckled green blending to mottled then matte green near edge of tile on red terra cotta clay.

USES
Decorative and sculptural.

FIRING RANGE
1940°F (1060°C)

PARTS DRY WEIGHT
Lead Bisilicate	55
Feldspar	25
Lilac Stain	10
China Clay	5
Whiting	5
+ Chromium Oxide sprayed	

DESCRIPTION
Satin/matte lime green with
dark blue speckling, blending
to darker blue then dry black
on white earthenware clay.

USES
Decorative and sculptural.

FIRING RANGE
1940°F (1060°C)

PARTS DRY WEIGHT
Lead Bisilicate	60
Feldspar	20
Lime Green Stain	10
China Clay	6
Whiting	4
+ Cobalt Carbonate sprayed	

DESCRIPTION
Matte black with speckled
green, blending to dry green
(where chromium oxide is
thickest on lower edge of tile)
on white earthenware clay.

USES
Decorative and sculptural.

FIRING RANGE
1940°F (1060°C)

PARTS DRY WEIGHT
Lead Bisilicate	53
Feldspar	27
Black Stain	10
China Clay	6
Whiting	4
+ Chromium Oxide sprayed	

DESCRIPTION
Dry black blending to
satin/matte dark blue then
to lime green speckled blue
on lower edge of red terra
cotta tile.

USES
Decorative and sculptural.

FIRING RANGE
1940°F (1060°C)

PARTS DRY WEIGHT
Lead Bisilicate	60
Feldspar	20
Lime Green Stain	10
China Clay	6
Whiting	4
+ Cobalt Carbonate sprayed	

Greens and Turquoises
OXIDIZED

DESCRIPTION
A smooth matte green, with warm red terra cotta clay body breaking through.

USES
Decorative and sculptural.

FIRING RANGE
1976°F (1080°C)
Soak time—30 minutes

PARTS DRY WEIGHT

Lead Bisilicate	47
Potash Feldspar	25
China Clay	16
Whiting	12
+ Chromium Oxide	3

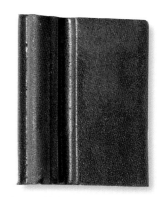

DESCRIPTION
Dry/matte dark green on red terra cotta clay which shows through on thinner glazed areas.

USES
Mainly sculptural.

FIRING RANGE
1976°F (1080°C)
Soak time—30 minutes

PARTS DRY WEIGHT

Lead Bisilicate	47
Potash Feldspar	25
China Clay	16
Whiting	12
+ Chromium Oxide	3
Rutile Oxide	1

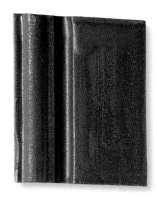

DESCRIPTION
Satin/ matte dark green/turquoise with red terra cotta colored clay breaking through on rims and edges.

USES
Decorative and sculptural.

FIRING RANGE
1976°F (1080°C)
Soak time—30 minutes

PARTS DRY WEIGHT

Lead Bisilicate	47
Potash Feldspar	25
China Clay	16
Whiting	12
+ Copper Oxide	2
Cobalt Carbonate	0.5

DESCRIPTION
A metallic glossy surface, green where glaze is thinner on white earthenware clay.

USES
Mainly decorative.

FIRING RANGE
2012°F (1100°C)

PARTS DRY WEIGHT
Lead Bisilicate	62
Cornish Stone	30
China Clay	3
Whiting	5
+ Copper Oxide	2
Cobalt Oxide	0.5

DESCRIPTION
Satin/matte black, blending to matte dark green on red terra cotta clay.

USES
Decorative and sculptural.

FIRING RANGE
1940°F (1060°C)

PARTS DRY WEIGHT
Lead Bisilicate	53
Feldspar	27
Black Stain	10
China Clay	6
Whiting	4
+ Chromium Oxide sprayed	

DESCRIPTION
Satin/gloss lilac/mottled green blending to silver/gray metallic on red terra cotta clay.

USES
Decorative and sculptural.

FIRING RANGE
1940°F (1060°C)

PARTS DRY WEIGHT
Lead Bisilicate	55
Feldspar	25
Lilac Stain	10
China Clay	5
Whiting	5
+ Copper Carbonate sprayed	

Black, White, and Metallic
OXIDIZED

DESCRIPTION
Matte vellum white/cream on white earthenware clay.

USES
For decorative and sculptural work. A good base for on-glaze colors.

FIRING RANGE
2012°F (1100°C)
Soak time—30 minutes

PARTS DRY WEIGHT
Lead Bisilicate	47
Potash Feldspar	25
China Clay	16
Whiting	12

DESCRIPTION
Glossy transparent white on white earthenware clay. Good general purpose earthenware glaze for use with colored slips, over- and underglaze stains and colors.

USES
Domestic and decorative.

FIRING RANGE
2012°F (1100°C)

PARTS DRY WEIGHT
Lead Bisilicate	62
Cornish Stone	30
Whiting	5
China Clay	3

DESCRIPTION
Satin/gloss white with speckled texture on surface on white earthenware clay. To avoid speckling on surface, materials should be resieved through a 120 sieve.

USES
Decorative and sculptural.

FIRING RANGE
1940°F (1060°C)

PARTS DRY WEIGHT
Lead Bisilicate	53
Feldspar	27
Tin Oxide	10
China Clay	6
Whiting	4

DESCRIPTION
A smooth glossy white, excellent covering, with just a hint of red terra cotta speckle, and edges and rims effectively showing through.

USES
Domestic and decorative.

FIRING RANGE
2012°F (1100°C)

PARTS DRY WEIGHT

Lead Bisilicate	60
Calcium Borate Frit	10
China Clay	10
Tin Oxide	10
Flint	5
Zirconium Silicate	5

DESCRIPTION
A speckled white on warm red terra cotta clay.

USES
Decorative and sculptural.

FIRING RANGE
1940°F (1060°C)

PARTS DRY WEIGHT

Lead Bisilicate	53
Feldspar	27
Tin Oxide	10
China Clay	6
Whiting	4

FENELLA MALLALIEU | THROWN BOWL

This bowl was dipped in glaze and then the rim was wiped clean and a contrasting color applied with a brush. It was fired to 1940°F (1060°C). The white glaze was as follows: Lead Sesquisilicate 74, China Clay 17, Flint 5, Whiting 4.

Black, White, and Metallic

OXIDIZED

DESCRIPTION
Satin/matte metallic blending
to green where thinly applied
on white earthenware clay.

USES
Mainly sculptural.

FIRING RANGE
2012°F (1100°C)

PARTS DRY WEIGHT
Lead Bisilicate	62
Cornish Stone	30
Whiting	5
China Clay	3
+ Copper Carbonate	3
Cobalt Carbonate	1

DESCRIPTION
Matte black to dry metallic
green at edges on red terra
cotta clay.

USES
Decorative and sculptural.

FIRING RANGE
1940°F (1060°C)

PARTS DRY WEIGHT
Lead Bisilicate	53
Feldspar	27
Yellow Stain	10
China Clay	6
Whiting	4
+ Copper Carbonate sprayed	

DESCRIPTION
Satin/matte black on red
terra cotta clay.

USES
Decorative and sculptural.

FIRING RANGE
1940°F (1060°C)

PARTS DRY WEIGHT
Lead Bisilicate	53
Feldspar	27
Black Stain	10
China Clay	6
Whiting	4
+ Manganese Dioxide sprayed	

DESCRIPTION

A smooth, satin black metallic on red terra cotta clay.

USES

Mainly sculptural.

FIRING RANGE

1976°F (1080°C)

PARTS DRY WEIGHT

Lead Bisilicate	58
Cornish Stone	30
China Clay	6
Whiting	6
+ Copper Oxide	2
Rutile Oxide	1
Cobalt Oxide	1

DESCRIPTION

Matte gray metallic, green where glaze is thinly applied on white earthenware clay.

USES

Mainly sculptural.

FIRING RANGE

2012°F (1100°C)

PARTS DRY WEIGHT

Lead Bisilicate	60
Cornish Stone	30
China Clay	5
Whiting	5
+ Chromium Oxide	1
Copper Oxide	1

DESCRIPTION

Satin/matte metallic, and glossy brown where glaze has been thinly applied on red terra cotta clay.

USES

Sculptural.

FIRING RANGE

1976°F (1080°C)

PARTS DRY WEIGHT

Lead Bisilicate	60
Cornish Stone	30
China Clay	5
Whiting	5
+ Chromium Oxide	1
Copper Oxide	1

Black, White, and Metallic
OXIDIZED

DESCRIPTION
A satin/gloss metallic and green on white earthenware clay.

USES
Decorative and sculptural.

FIRING RANGE
2012°F (1100°C)

PARTS DRY WEIGHT
Lead Bisilicate	58
Cornish Stone	30
China Clay	6
Whiting	6
+ Copper Oxide	2
Cobalt Oxide	1

DESCRIPTION
Satin, smooth dense metallic, hint of green on white earthenware clay.

USES
Mainly sculptural.

FIRING RANGE
2012°F (1100°C)

PARTS DRY WEIGHT
Lead Bisilicate	62
Cornish Stone	30
Whiting	5
China Clay	3
+ Rutile Oxide	3
Copper Carbonate	3

DESCRIPTION
Satin/gloss metallic, with hint of green on red terra cotta clay.

USES
Decorative and sculptural.

FIRING RANGE
1976°F (1080°C)

PARTS DRY WEIGHT
Lead Bisilicate	58
Cornish Stone	30
China Clay	6
Whiting	6
+ Copper Oxide	2
Cobalt Oxide	1

DESCRIPTION
Semi-gloss gray with dark
speckle blending to black where
more thickly applied on white
earthenware clay.

USES
Mainly decorative.

FIRING RANGE
2012°F (1100°C)

PARTS DRY WEIGHT
Lead Bisilicate	62
Cornish Stone	30
Whiting	5
China Clay	3
+ Manganese Dioxide	4
Cobalt Carbonate	0.5

DESCRIPTION
A satin/matte dark red/brown
blending to a dark speckled
lilac on red terra cotta clay.

USES
Decorative and sculptural.

FIRING RANGE
1940°F (1060°C)

PARTS DRY WEIGHT
Lead Bisilicate	53
Feldspar	27
Tin Oxide	10
China Clay	6
Whiting	4
+ Manganese Dioxide sprayed	

DESCRIPTION
Semi-gloss speckled lilac
blending to black/metallic on
red terra cotta clay.

USES
Decorative and sculptural.

FIRING RANGE
1940°F (1060°C)

PARTS DRY WEIGHT
Lead Bisilicate	53
Feldspar	27
Lilac Stain	10
China Clay	6
Whiting	4
+ Manganese Dioxide sprayed	

Black, White, and Metallic
OXIDIZED

DESCRIPTION
Satin/gloss black blending to
dry metallic toward lower edge
where manganese is thickest on
white earthenware clay.

USES
Decorative and sculptural.

FIRING RANGE
1940°F (1060°C)

PARTS DRY WEIGHT
Lead Bisilicate	53
Feldspar	27
Black Stain	10
China Clay	6
Whiting	4
+ Manganese Dioxide sprayed	

DESCRIPTION
Satin/matte black blending to
dry metallic on edge where
cobalt is thicker on red
terra cotta clay.

USES
Decorative and sculptural.

FIRING RANGE
1940°F (1060°C)

PARTS DRY WEIGHT
Lead Bisilicate	53
Feldspar	27
Black Stain	10
China Clay	6
Whiting	4
+ Cobalt Carbonate sprayed	

DESCRIPTION
Semi-gloss dark blue on lilac
blending to dark blue dry
metallic surface on red
terra cotta clay.

USES
Decorative and sculptural.

FIRING RANGE
1940°F (1060°C)

PARTS DRY WEIGHT
Lead Bisilicate	50
Feldspar	20
China Clay	10
Whiting	10
Yellow Stain	10
+ Cobalt Carbonate sprayed	

DESCRIPTION
Satin/matte black on red
terra cotta clay.

USES
Decorative and sculptural.

FIRING RANGE
1940°F (1060°C)

PARTS DRY WEIGHT
Lead Bisilicate	53
Feldspar	27
Black Stain	10
China Clay	6
Whiting	4

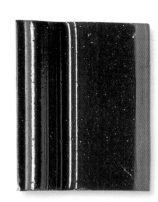

DESCRIPTION
Satin/matte black on red
terra cotta clay. (Slight "dry
mottling" from red iron
sprayed over.)

USES
Decorative and sculptural.

FIRING RANGE
1940°F (1060°C)

PARTS DRY WEIGHT
Lead Bisilicate	53
Feldspar	27
Black Stain	10
China Clay	6
Whiting	4
+ Red Iron Oxide sprayed	

DAVID JONES I VASE
David Jones raku-fires his pots with varied degrees of post-firing
reduction. The piece illustrated shows his use of resists (masking
tape) and sprayed glazes. He uses a base glaze of: Alkaline Frit
85, China Clay 10, Bentonite 5, with the following additions:
White = + Tin Oxide 7. Turquoise = + Copper Carbonate 1 and
Tin Oxide 0.5. Silver = + Silver Nitrate 1. Blue = + Cobalt
Oxide 2.5. Purple= + Gold Chloride 0.25.
Height 12 in (30 cm).

Black, White, and Metallic
OXIDIZED

DESCRIPTION
Semi-gloss dark brown
blending to black/metallic
where more thickly applied on
red terra cotta clay.

USES
Mainly decorative.

FIRING RANGE
1976°F (1080°C)

PARTS DRY WEIGHT
Lead Bisilicate	62
Cornish Stone	30
Whiting	5
China Clay	3
+ Manganese Dioxide	4
Cobalt Carbonate	1
Rutile Oxide	1

DESCRIPTION
Gloss, dark brown/black
blending to brown where thinly
applied on white earthenware
clay.

USES
Mainly decorative.

FIRING RANGE
2012°F (1100°C)

PARTS DRY WEIGHT
Lead Bisilicate	62
Cornish Stone	30
Whiting	5
China Clay	3
+ Manganese Dioxide	4
Cobalt Carbonate	1
Rutile Oxide	1

DESCRIPTION
A glossy dark brown/black on
red terra cotta clay.

USES
Domestic and decorative.

FIRING RANGE
1976°F (1080°C)

PARTS DRY WEIGHT
Lead Bisilicate	62
Cornish Stone	30
Whiting	5
China Clay	3
+ Rutile Oxide	3
Cobalt Oxide	2

DESCRIPTION
A glossy dark brown on red terra cotta clay (iron speckle still in evidence).

USES
Domestic and decorative.

FIRING RANGE
1976°F (1080°C)

PARTS DRY WEIGHT

Lead Bisilicate	60
Cornish Stone	30
China Clay	5
Whiting	5
+ Cobalt Carbonate	2
Red Iron Oxide	1

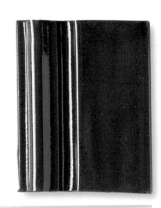

DESCRIPTION
A rich, dark honey brown on red terra cotta clay.

USES
Mainly decorative.

FIRING RANGE
1976°F (1080°C)

PARTS DRY WEIGHT

Lead Bisilicate	62
Cornish Stone	30
Whiting	5
China Clay	3
+ Manganese Dioxide	4
Cobalt Carbonate	0.5

DESCRIPTION
A glossy black/metallic on red terra cotta clay.

USES
Mainly decorative.

FIRING RANGE
1976°F (1080°C)

PARTS DRY WEIGHT

Lead Bisilicate	62
Cornish Stone	30
Whiting	5
China Clay	3
+ Copper Oxide	2
Cobalt Oxide	0.5

MAJOLICA

Majolica is the Italian name for decorated tin-glazed earthenware pottery that has a long and varied tradition both in Europe and further afield. The method offers potters the opportunity to decorate their wares by painting directly onto the pot in almost the same way as an artist will paint on paper. The following is a description of potter Rob Bibby's technique for majolica.

METHOD

Pots are biscuit fired to 1832°F (1000°C), then glazed with a white tin glaze, which is usually left for about half a day to dry.

White Glaze Recipe

Lead Bisilicate	60
Calcium Borate Frit	10
China Clay	10
Tin Oxide	10
Flint	5
Zirconium Silicate	5

The color is sponged or brushed over the glaze, which provides an absorbent white surface on which to paint. A flat, wide brush is usually used, and the color variation is achieved by dipping the brush into more than one color at a time. **The order of the glaze stains listed in the recipes is the order in which the brush is dipped into the colors.** The color variation is effected according to how much color is taken up by the brush. The colors used are glaze stains that are purchased in powder form. To help the color blend with the white glaze, the glaze stain is mixed with clear glaze.

For convenience this mix is by volume: powdered glaze stain (1 part) to liquid clear glaze (3 parts). This mixture is then diluted with water to a working consistency.

Clear Glaze Recipe

Lead Bisilicate	68
Calcium Borate Frit	12
China Clay	12
Flint	8

The tiles on the following pages have two brush marks: The top one is the mixture of clear glaze with the glaze stain and/or oxide listed in the recipe. The corner of the brush has also been dipped in a mixture of Crocus Martis and Cobalt Carbonate. The lower brush mark is just the mixture of clear glaze with the listed stain/oxide.

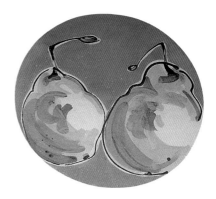

WYNNE WILBUR | MAJOLICA DISH

Majolica on terra cotta. Lines were trailed with a majolica glaze and then color was brushed on using majolica stain and commercial colors.

Majolica Naturals and Browns

OXIDIZED

DESCRIPTION
Top: Pale blue, yellow/pink with slight blue speckling.
Bottom: Brown blending into white/cream.

USES
Domestic and decorative.

FIRING RANGE
2012°F (1100°C)

PARTS DRY WEIGHT
Base: White Glaze (p.82) on white earthenware clay

Top: Clear Glaze (p.82)
+ Iron Oxide
+ Manganese Dioxide
+ brush dipped into a mixture
　 of Crocus Martis and Cobalt
　 Carbonate
Bottom: As top, without Crocus Martis and Cobalt Carbonate

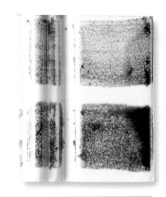

DESCRIPTION
Top: Brown and blue speckled surface.
Bottom: As above with less blue, more brown.

USES
Domestic and decorative.

FIRING RANGE
2012°F (1100°C)

PARTS DRY WEIGHT
Base: White Glaze (p.82) on red earthenware clay

Top: Clear Glaze (p.82)
+ Iron Oxide
+ Orange Brown Glaze Stain
+ brush dipped into a mixture
　 of Crocus Martis and Cobalt
　 Carbonate
Bottom: As top, without Crocus Martis and Cobalt Carbonate

DESCRIPTION
Top: Yellow/green blending with brown/beige.
Bottom: Yellow/brown/blue blend.

USES
Domestic and decorative.

FIRING RANGE
2012°F (1100°C)

PARTS DRY WEIGHT
Base: White Glaze (p.82) on white earthenware clay

Top: Clear Glaze (p.82)
+ Iron Oxide
+ Yellow Glaze Stain
+ Manganese Dioxide
+ brush dipped into a mixture
　 of Crocus Martis and Cobalt
　 Carbonate
Bottom: As top, without Crocus Martis and Cobalt Carbonate

Majolica Naturals and Browns

OXIDIZED

DESCRIPTION
Top: Orange/brown blending with dark blue/black.
Bottom: Orange/brown with white and slight blue speckling.

USES
Domestic and decorative.

FIRING RANGE
2012°F (1100°C)

PARTS DRY WEIGHT
Base: White Glaze (p.82) on white earthenware clay

Top: Clear Glaze (p.82)
+ Iron Oxide
+ Orange Brown Glaze Stain
+ brush dipped into a mixture of Crocus Martis and Cobalt Carbonate

Bottom: As top, without Crocus Martis and Cobalt Carbonate

DESCRIPTION
Top: Green/brown blending with blue/yellow.
Bottom: Pale yellow blending with orange/brown.

USES
Domestic and decorative.

FIRING RANGE
2012°F (1100°C)

PARTS DRY WEIGHT
Base: White Glaze (p.82) on red earthenware clay

Top: Clear Glaze (p.82)
+ Iron Oxide
+ Orange Brown Glaze Stain
+ Yellow Glaze Stain
+ brush dipped into a mixture of Crocus Martis and Cobalt Carbonate

Bottom: As top, without Crocus Martis and Cobalt Carbonate

DESCRIPTION
Top: Pale blue blending to purple/brown.
Bottom: Pale blue with yellow/brown tint.

USES
Domestic and decorative.

FIRING RANGE
2012°F (1100°C)

PARTS DRY WEIGHT
Base: White Glaze (p.82) on red earthenware clay

Top: Clear Glaze (p.82)
+ Iron Oxide
+ brush dipped into a mixture of Crocus Martis and Cobalt Carbonate

Bottom: As top, without Crocus Martis and Cobalt Carbonate

DESCRIPTION
Top: Pale mustard yellow to dark purple/brown blend.
Bottom: Mainly dark brown with mustard yellow on edges, both with evidence of white underglaze showing.

USES
Domestic and decorative.

FIRING RANGE
2012°F (1100°C)

PARTS DRY WEIGHT
Base: White Glaze (p.82) on white earthenware clay

Top: Clear Glaze (p.82)
+ Iron Oxide
+ Crocus Martis
+ brush dipped into a mixture of Crocus Martis and Cobalt Carbonate

Bottom: As top, without additional Crocus Martis and Cobalt Carbonate

DESCRIPTION
Top: Dark brown/black with hints of speckled white just showing through.
Bottom: As above but with more white showing through.

USES
Domestic and decorative.

FIRING RANGE
2012°F (1100°C)

PARTS DRY WEIGHT
Base: White Glaze (p.82) on red earthenware clay

Top: Clear Glaze (p.82)
+ Iron Oxide
+ Crocus Martis
+ brush dipped into a mixture of Crocus Martis and Cobalt Carbonate

Bottom: As top, without additional Crocus Martis and Cobalt Carbonate

DESCRIPTION
Top: Dark purple/brown blending with pale blue.
Bottom: Brown/beige blending with white/cream.

USES
Domestic and decorative.

FIRING RANGE
2012°F (1100°C)

PARTS DRY WEIGHT
Base: White Glaze (p.82) on red earthenware clay

Top: Clear Glaze (p.82)
+ Iron Oxide
+ Manganese Dioxide
+ brush dipped into a mixture of Crocus Martis and Cobalt Carbonate

Bottom: As top, without Crocus Martis and Cobalt Carbonate

Majolica Yellows and Oranges
OXIDIZED

DESCRIPTION
Top: A yellow/green and blue blend with brown/metallic brush mark.
Bottom: As above but more yellow/green with a blue speckle.

USES
Domestic and decorative.

FIRING RANGE
2012°F (1100°C)

PARTS DRY WEIGHT
Base: White Glaze (p.82) on white earthenware clay

Top: Clear Glaze (p.82)
+ Iron Oxide
+ Yellow Glaze Stain
+ brush dipped into a mixture of Crocus Martis and Cobalt Carbonate

Bottom: As top, without Crocus Martis and Cobalt Carbonate

DESCRIPTION
Top: Yellow/green blending with blue/brown.
Bottom: Green/yellow with slight blue speckle.

USES
Domestic and decorative.

FIRING RANGE
2012°F (1100°C)

PARTS DRY WEIGHT
Base: White Glaze (p.82) on white earthenware clay

Top: Clear Glaze (p.82)
+ Yellow Glaze Stain
+ brush dipped into a mixture of Crocus Martis and Cobalt Carbonate

Bottom: As top, without Crocus Martis and Cobalt Carbonate

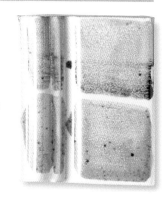

DESCRIPTION
Top: Pale yellow blending with dark brown/metallic.
Bottom: Pale yellow with slight blue speckling.

USES
Domestic and decorative.

FIRING RANGE
2012°F (1100°C)

PARTS DRY WEIGHT
Base: White Glaze (p.82) on red earthenware clay

Top: Clear Glaze (p.82)
+ Yellow Glaze Stain
+ brush dipped into a mixture of Crocus Martis and Cobalt Carbonate

Bottom: As top, without Crocus Martis and Cobalt Carbonate

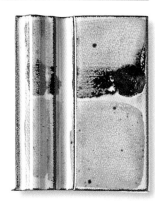

DESCRIPTION
Top: Brown/pale blue blending.
Bottom: Yellow/green with brown speckling.

USES
Domestic and decorative.

FIRING RANGE
2012°F (1100°C)

PARTS DRY WEIGHT
Base: White Glaze (p.82) on red earthenware clay

Top: Clear Glaze (p.82)
+ Iron Oxide
+ Yellow Glaze Stain
+ brush dipped into a mixture of Crocus Martis and Cobalt Carbonate

Bottom: As top, without Crocus Martis and Cobalt Carbonate

DESCRIPTION
Top: Yellow/green blending with blue/brown.
Bottom: Yellow/green/brown blend.

USES
Domestic and decorative.

FIRING RANGE
2012°F (1100°C)

PARTS DRY WEIGHT
Base: White Glaze (p.82) on red earthenware clay

Top: Clear Glaze (p.82)
+ Yellow Glaze Stain
+ Iron Oxide
+ brush dipped into a mixture of Crocus Martis and Cobalt Carbonate

Bottom: As top, without Crocus Martis and Cobalt Carbonate

DESCRIPTION
Top: Yellow/blue blending with dark brown/metallic.
Bottom: Red/orange and yellow blend.

USES
Domestic and decorative.

FIRING RANGE
2012°F (1100°C)

PARTS DRY WEIGHT
Base: White Glaze (p.82) on white earthenware clay

Top: Clear Glaze (p.82)
+ Yellow Glaze Stain
+ Red Glaze stain
+ brush dipped into a mixture of Crocus Martis and Cobalt Carbonate

Bottom: As top, without Crocus Martis and Cobalt Carbonate

Majolica Reds and Purples

OXIDIZED

DESCRIPTION
Top: Pink/red/dark brown blend.
Bottom: Mainly red with some white speckling showing through.

USES
Domestic and decorative.

FIRING RANGE
2012°F (1100°C)

PARTS DRY WEIGHT
Base: White Glaze (p.82) on white earthenware clay

Top: Clear Glaze (p.82)
+ Red Glaze Stain
+ brush dipped into a mixture of Crocus Martis and Cobalt Carbonate

Bottom: As top, without Crocus Martis and Cobalt Carbonate

DESCRIPTION
Top: Pink/red/brown blend.
Bottom: Mainly red with some white speckle showing.

USES
Domestic and decorative.

FIRING RANGE
2012°F (1100°C)

PARTS DRY WEIGHT
Base: White Glaze (p.82) on red earthenware clay

Top: Clear Glaze (p.82)
+ Red Glaze Stain
+ brush dipped into a mixture of Crocus Martis and Cobalt Carbonate

Bottom: As top, without Crocus Martis and Cobalt Carbonate

DESCRIPTION
Top: Red with white speckle with blue tinge.
Bottom: Mainly red with some white speckle showing through.

USES
Domestic and decorative.

FIRING RANGE
2012°F (1100°C)

PARTS DRY WEIGHT
Base: White Glaze (p.82) on white earthenware clay

Top: Clear Glaze (p.82)
+ Red Glaze Stain
+ Cobalt Carbonate
+ brush dipped into a mixture of Crocus Martis and Cobalt Carbonate

Bottom: As top, without additional Crocus Martis and Cobalt Carbonate

DESCRIPTION
Top: Pink/red blending with white and brown.
Bottom: As above with less brown.

USES
Domestic and decorative.

FIRING RANGE
2012°F (1100°C)

PARTS DRY WEIGHT
Base: White Glaze (p.82) on red earthenware clay

Top: Clear Glaze (p.82)
+ Iron Oxide
+ Red Glaze Stain
+ brush dipped into a mixture of Crocus Martis and Cobalt Carbonate

Bottom: As top, without Crocus Martis and Cobalt Carbonate

DESCRIPTION
Top: Orange/yellow blending with dark brown.
Bottom: Red/yellow/orange blend.

USES
Domestic and decorative.

FIRING RANGE
2012°F (1100°C)

PARTS DRY WEIGHT
Base: White Glaze (p.82) on red earthenware clay

Top: Clear Glaze (p.82)
+ Yellow Glaze Stain
+ Red Glaze Stain
+ brush dipped into a mixture of Crocus Martis and Cobalt Carbonate

Bottom: As top, without Crocus Martis and Cobalt Carbonate

DESCRIPTION
Top: Red/brown/black with white speckling.
Bottom: Red/brown blend with some white speckling showing through.

USES
Domestic and decorative.

FIRING RANGE
2012°F (1100°C)

PARTS DRY WEIGHT
Base: White Glaze (p.82) on red earthenware clay

Top: Clear Glaze (p.82)
+ Red Glaze Stain
+ Iron Oxide
+ brush dipped into a mixture of Crocus Martis and Cobalt Carbonate

Bottom: As top, without Crocus Martis and Cobalt Carbonate

Majolica Reds and Purples

OXIDIZED

DESCRIPTION
Top: Red/blue and black with even white speckle.
Bottom: Red/pink and blue blend.

USES
Domestic and decorative.

FIRING RANGE
2012°F (1100°C)

PARTS DRY WEIGHT
Base: White Glaze (p.82) on white earthenware clay

Top: Clear Glaze (p.82)
+ Red Glaze Stain
+ Iron Oxide
+ Sky Blue Glaze Stain
+ brush dipped into a mixture of Crocus Martis and Cobalt Carbonate

Bottom: As top, without Crocus Martis and Cobalt Carbonate

DESCRIPTION
Top: Red/blue/black blend.
Bottom: Mainly red and blue with white speckling.

USES
Domestic and decorative.

FIRING RANGE
2012°F (1100°C)

PARTS DRY WEIGHT
Base: White Glaze (p.82) on white earthenware clay

Top: Clear Glaze (p.82)
+ Red Glaze Stain
+ Iron Oxide
+ Cobalt Carbonate
+ brush dipped into a mixture of Crocus Martis and Cobalt Carbonate

Bottom: As top, without additional Crocus Martis and Cobalt Carbonate

DESCRIPTION
Top: Red/pink blending to dark brown on edges.
Bottom: Red/pink/blue blend.

USES
Domestic and decorative.

FIRING RANGE
2012°F (1100°C)

PARTS DRY WEIGHT
Base: White Glaze (p.82) on red earthenware clay

Top: Clear Glaze (p.82)
+ Red Glaze Stain
+ Sky Blue Glaze Stain
+ brush dipped into a mixture of Crocus Martis and Cobalt Carbonate

Bottom: As top, without Crocus Martis and Cobalt Carbonate

DESCRIPTION

Top: Pink/red/blue and green blend.
Bottom: Pink/red and turquoise blend.

USES

Domestic and decorative.

FIRING RANGE

2012°F (1100°C)

PARTS DRY WEIGHT

Base: White Glaze (p.82) on red earthenware clay

Top: Clear Glaze (p.82)
+ Red Glaze Stain
+ Iron Oxide
+ Sky Blue Glaze Stain
+ brush dipped into a mixture of Crocus Martis and Cobalt Carbonate

Bottom: As top, without Crocus Martis and Cobalt Carbonate

DESCRIPTION

Top: Black/brown with white speckle.
Bottom: Mainly red with some white and blue speckling.

USES

Domestic and decorative.

FIRING RANGE

2012°F (1100°C)

PARTS DRY WEIGHT

Base: White Glaze (p.82) on red earthenware clay

Top: Clear Glaze (p.82)
+ Red Glaze Stain
+ Cobalt Carbonate
+ brush dipped into a mixture of Crocus Martis and Cobalt Carbonate

Bottom: As top, without additional Crocus Martis and Cobalt Carbonate

ROB BIBBY | BOWL

An example of Rob Bibby's very "painterly" approach. His working methods are detailed on page 82. He uses a majolica "in-glaze" painting over a base tin glaze. Fired to 2012°F (1100°C) in an electric kiln.
Diameter 9 in (23 cm).

Majolica Blues
OXIDIZED

DESCRIPTION
Top: Pale blue/white blend with hint of black/green.
Bottom: Slightly paler version of top.

USES
Domestic and decorative.

FIRING RANGE
2012°F (1100°C)

PARTS DRY WEIGHT
Base: White Glaze (p.82) on white earthenware

Top: Clear Glaze (p.82)
+ Black Glaze Stain
+ brush dipped into a mixture of Crocus Martis and Cobalt Carbonate

Bottom: As top, without Crocus Martis and Cobalt Carbonate

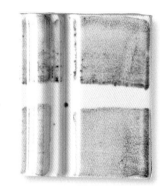

DESCRIPTION
Top: Pale blue with green speckle and brown/metallic brush mark.
Bottom: Pale blue with yellow/brown tint with more purple/brown.

USES
Domestic and decorative.

FIRING RANGE
2012°F (1100°C)

PARTS DRY WEIGHT
Base: White Glaze (p.82) on white earthenware

Top: Clear Glaze (p.82)
+ Iron Oxide
+ Orange Brown Glaze Stain
+ brush dipped into a mixture of Crocus Martis and Cobalt Carbonate

Bottom: As top, without Crocus Martis and Cobalt Carbonate

DESCRIPTION
Top: Pale blue to dark brown "shore line" blend.
Bottom: Pale blue/white speckled blend.

USES
Domestic and decorative.

FIRING RANGE
2012°F (1100°C)

PARTS DRY WEIGHT
Base: White Glaze (p.82) on red earthenware

Top: Clear Glaze (p.82)
+ Black Glaze Stain
+ brush dipped into a mixture of Crocus Martis and Cobalt Carbonate

Bottom: As top, without Crocus Martis and Cobalt Carbonate

DESCRIPTION

Top: Blue with white speckle blending to dark brown/black.
Bottom: Mainly blue with white even speckling.

USES

Domestic and decorative.

FIRING RANGE

2012°F (1100°C)

PARTS DRY WEIGHT

Base: White Glaze (p.82) on white earthenware

Top: Clear Glaze (p.82)
+ Sky Blue Glaze Stain
+ brush dipped into a mixture of Crocus Martis and Cobalt Carbonate

Bottom: As top, without Crocus Martis and Cobalt Carbonate

DESCRIPTION

Top: Pale blue blending to dark brown.
Bottom: Even blue with some white speckling.

USES

Domestic and decorative.

FIRING RANGE

2012°F (1100°C)

PARTS DRY WEIGHT

Base: White Glaze (p.82) on red earthenware

Top: Clear Glaze (p.82)
+ Sky Blue Glaze Stain
+ brush dipped into a mixture of Crocus Martis and Cobalt Carbonate

Bottom: As top, without Crocus Martis and Cobalt Carbonate

DESCRIPTION

Top: Pale blue with hint of green/brown.
Bottom: Stronger blue with hint of pink/red.

USES

Domestic and decorative.

FIRING RANGE

2012°F (1100°C)

PARTS DRY WEIGHT

Base: White Glaze (p.82) on white earthenware

Top: Clear Glaze (p.82)
+ Cobalt Glaze Stain
+ Red Glaze Stain
+ brush dipped into a mixture of Crocus Martis and Cobalt Carbonate

Bottom: As top, without Crocus Martis and Cobalt Carbonate

Majolica Blues
OXIDIZED

DESCRIPTION
Top: Green/blue to dark brown/black blend.
Bottom: Mainly green/blue blend.

USES
Domestic and decorative.

FIRING RANGE
2012°F (1100°C)

PARTS DRY WEIGHT
Base: White Glaze (p.82) on white earthenware

Top: Clear Glaze (p.82)
+ Green Glaze Stain
+ Cobalt Carbonate
+ brush dipped into a mixture of Crocus Martis and Cobalt Carbonate

Bottom: As top, without additional Crocus Martis and Cobalt Carbonate

DESCRIPTION
Top: Green/blue white speckled blend.
Bottom: Green/blue/turquoise blend.

USES
Domestic and decorative.

FIRING RANGE
2012°F (1100°C)

PARTS DRY WEIGHT
Base: White Glaze (p.82) on white earthenware

Top: Clear Glaze (p.82)
+ Sky Blue Glaze Stain
+ Green Glaze Stain
+ brush dipped into a mixture of Crocus Martis and Cobalt Carbonate

Bottom: As top, without Crocus Martis and Cobalt Carbonate

DESCRIPTION
Top: Even mid blue.
Bottom: Blue/turquoise blend.

USES
Domestic and decorative.

FIRING RANGE
2012°F (1100°C)

PARTS DRY WEIGHT
Base: White Glaze (p.82) on red earthenware

Top: Clear Glaze (p.82)
+ Sky Blue Glaze Stain
+ Cobalt Carbonate
+ brush dipped into a mixture of Crocus Martis and Cobalt Carbonate

Bottom: As top, without additional Crocus Martis and Cobalt Carbonate

DESCRIPTION
Top: Cobalt blue blending to black.
Bottom: Cobalt blue, darker where gathering thicker.

USES
Domestic and decorative.

FIRING RANGE
2012°F (1100°C)

PARTS DRY WEIGHT
Base: White Glaze (p.82) on white earthenware

Top: Clear Glaze (p.82)
+ Cobalt Carbonate
+ brush dipped into a mixture of Crocus Martis and Cobalt Carbonate

Bottom: As top, without additional Crocus Martis and Cobalt Carbonate

DESCRIPTION
Top: Even cobalt blue.
Bottom: As above.

USES
Domestic and decorative.

FIRING RANGE
2012°F (1100°C)

PARTS DRY WEIGHT
Base: White Glaze (p.82) on red earthenware

Top: Clear Glaze (p.82)
+ Cobalt Carbonate
+ brush dipped into a mixture of Crocus Martis and Cobalt Carbonate

Bottom: As top, without additional Crocus Martis and Cobalt Carbonate

DESCRIPTION
Top: Pale blue/turquoise to dark brown blend.
Bottom: Red/pink/blue blend.

USES
Domestic and decorative.

FIRING RANGE
2012°F (1100°C)

PARTS DRY WEIGHT
Base: White Glaze (p.82) on red earthenware

Top: Clear Glaze (p.82)
+ Sky Blue Glaze Stain
+ Red Glaze Stain
+ brush dipped into a mixture of Crocus Martis and Cobalt Carbonate

Bottom: As top, without Crocus Martis and Cobalt Carbonate

Majolica Greens and Turquoises

OXIDIZED

DESCRIPTION
Top: Blue/green blending with dark brown/metallic.
Bottom: Green/yellow with blue speckling.

USES
Domestic and decorative.

FIRING RANGE
2012°F (1100°C)

PARTS DRY WEIGHT
Base: White Glaze (p.82) on white earthenware

Top: Clear Glaze (p.82)
+ Yellow Glaze Stain
+ Orange Brown Glaze Stain
+ brush dipped into a mixture of Crocus Martis and Cobalt Carbonate

Bottom: As top, without Crocus Martis and Cobalt Carbonate

DESCRIPTION
Top: Yellow/blue blending with dark brown.
Bottom: Yellow/orange/green blend.

USES
Domestic and decorative.

FIRING RANGE
2012°F (1100°C)

PARTS DRY WEIGHT
Base: White Glaze (p.82) on white earthenware

Top: Clear Glaze (p.82)
+ Iron Oxide
+ Yellow Glaze Stain
+ brush dipped into a mixture of Crocus Martis and Cobalt Carbonate

Bottom: As top, without Crocus Martis and Cobalt Carbonate

DESCRIPTION
Top: Yellow/green mottled with pale blue to dark green blend.
Bottom: Green/yellow blend.

USES
Domestic and decorative.

FIRING RANGE
2012°F (1100°C)

PARTS DRY WEIGHT
Base: White Glaze (p.82) on white earthenware

Top: Clear Glaze (p.82)
+ Iron Oxide
+ Green Glaze Stain
+ Yellow Glaze Stain
+ brush dipped into a mixture of Crocus Martis and Cobalt Carbonate

Bottom: As top, without Crocus Martis and Cobalt Carbonate

DESCRIPTION
Top: Green/yellow to dark brown blend.
Bottom: Pale green/yellow blend.

USES
Domestic and decorative.

FIRING RANGE
2012°F (1100°C)

PARTS DRY WEIGHT
Base: White Glaze (p.82) on red earthenware

Top: Clear Glaze (p.82)
+ Iron Oxide
+ Green Glaze Stain
+ Yellow Glaze Stain
+ brush dipped into a mixture of Crocus Martis and Cobalt Carbonate

Bottom: As top, without Crocus Martis and Cobalt Carbonate

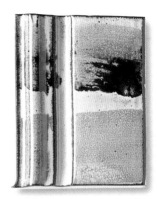

DESCRIPTION
Top: Green/pale blue to dark brown blend.
Bottom: Green with speckled to even pale blue blend.

USES
Domestic and decorative.

FIRING RANGE
2012°F (1100°C)

PARTS DRY WEIGHT
Base: White Glaze (p.82) on red earthenware

Top: Clear Glaze (p.82)
+ Iron Oxide
+ Green Glaze Stain
+ brush dipped into a mixture of Crocus Martis and Cobalt Carbonate

Bottom: As top, without Crocus Martis and Cobalt Carbonate

POSEY BACOPOULES I OVAL BOX
Lidded decorative piece with majolica glaze on terra cotta clay, thrown, altered, and assembled. Stain colors used include black, neutral, charcoal gray, blue, and copper green.
Size: 5 x 8 x 4 in (12 x 20 x 10 cm).

Majolica Greens and Turquoises

OXIDIZED

DESCRIPTION
Top: Green/pale blue to dark brown blend.
Bottom: Green/pale blue speckle blend.

USES
Domestic and decorative.

FIRING RANGE
2012°F (1100°C)

PARTS DRY WEIGHT
Base: White Glaze (p.82) on white earthenware

Top: Clear Glaze (p.82)
+ Iron Oxide
+ Green Glaze Stain
+ brush dipped into a mixture of Crocus Martis and Cobalt Carbonate

Bottom: As top, without Crocus Martis and Cobalt Carbonate

DESCRIPTION
Top: Green and blue with white speckling.
Bottom: Green and turquoise blue blend.

USES
Domestic and decorative.

FIRING RANGE
2012°F (1100°C)

PARTS DRY WEIGHT
Base: White Glaze (p.82) on white earthenware

Top: Clear Glaze (p.82)
+ Iron Oxide
+ Green Glaze Stain
+ Sky Blue Glaze Stain
+ brush dipped into a mixture of Crocus Martis and Cobalt Carbonate

Bottom: As top, without Crocus Martis and Cobalt Carbonate

DESCRIPTION
Top: Pale green with brushed dark brown blend.
Bottom: Pale green lightened by the white base glaze showing through.

USES
Domestic and decorative.

FIRING RANGE
2012°F (1100°C)

PARTS DRY WEIGHT
Base: White Glaze (p.82) on red earthenware

Top: Clear Glaze (p.82)
+ Iron Oxide
+ Green Glaze Stain
+ Sky Blue Glaze Stain
+ brush dipped into a mixture of Crocus Martis and Cobalt Carbonate

Bottom: As top, without Crocus Martis and Cobalt Carbonate

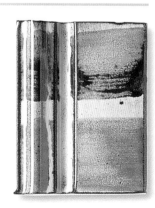

DESCRIPTION
Top: Copper green to dark metallic blend.
Bottom: As above.

USES
Domestic and decorative.

FIRING RANGE
2012°F (1100°C)

PARTS DRY WEIGHT
Base: White Glaze (p.82) on white earthenware

Top: Clear Glaze (p.82)
+ Iron Oxide
+ Copper Oxide
+ brush dipped into a mixture of Crocus Martis and Cobalt Carbonate

Bottom: As top, without Crocus Martis and Cobalt Carbonate

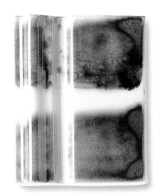

DESCRIPTION
Top: Dark brown with "sky" of green.
Bottom: Mainly green with a hint of turquoise.

USES
Domestic and decorative.

FIRING RANGE
2012°F (1100°C)

PARTS DRY WEIGHT
Base: White Glaze (p.82) on red earthenware

Top: Clear Glaze (p.82)
+ Iron Oxide
+ Dark Green Glaze Stain
+ brush dipped into a mixture of Crocus Martis and Cobalt Carbonate

Bottom: As top, without Crocus Martis and Cobalt Carbonate

DESCRIPTION
Top: Green/blue with dark brown on edges.
Bottom: Mainly blue with hint of green.

USES
Domestic and decorative.

FIRING RANGE
2012°F (1100°C)

PARTS DRY WEIGHT
Base: White Glaze (p.82) on red earthenware

Top: Clear Glaze (p.82)
+ Iron Oxide
+ Green Glaze Stain
+ Cobalt Carbonate
+ brush dipped into a mixture of Crocus Martis and Cobalt Carbonate

Bottom: As top, without Crocus Martis and Cobalt Carbonate

Majolica Black, White, and Metallic

OXIDIZED

DESCRIPTION
Top: Pale blue with brown/purple blending.
Bottom: Pale blue with yellow/brown tint.

USES
Domestic and decorative.

FIRING RANGE
2012°F (1100°C)

PARTS DRY WEIGHT
Base: White Glaze (p.82) on white earthenware

Top: Clear Glaze (p.82)
+ Iron Oxide
+ brush dipped into a mixture of Crocus Martis and Cobalt Carbonate

Bottom: As top, without Crocus Martis and Cobalt Carbonate

DESCRIPTION
Top: Gray/brown to black blend with speckled white showing through.
Bottom: Gray to black blend.

USES
Domestic and decorative.

FIRING RANGE
2012°F (1100°C)

PARTS DRY WEIGHT
Base: White Glaze (p.82) on white earthenware

Top: Clear Glaze (p.82)
+ Cobalt Carbonate
+ Iron Oxide
+ Manganese Dioxide
+ brush dipped into a mixture of Crocus Martis and Cobalt Carbonate

Bottom: As top, without Crocus Martis and Cobalt Carbonate

DESCRIPTION
Top: Mauve to dark brown/metallic "splodge" blend.
Bottom: Mauve and speckled white blend.

USES
Domestic and decorative.

FIRING RANGE
2012°F (1100°C)

PARTS DRY WEIGHT
Base: White Glaze (p.82) on white earthenware

Top: Clear Glaze (p.82)
+ Manganese Dioxide
+ brush dipped into a mixture of Crocus Martis and Cobalt Carbonate

Bottom: As top, without additional Crocus Martis and Cobalt Carbonate

DESCRIPTION
Top: Dark brown/black to pale blue/green blend.
Bottom: As above.

USES
Domestic and decorative.

FIRING RANGE
2012°F (1100°C)

PARTS DRY WEIGHT
Base: White Glaze (p.84) on white earthenware

Top: Clear Glaze (p.84)
+ Cobalt Carbonate
+ Crocus Martis
+ brush dipped into a mixture of Crocus Martis and Cobalt Carbonate

Bottom: As top, without additional Crocus Martis and Cobalt Carbonate

DESCRIPTION
Top: Mainly dark brown/black with hint of white base glaze showing through.
Bottom: Pale blue to speckled then dark brown on edges.

USES
Domestic and decorative.

FIRING RANGE
2012°F (1100°C)

PARTS DRY WEIGHT
Base: White Glaze (p.82) on red earthenware

Top: Clear Glaze (p.82)
+ Cobalt Carbonate
+ Crocus Martis
+ brush dipped into a mixture of Crocus Martis and Cobalt Carbonate

Bottom: As top, without additional Crocus Martis and Cobalt Carbonate

DESCRIPTION
Top: Mainly brown with some white base glaze in evidence.
Bottom: Same as above.

USES
Domestic and decorative.

FIRING RANGE
2012°F (1100°C)

PARTS DRY WEIGHT
Base: White Glaze (p.82) on red earthenware

Top: Clear Glaze (p.82)
+ Cobalt Carbonate
+ Iron Oxide
+ Manganese Dioxide
+ brush dipped into a mixture of Crocus Martis and Cobalt Carbonate

Bottom: As top, without additional Crocus Martis and Cobalt Carbonate

RAKU

Raku has its origins in the 16th-century tea ceremonies of Japan. The greatest of the tea masters was Seno-Rikyu (1522–91). He established the concept of "Wabi," which translates as "austerity" or "simplicity." Rikyu commissioned Chojiro to make raku ware, which he felt best represented the idea of "Wabi" and was most fitting for tea ceremony use. Since then, raku has evolved into the exciting practice currently being explored by many potters.

Clays that withstand the shock of rapid heating and cooling are best used for this process. These clays tend to have an open structure achieved by the addition of grog or sand, and remain porous after both the bisque and the glaze firings.

After biscuit firing at 1922°F (1050°C), the work is glazed (see page 20). Any glaze that will stay on a pot during the firing process is a raku glaze. The usual temperature range for raku is from 1472°F to 2012°F (800°C to 1100°C). The pots can be fired in a raku kiln, or ones adapted from old and recycled electric kilns, fiber-lined fridges, etc.

Once the required temperature is reached, or the glaze has melted and matured, the pots are removed from the kiln with tongs and placed into bins of combustible materials, such as sawdust and/or wood shavings. Large-scale work can be reduced inside the kiln,

STEPHEN MURFITT | TALL RAKU POT?
Glazes were brushed and sprayed before the pots were raku-fired to 1796°F (980°C), followed by a post-firing reduction in sawdust and wood shavings

by the introduction of combustible materials to the kiln chamber after the kiln has been "crash cooled" down to about 1292°F (700°C). This post-firing reduction creates a number of effects, including metallic lusters, crackle glazes, and smoked, carbonized and blackened surfaces.

N.B. The clay used for the illustrated tiles was Scarva Earthstone S40. They were all biscuit fired within the range 1832–1922°F (1000–1051°C) and glaze fired within the range of 1742–1796°F (940–980°C).

CAUTION
Raku kilns must be fired outdoors because smoke and gases are generated when placing the piece into the combustible materials for reduction.

Protective clothing must always be worn e.g. mask (for vapor), goggles (sparks, flames, heat etc.), stout shoes/boots and heat resistant gloves/gauntlets (see page 17).

DESCRIPTION
"Pin-holed" and speckled
matte white.

USES
Decorative and sculptural.

FIRING RANGE
1760-1814°F (960-990°C)
+ post-firing reduction—1 hour

PARTS DRY WEIGHT

Borax Frit	75
Ball Clay	10
Flint	10
Tin Oxide	4
Bentonite	1
+ Venadium Oxide	2

DESCRIPTION
Satin/matte, pink/white
surface.

USES
Decorative and sculptural.

FIRING RANGE
1742–1778°F (950–970°C)
+ post-firing reduction—1 hour

PARTS DRY WEIGHT

Borax Frit	75
Ball Clay	10
Flint	10
Tin Oxide	4
Bentonite	1
+ Manganese Oxide	1

DESCRIPTION
Satin, smooth white, and
slightly iridescent.

USES
Decorative and sculptural.

FIRING RANGE
1760–1796°F (960–980°C)
+ post-firing reduction—1 hour

PARTS DRY WEIGHT

Borax Frit	80
China Clay	10
Flint	5
Tin Oxide	4
Bentonite	1
+ Nickel Oxide	1

Raku
REDUCED

DESCRIPTION
Smooth gloss glaze, white crackle (small).

USES
Decorative and sculptural.

FIRING RANGE
1742–1796°F (950–980°C)
+ post-firing reduction—at least 1 hour

PARTS DRY WEIGHT
Alkaline Frit	68
Borax Frit	25
Tin Oxide	5
Bentonite	2

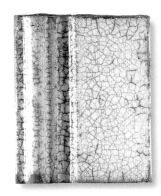

DESCRIPTION
Satin/matte, white with small crackle on surface.

USES
Decorative and sculptural.

FIRING RANGE
1760–1796°F (960–980°C)
+ post-firing reduction—1 hour

PARTS DRY WEIGHT
Alkaline Frit	65
Borax Frit	20
China Clay	10
Tin Oxide	4
Bentonite	1
+ Venadium Oxide	4

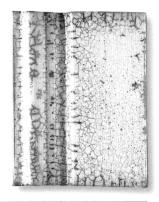

DESCRIPTION
Gloss, smooth white crackled surface.

USES
Decorative and sculptural.

FIRING RANGE
1742–1796°F (950–980°C)
+ post-firing reduction—1 hour

PARTS DRY WEIGHT
Alkaline Frit	90
China Clay	6
Tin Oxide	4
Bentonite	2

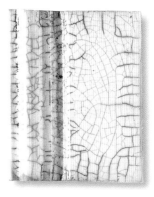

DESCRIPTION
Gloss surface, large white crackle.

USES
Decorative and sculptural.

FIRING RANGE
1742–1796°F (950–980°C) + post-firing reduction—at least 1 hour

PARTS DRY WEIGHT

Alkaline Frit	86
China Clay	8
Tin Oxide	4
Bentonite	2

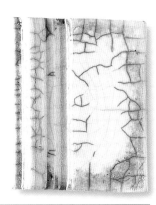

DESCRIPTION
Semi matte/satin, variegated white crackle.

USES
Decorative and sculptural.

FIRING RANGE
1778–1832°F (970–1000°C) + post-firing reduction—1 hour

PARTS DRY WEIGHT

Alkaline Frit	86
Ball Clay	6
Whiting	6
Bentonite	2
+ Uranium Substitute	1

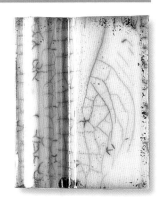

STEPHEN MURFITT I RAKU-FIRED CRACKLE POT

Hand built using a mixture of earthstone hand-building body and a standard white, stoneware clay. After a bisque firing of 1904°F (1040°C) in an electric kiln, a layer of an alkaline-frit base glaze was brushed on. A thin coat of the same glaze was then sprayed over the top of the form. A raku firing to 1742°F (950°C) was followed by two hours of post-firing reduction in a mixture of sawdust and wood shavings. (The larger the pot, the longer the period of reduction.) Diameter 18 in (45 cm).

Raku
REDUCED

DESCRIPTION
Satin, smooth, pale yellow, and slight crackle.

USES
Decorative and sculptural.

FIRING RANGE
1742–1778°F (950–970°C)
+ post-firing reduction—1 hour

PARTS DRY WEIGHT
Borax Frit	60
Alkaline Frit	25
Flint	10
Tin Oxide	4
Bentonite	1
+ Uranium Substitute	1

DESCRIPTION
Satin/gloss, pink/purple crackled surface.

USES
Decorative and sculptural.

FIRING RANGE
1760–1796°F (960–980°C)
+ post-firing reduction—1 hour

PARTS DRY WEIGHT
Alkaline Frit	68
Borax Frit	25
Tin Oxide	5
Bentonite	2
+ Manganese Oxide	3

DESCRIPTION
Satin/gloss, blue crackled surface.

USES
Decorative and sculptural.

FIRING RANGE
1742–1796°F (950–980°C)
+ post-firing reduction—1 hour

PARTS DRY WEIGHT
Alkaline Frit	90
China Clay	5
Tin Oxide	4
Bentonite	2
+ Cobalt Oxide	4

DESCRIPTION
Satin/gloss smooth, light blue, and lustered surface.

USES
Decorative and sculptural.

FIRING RANGE
1778–1814°F (970–990°C)
+ post-firing reduction—1 hour

PARTS DRY WEIGHT
Soft Borax Frit	75
Flint	10
Ball Clay	10
Tin Oxide	4
Bentonite	1
+ Copper Carbonate	4
Cobalt Oxide	2

DESCRIPTION
Gloss, blue/green, large crackled and slightly lustered surface.

USES
Decorative and sculptural.

FIRING RANGE
1742–1778°F (950–970°C)
+ post-firing reduction—1 hour

PARTS DRY WEIGHT
Alkaline Frit	80
Ball Clay	10
Flint	5
Tin Oxide	4
Bentonite	1
+ Copper Carbonate	4
Cobalt Oxide	1

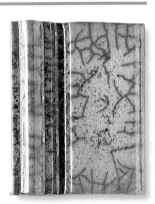

DESCRIPTION
Gloss, turquoise/green crackled surface.

USES
Decorative and sculptural.

FIRING RANGE
1742–1778°F (950–970°C)
+ post-firing reduction—1 hour

PARTS DRY WEIGHT
Alkaline Frit	90
China Clay	5
Tin Oxide	4
Bentonite	1
+ Black Copper Oxide	3

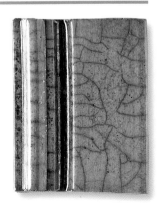

Raku
REDUCED

DESCRIPTION
Satin, smooth, light blue
iridescent surface.

USES
Decorative and sculptural.

FIRING RANGE
1742–1778°F (950–970°C)
+ post-firing reduction—1 hour

PARTS DRY WEIGHT

Borax Frit	80
Ball Clay	15
Tin Oxide	4
Bentonite	1
+ Cobalt Oxide	1

DESCRIPTION
Satin, smooth, light blue/gray,
and slight lustrous surface.

USES
Decorative and sculptural.

FIRING RANGE
1760–1796°F (960–980°C)
+ post-firing reduction—1 hour

PARTS DRY WEIGHT

Alkaline Frit	70
Borax Frit	20
Whiting	5
Tin Oxide	4
Bentonite	1
+ Red Copper Oxide	4
Nickel Oxide	3
Venadium Oxide	3

DESCRIPTION
Satin, smooth, slight turquoise
luster.

USES
Decorative and sculptural.

FIRING RANGE
1796–1832°F (980–1000°C)
+ post-firing reduction—1 hour

PARTS DRY WEIGHT

Borax Frit	70
Ball Clay	12
Flint	12
Tin Oxide	4
Bentonite	2
+ Cobalt Carbonate	3
Copper Carbonate	3

DESCRIPTION
Satin/gloss, green/turquoise
lustered surface.

USES
Decorative and sculptural.

FIRING RANGE
1742–1778°F (950–970°C)
+ post-firing reduction—1 hour

PARTS DRY WEIGHT

Borax Frit	80
Flint	10
China Clay	5
Tin Oxide	4
Bentonite	1
+ Copper Carbonate	5

DESCRIPTION
Satin, matte green/turquoise,
crackled and lustered surface.

USES
Decorative and sculptural.

FIRING RANGE
1742–1778°F (950–970°C)
+ post-firing reduction—1 hour

PARTS DRY WEIGHT

Alkaline Frit	75
China Clay	10
Flint	10
Tin Oxide	4
Bentonite	1
+ Copper Carbonate	6

DAVID JONES I RAKU FORM

Hand-built and raku-fired form. An
alkaline-frit base glaze was applied
with additions as detailed on page
79. Silver nitrate is used to give
a lustrous metallic surface.
Diameter 14 in (36 cm).

Raku
REDUCED

DESCRIPTION
Smooth satin, lustrous surface, variegated pinks/yellow.

USES
Decorative and sculptural.

FIRING RANGE
1742–1778°F (950–970°C)
+ post-firing reduction—1 hour

PARTS DRY WEIGHT
Borax Frit	75
Ball Clay	10
Flint	10
Tin Oxide	4
Bentonite	1
+ Venadium Oxide	4
Nickel Oxide	4
Manganese Oxide	4

DESCRIPTION
Satin pink, smooth, lustrous surface.

USES
Decorative and sculptural.

FIRING RANGE
1742–1796°F (950–980°C)
+ post-firing reduction—1 hour

PARTS DRY WEIGHT
Alkaline Frit	80
China Clay	7
Whiting	7
Tin Oxide	4
Bentonite	2
+ Copper Oxide	2
Black iron Oxide	2
Red Iron Oxide	2
Rutile Oxide	2
Manganese Oxide	2

DESCRIPTION
Smooth satin, lustrous green glaze.

USES
Decorative and sculptural.

FIRING RANGE
1760–1796°F (960–980°C)
+ post-firing reduction—1 hour

PARTS DRY WEIGHT
Soft Borax Frit	85
Flint	10
Tin Oxide	4
+ Copper Carbonate	5
Bentonite	1

DESCRIPTION
Dry, lustered, and iridescent.

USES
Decorative and sculptural.

FIRING RANGE
1796–1850°F (980–1010°C)
+ post-firing reduction—1 hour

PARTS DRY WEIGHT

Alkaline Frit	35
Borax Frit	35
Ball Clay	20
Flint	9
Bentonite	1
+ Black Copper Oxide	3
Venadium Oxide	3
Manganese Oxide	3
Uranium Substitute	3

DESCRIPTION
Matte slate gray with
pink/yellow tinge.

USES
Decorative and sculptural.

FIRING RANGE
1778–1814°F (970–990°C)
+ post-firing reduction—1 hour

PARTS DRY WEIGHT

Borax Frit	70
Whiting	9
Ball Clay	9
Bentonite	2
+ Manganese Oxide	2
Venadium Oxide	2
Black Iron Oxide	2
Red Iron Oxide	2

DESCRIPTION
Matte/dry dark metallic
surface.

USES
Decorative and sculptural.

FIRING RANGE
1778–1832°F (970–1000°C)
+ post-firing reduction—1 hour

PARTS DRY WEIGHT

Borax Frit	64
Ball Clay	12
Flint	12
Bentonite	2
+ Nickel Oxide	4
Venadium Oxide	2
Black Iron Oxide	2
Rutile Oxide	2

Raku
REDUCED

DESCRIPTION
Smooth satin, green, and slightly iridescent glaze.

USES
Decorative and sculptural.

FIRING RANGE
1760–1796°F (960–980°C)
+ post-firing reduction—1 hour

PARTS DRY WEIGHT
Soft Borax Frit	75
Whiting	10
Ball Clay	10
Tin Oxide	4
Bentonite	1
+ Copper Carbonate	4
Venadium	3
Black Iron	3

DESCRIPTION
Matte metallic/lustered surface with yellow tinges.

USES
Decorative and sculptural.

FIRING RANGE
1796–1832°F (980–1000°C)
+ post-firing reduction—1 hour

PARTS DRY WEIGHT
Alkaline Frit	50
Borax Frit	20
Ball Clay	15
Flint	10
Tin Oxide	4
Bentonite	2
+ Manganese Oxide	4
Copper Oxide Black	4
Uranium Substitute	2
Venadium Oxide	2
Red Iron Oxide	2

DESCRIPTION
Smooth/matte lustered surface.

USES
Decorative and sculptural.

FIRING RANGE
1742–1796°F (950–980°C)
+ post-firing reduction—1 hour

PARTS DRY WEIGHT
Borax Frit	60
Ball Clay	12
Flint	12
Tin Oxide	4
Bentonite	2
+ Red Copper Oxide	5
Manganese Oxide	3
Nickel Oxide	2

DESCRIPTION
Matte/dry dark metallic surface.

USES
Decorative and sculptural.

FIRING RANGE
1778–1832°F (970–1000°C)
+ post-firing reduction—1 hour

PARTS DRY WEIGHT

Borax Frit	64
Ball Clay	12
Flint	12
Bentonite	2
+ Nickel Oxide	4
Venadium Oxide	2
Black Iron Oxide	2
Rutile Oxide	2

DESCRIPTION
Gloss, turquoise luster glaze.

USES
Decorative and sculptural.

FIRING RANGE
1724–1760°F (940–960°C)
+ post-firing reduction—1 hour

PARTS DRY WEIGHT

Alkaline Frit	94
China Clay	4
Bentonite	2
+ Black Copper Oxide	3

STEPHEN MURFITT I RAKU POT

The form was hand built using a mixture of earthstone hand-building body and a standard white, stoneware clay. After bisque firing to 1904°F (1040°C), a thin coat of manganese and copper oxides was brushed over the pot. Then a thin layer of glaze was sprayed over the mixture of oxides. This glaze, a mixture of borax and high alkaline frits, is also high in clay content—around 40 percent. This can be ball clay, china clay, etc. The increase in clay content "mattes out" the surface.

LUSTER

Commercial lusters are supplied as a liquid and are applied as a thin layer on to an already glazed surface. The iridescent types of luster, such as mother-of-pearl, need the thinnest application; rather like painting on a thin layer of varnish. If using a banding wheel it can be helpful to place the pot on a board, so that the pot can be lifted off while the luster is still wet. When dry, after several hours, the work can be handled for packing in the kiln, but some care and cleanliness is needed to avoid fingermarks. The precious metal lusters such as the gold and platinum are opaque and need a thicker application.

The luster effect is produced by depositing a layer of metal onto the glaze surface. The thickness for the iridescent lusters is between 0.1 and 1.0 micron, and for the opaque metal lusters it is between 1 and 20 microns. The resin in the luster creates a locally reducing atmosphere as the work is heated up. The smell is quite unpleasant as this burns off, and adequate ventilation needs to be provided.

The quality and lustrousness depends very much on the surface of the underlying glaze. Very smooth and shiny glazes give the brightest, most reflective result. Over satin and matte glazes, there is a more subdued and subtle effect.

There is a temperature "window" rather than a definitive temperature for firing lusters. The work needs to be heated high enough so that the underlying glaze softens and the luster "sticks" to the glaze; otherwise the luster will rub off. After firing, this can be tested by rubbing with a soft cloth. If fired too high, though, the glaze may begin to "sinter," producing a roughened surface. Lusters used over earthenware glazes are typically fired in the region of 1328–1454°F (720–790°C). In the case of using lusters over stoneware glazes, however, it may be necessary to fire slightly higher than this, even up to 1580°F (860°C) in some cases.

Large pieces of work are susceptible to thermal shock and can crack, so a gentle start to the firing is needed.

SUSAN TUTTON | LUSTERED POT
Hand-built form burnished at the leatherhard stage, then bisque fired in an electric kiln. Gold luster was applied with sponges to build layers. The pot was then fired to 1436°F (780°C), followed by a sawdust firing that creates its own random markings.

DESCRIPTION
Mother-of-pearl luster. Smooth, shiny, iridescent, and reflective.

USES
For use on decorative ware.

FIRING RANGE
1454°F (790°C)

PARTS DRY WEIGHT
Mother-of-pearl: Hernaeus
  N 472
Brushed onto leadless
  transparent glaze:
  W.G. Ball's G3293

DESCRIPTION
Yellow mother-of-pearl luster. Smooth, shiny, iridescent, and reflective.

USES
For use on decorative ware.

FIRING RANGE
1454°F (790°C)

PARTS DRY WEIGHT
Yellow mother-of-pearl luster:
  Hernaeus N 633
Brushed onto leadless
  transparent glaze:
  W.G. Ball's G3293

DESCRIPTION
Pink luster. Smooth, shiny, iridescent.

USES
For use on decorative ware.

FIRING RANGE
1454°F (790°C)

PARTS DRY WEIGHT
Pink luster: Hernaeus, Iris
  Lilac N 513
Brushed onto leadless
  transparent glaze:
  W.G. Ball's G3293

Luster
OXIDIZED

DESCRIPTION
Light blue luster. Smooth, shiny, iridescent, and reflective.

USES
For use on decorative ware.

FIRING RANGE
1454°F (790°C)

PARTS DRY WEIGHT
Light blue luster: Hernaeus
  LUE 69-B
Brushed onto leadless
  transparent glaze:
  W.G. Ball's G3293

DESCRIPTION
Light green luster. Smooth, shiny, and reflective.

USES
For use on decorative ware.

FIRING RANGE
1454°F (790°C)

PARTS DRY WEIGHT
Light green luster: Mathey LLC
  04793
Brushed onto leadless
  transparent glaze:
  W.G. Ball's G3293

DESCRIPTION
Gray luster. Smooth, shiny, and reflective.

USES
For use on decorative ware.

FIRING RANGE
1454°F (790°C)

PARTS DRY WEIGHT
Gray luster: Hernaeus N 543
Brushed onto leadless
  transparent glaze:
  W.G. Ball's G3293

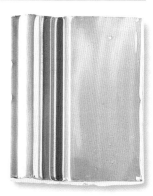

DESCRIPTION
Amber luster. Smooth, shiny,
and reflective.

USES
For use on decorative ware.

FIRING RANGE
1454°F (790°C)

PARTS DRY WEIGHT
Amber luster: Hernaeus
  N 493/A
Brushed onto leadless
  transparent glaze:
  W.G. Ball's G3293

DESCRIPTION
Turquoise green luster. Smooth,
shiny, iridescent, and reflective.

USES
For use on decorative ware.

FIRING RANGE
1454°F (790°C)

PARTS DRY WEIGHT
Turquoise green luster:
  Hernaeus N 518
Brushed onto leadless
  transparent glaze:
  W.G. Ball's G3293

TONY LAVERICK | SLABBED SQUARE BOWL

This piece was slab built in porcelain. Colored slips and stains were applied and the
piece was fired to 2318°F (1270°C) in an oxidizing atmosphere.
Lusters were then applied and the
piece was re-fired to 1382°F
(750°C) to create a richly colored
surface with areas of gold luster.
Diameter 20 in (50 cm).

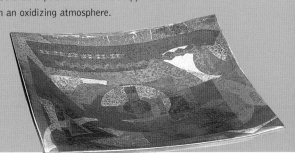

Luster
OXIDIZED

DESCRIPTION
Carmine luster. Smooth, shiny, and reflective.

USES
For use on decorative ware.

FIRING RANGE
1454°F (790°C)

PARTS DRY WEIGHT
Carmine luster: Hernaeus
   N 496
Brushed onto leadless
   transparent glaze:
   W.G. Ball's G3293

DESCRIPTION
Dark blue luster. Smooth, shiny, iridescent, and reflective.

USES
For use on decorative ware.

FIRING RANGE
1454°F (790°C)

PARTS DRY WEIGHT
Dark blue luster: Hernaeus
   N 401
Brushed onto leadless
   transparent glaze:
   W.G. Ball's G3293

DESCRIPTION
Dark green luster. Smooth and shiny, reflective, iridescent.

USES
For use on decorative ware.

FIRING RANGE
1454°F (790°C

PARTS DRY WEIGHT
Dark green luster: Mathey
   LLC 04762
Brushed onto leadless
   transparent glaze:
   W.G. Ball's G3293

DESCRIPTION
Bright gold luster. Smooth,
shiny and reflective.

USES
For use on decorative ware.

FIRING RANGE
1454°F (790°C)

PARTS DRY WEIGHT
Bright gold luster ref:
    Hernaeus GGE FE-3-6%
Brushed onto leadless
    transparent glaze:
    W.G. Ball's G3293

DESCRIPTION
Purple luster. Smooth, shiny,
iridescent, and reflective.

USES
For use on decorative ware.

FIRING RANGE
1454°F (790°C)

PARTS DRY WEIGHT
Purple luster ref: Hernaeus
    N 495
Brushed onto leadless
    transparent glaze:
    W.G. Ball's G3293

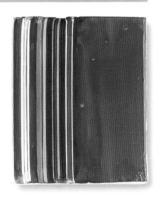

DESCRIPTION
Bright platinum luster. Smooth,
shiny, and reflective.

USES
For use on decorative ware.

FIRING RANGE
1454°F (790°C)

PARTS DRY WEIGHT
Bright platinum luster:
    Hernaeus GPE BP-38
Brushed onto leadless
    transparent glaze:
    W.G. Ball's G3293

Stoneware

The tiles in this section were made from Scarva Earthstone S5 Original. This is a versatile white/off-white throwing and hand-building clay. It is suitable for all types of high earthenware and stoneware firing, including salt and soda. All the tiles had an initial biscuit firing to 1859°F (1015°C).

The name "stoneware" comes from the dense, hard, impervious nature of the fired body. It is a vitrified (non-porous) ware that matures within the temperature range of about 2192–2372°F (1200–1300°C).

The body and glaze mature at the same time to form an integrated body-glaze layer. The formulation of stoneware bodies is simpler than earthenware, as the higher temperature used makes less flux necessary. The difference between earthenware and stoneware is often given as depending on the porosity of the body. There are many porous stonewares

TOM COLEMAN I VASE
Thrown and altered piece. Multiple underglazes were sprayed on green ware and fired in oxidation to 2192°F (1200°C). A colored crackle slip was applied and the piece re-fired to 2012°F (1100°C).

EMILY MYERS I VASES
These three pots were thrown and then facets were cut. They were glazed in a barium-based glaze containing 6 percent rutile oxide.

ASHLEY HOWARD |
LIDDED JAR

Thrown and altered vessel, fired to 2228°F (1220°C) in an oxidizing atmosphere. A slip containing copper oxide was applied to the surface and covered with a barium glaze.

with well-integrated body-glaze layers in which the quality of the glaze is derived from the body beneath. Because of this "body-glaze" integration at the higher temperature range associated with stoneware, the resulting color range does usually tend to be softer and more muted than earthenware. The heat works within the kiln, creating this body-glaze integration, burning out/fusing the glaze ingredients that remain stable at the earthenware temperature range, providing the potential for a more vivid color palette. However, as this book clearly demonstrates, the use of commercial glaze colors and stains makes possible a wide range of brilliant colors at any of the temperatures used to fire pottery today.

MARK JUDSON | THROWN BOWL

The clay body is white St. Thomas. A wax resist was applied and stoneware glazes poured and sprayed over the surface, covered in areas by manganese oxide. This combination, with a firing temperature of 2336°F (1280°C) + a 30-minute soak, has resulted in a dramatic mix on the interior of the bowl.

Naturals and Browns
OXIDIZED

DESCRIPTION
Satin/gloss, transparent with some surface crazing.

USES
Mainly decorative ware; works well in combination with coloring oxides.

FIRING RANGE
2354°F (1290°C)
Soak time—1 hour

PARTS DRY WEIGHT
Potash Feldspar	58
Quartz	18
Bone Ash	8
China Clay	8
Talc	8
+ Yellow Ocher	5

DESCRIPTION
Satin, transparent with slight crazing.

USES
Decorative and domestic.

FIRING RANGE
2354°F (1290°C)
Soak time—1 hour

PARTS DRY WEIGHT
Quartz	41
Potash Feldspar	34
Whiting	16
China Clay	9
+ Yellow Ocher	10

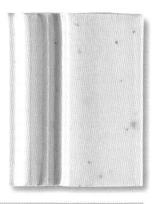

DESCRIPTION
High gloss, transparent with white flecks. Some crazing evident.

USES
Decorative. Works well in combination with oxide decoration, particularly iron.

FIRING RANGE
2354°F (1290°C)
Soak time—1 hour

PARTS DRY WEIGHT
Potash Feldspar	60
Dolomite	20
Quartz	15
China Clay	5
+ Titanium Dioxide	3

DESCRIPTION
Satin/matte, opaque
cream/gray.

USES
Domestic and decorative.

FIRING RANGE
2354°F (1290°C)
Soak time—1 hour

PARTS DRY WEIGHT
Potash Feldspar	45
Dolomite	22
Quartz	16
Zirconium Silicate	11
China Clay	6
+ Chrome Oxide	1

DESCRIPTION
Satin/matte, opaque cream
"oatmeal."

USES
Domestic and decorative.

FIRING RANGE
2354°F (1290°C)
Soak time—1 hour

PARTS DRY WEIGHT
Potash Feldspar	45
Dolomite	22
Quartz	16
Zirconium Silicate	11
China Clay	6
+ Zinc Oxide	2
Chrome Oxide	1

DESCRIPTION
High gloss, semi-transparent
light brown. Some crazing and
breaking to white on rims and
edges.

USES
Decorative.

FIRING RANGE
2354°F (1290°C)
Soak time—1 hour

PARTS DRY WEIGHT
Cornish Stone	28
Quartz	20
Dolomite	18
Whiting	16
China Clay	12
Bone Ash	4
Tin Oxide	2
+ Manganese Dioxide	1

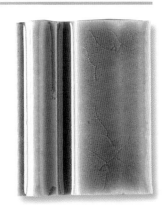

Naturals and Browns
OXIDIZED

DESCRIPTION
Glossy mottled crystalline light ocher. Can be used on porcelain and stoneware bodies.

USES
Domestic and decorative.

FIRING RANGE
2264–2336°F (1240–1280°C)

PARTS DRY WEIGHT
Potash Feldspar	33
Talc	21
Quartz	16
China Clay	15
Whiting	12
Zinc Oxide	3
+ Vanadium Pentoxide	6
Titanium Dioxide	5

DESCRIPTION
Satin, smooth ocher/speckled gray. Can be used on porcelain and stoneware bodies.

USES
Domestic and decorative.

FIRING RANGE
2264–2336°F (1240–1280°C)

PARTS DRY WEIGHT
Potash Feldspar	33
Talc	21
Quartz	16
China Clay	15
Whiting	12
Zinc Oxide	3
+ Titanium Dioxide	10
Vanadium Pentoxide	3

DESCRIPTION
Satin, smooth opaque ocher. Can be used on porcelain and stoneware bodies.

USES
Domestic and decorative.

FIRING RANGE
2264–2336°F (1240–1280°C)

PARTS DRY WEIGHT
Potash Feldspar	33
Talc	21
Quartz	16
China Clay	15
Whiting	12
Zinc Oxide	3
+ Titanium Dioxide	7.5
Chrome Oxide	2
Tin Oxide	2

DESCRIPTION

Smooth satin speckled ocher.
Can be used on porcelain and
stoneware bodies.

USES

Domestic and decorative.

FIRING RANGE

2264–2336°F (1240–1280°C)

PARTS DRY WEIGHT

Potash Feldspar	33
Talc	21
Quartz	16
China Clay	15
Whiting	12
Zinc Oxide	3
+ Titanium Dioxide	5
Manganese Dioxide	4
Tin Oxide	2

DESCRIPTION

High gloss, semi-transparent
mid brown with crazing.
Breaking to white/beige on
rims and edges.

USES

Decorative.

FIRING RANGE

2354°F (1290°C)
Soak time—1 hour

PARTS DRY WEIGHT

Cornish Stone	28
Quartz	20
Dolomite	18
Whiting	16
China Clay	12
Bone Ash	4
Tin Oxide	2
+ Manganese Dioxide	2

EMILY MYERS | THROWN AND CUT FORMS
These three pots were wheel thrown and then facets were
wire-cut. The clay was Keuper Red stoneware clay, and
they were glazed in a barium-based glaze containing
6 percent rutile oxide. Height 10–12 in (25–30 cm).

Naturals and Browns

OXIDIZED

DESCRIPTION
Satin/gloss, semi-transparent with iron speckles.

USES
Decorative.

FIRING RANGE
2354°F (1290°C)
Soak time—1 hour

PARTS DRY WEIGHT
Potash Feldspar	58
Quartz	18
Bone Ash	8
China Clay	8
Talc	8
+ Iron Oxide Spangles	5

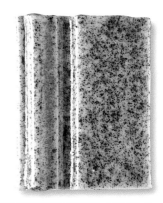

DESCRIPTION
Glossy mottled light ocher/brown. Can be used on porcelain and stoneware bodies.

USES
Domestic and decorative.

FIRING RANGE
2264–2336°F (1240–1280°C)

PARTS DRY WEIGHT
Potash Feldspar	33
Talc	21
Quartz	16
China Clay	15
Whiting	12
Zinc Oxide	3
+ Titanium Dioxide	7.5
Vanadium Pentoxide	6
Tin Oxide	2

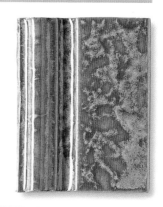

DESCRIPTION
Satin/gloss, crystalline yellow brown. Can be used on porcelain and stoneware bodies.

USES
Domestic and decorative.

FIRING RANGE
2264–2336°F (1240–1280°C)

PARTS DRY WEIGHT
Potash Feldspar	33
Talc	21
Quartz	16
China Clay	15
Whiting	12
Zinc Oxide	3
+ Titanium Dioxide	5
Red Iron Oxide	4

DESCRIPTION
Satin, smooth mottled yellow.
Can be used on porcelain and
stoneware bodies.

USES
Domestic and decorative.

FIRING RANGE
2264–2336°F (1240–1280°C)

PARTS DRY WEIGHT
Potash Feldspar	33
Talc	21
Quartz	16
China Clay	15
Whiting	12
Zinc Oxide	3
+ Titanium Dioxide	5
Red Iron Oxide	4

DESCRIPTION
Satin, dark brown, breaking to
light brown.

USES
Domestic and decorative.

FIRING RANGE
2354°F (1290°C)
Soak time—1 hour

PARTS DRY WEIGHT
Quartz	41
China Clay	35
Whiting	24
+ Rutile	5
Crocus Martis	3

DESCRIPTION
Satin/gloss, dark green mottled
semi-transparent.

USES
Domestic and decorative.

FIRING RANGE
2354°F (1290°C)
Soak time—1 hour

PARTS DRY WEIGHT
Quartz	41
Potash Feldspar	34
Whiting	16
China Clay	9
+ Iron Spangles	5

Naturals and Browns
OXIDIZED

DESCRIPTION
Satin/gloss, white/dark brown "leopard skin" effect.

USES
Domestic, decorative, and sculptural.

FIRING RANGE
2354°F (1290°C)
Soak time—1 hour

PARTS DRY WEIGHT
Mix 50/50 Recipes A and B

Recipe A
Potash Feldspar	45
Dolomite	22
Quartz	16
Zirconium Silicate	11

Recipe B
Quartz	41
Potash Feldspar	34
Whiting	16
China Clay	9

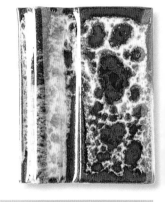

DESCRIPTION
Satin/gloss, red brown/white "leopard skin" effect.

USES
Domestic, decorative, or sculptural.

FIRING RANGE
2354°F (1290°C)
Soak time—1 hour

PARTS DRY WEIGHT
Mix 50/50 Recipes A and B

Recipe A
Potash Feldspar	45
Dolomite	22
Quartz	16
Zirconium Silicate	11
China Clay	6

Recipe B
Potash Feldspar	58
Quartz	18
China Clay	8
Bone Ash	8
Talc	8

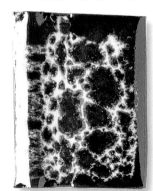

DESCRIPTION
Brown/white/ black gloss, "leopard skin" effect.

USES
Domestic, decorative, and sculptural.

FIRING RANGE
2354°F (1290°C)
Soak time—1 hour

PARTS DRY WEIGHT
Mix ⅓ each of recipes A, B, C

Recipe A
Potash Feldspar	45
Dolomite	22
Quartz	16
Zirconium Silicate	11
China Clay	6

Recipe B
Potash Feldspar	58
Quartz	18
China Clay	8
Bone Ash	8
Talc	8

Recipe C
Quartz	41
Potash Feldspar	34
Whiting	16
China Clay	9

DESCRIPTION
Satin/gloss, textured dark green and white with red iron speckle.

USES
Domestic and decorative.

FIRING RANGE
2354°F (1290°C)
Soak time—1 hour

PARTS DRY WEIGHT

Potash Feldspar	58
Quartz	18
Bone Ash	8
China Clay	8
Talc	8
+ Iron Oxide Spangles	10

DESCRIPTION
Satin/gloss, rust red mottled with black.

USES
Domestic and decorative.

FIRING RANGE
2354°F (1290°C)
Soak time—1 hour

PARTS DRY WEIGHT

Potash Feldspar	58
Quartz	18
Bone Ash	8
China Clay	8
Talc	8
+ Red Iron Oxide	10

DESCRIPTION
High gloss, red/brown and black mottled.

USES
Domestic and decorative.

FIRING RANGE
2354°F (1290°C)
Soak time—1 hour

PARTS DRY WEIGHT
Mix 50/50 Recipes A and B

Recipe A

Potash Feldspar	58
Quartz	18
China Clay	8
Bone Ash	8
Talc	8

Recipe B

Quartz	41
Potash Feldspar	34
Whiting	16
China Clay	9

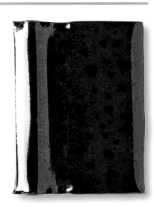

Naturals and Browns
OXIDIZED

DESCRIPTION
High gloss, green/brown mottle with blue/white, breaking to light green/brown on rims and edges.

USES
Domestic and decorative.

FIRING RANGE
2354°F (1290°C)
Soak time—1 hour

PARTS DRY WEIGHT
Potash Feldspar	45
Quartz	20
Whiting	20
China Clay	10
Tin Oxide	5
+ Titanium Dioxide	2
Red Iron Oxide	0.5
Nickel Oxide	0.5

DESCRIPTION
Satin, mottled yellow/brown, breaking to yellow on edges where thin.

USES
Domestic and decorative.

FIRING RANGE
2354°F (1290°C)
Soak time—1 hour

PARTS DRY WEIGHT
Feldspar	46
Dolomite	23
Quartz	15
Zircon	11
China Clay	5
+ Copper Carbonate	2
Nickel Oxide	2

DESCRIPTION
High gloss, mottled red/brown.

USES
Domestic and decorative.

FIRING RANGE
2354°F (1290°C)
Soak time—1 hour

PARTS DRY WEIGHT
Potash Feldspar	58
Quartz	18
Bone Ash	8
China Clay	8
Talc	8
+ Crocus Martis	5

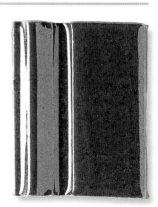

DESCRIPTION
High gloss, dark brown/black, breaking to semi-transparent on rims and edges.

USES
Domestic.

FIRING RANGE
2354°F (1290°C)
Soak time—1 hour

PARTS DRY WEIGHT
Quartz	41
Potash Feldspar	34
Whiting	16
China Clay	9
+ Red Iron Oxide	5

DESCRIPTION
High gloss, dark brown/black, breaking to light brown on rims and edges.

USES
Domestic.

FIRING RANGE
2354°F (1290°C)
Soak time—1 hour

PARTS DRY WEIGHT
Quartz	41
Potash Feldspar	34
Whiting	16
China Clay	9
+ Crocus Martis	5

DESCRIPTION
High gloss, mottled black/brown.

USES
Domestic.

FIRING RANGE
2354°F (1290°C)
Soak time—1 hour

PARTS DRY WEIGHT
Potash Feldspar	58
Quartz	18
Bone Ash	8
China Clay	8
Talc	8
+ Red Iron Oxide	5

Yellows and Oranges
OXIDIZED

DESCRIPTION
Satin semi-opaque gloss, breaking to transparent where thin on edges. Slight blue speckle.

USES
Mainly domestic.

FIRING RANGE
2354°F (1290°C)
Soak time—1 hour

PARTS DRY WEIGHT
Cornish Stone	28
Quartz	20
Dolomite	18
Whiting	16
China Clay	12
Bone Ash	4
Tin Oxide	2
+ Tin Oxide	3

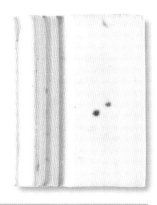

DESCRIPTION
Satin/gloss, pearl white, breaking to transparent on edges.

USES
Domestic and decorative.

FIRING RANGE
2354°F (1290°C)
Soak time—1 hour

PARTS DRY WEIGHT
Potash Feldspar	60
Dolomite	20
Quartz	15
China Clay	5
+ Rutile	5

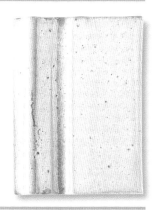

DESCRIPTION
Satin/gloss, semi-transparent pearl. Slight red speckling.

USES
Mainly on domestic ware.

FIRING RANGE
2354°F (1290°C)
Soak time—1 hour

PARTS DRY WEIGHT
Potash Feldspar	60
Dolomite	20
Quartz	15
China Clay	5
+ Rutile	4

DESCRIPTION
Matte, opaque cream/yellow.

USES
Decorative.

FIRING RANGE
2354°F (1290°C)
Soak time—1 hour

PARTS DRY WEIGHT
Quartz	41
China Clay	35
Whiting	24
+ Rutile	5

DESCRIPTION
Satin, cream, breaking to
yellow on edges.

USES
Domestic and decorative.

FIRING RANGE
2354°F (1290°C)
Soak time—1 hour

PARTS DRY WEIGHT
Potash Feldspar	60
Dolomite	20
Quartz	15
China Clay	5
+ Titanium Dioxide	5

DESCRIPTION
Glossy light yellow. Can be used
on porcelain and stoneware
bodies.

USES
Domestic and decorative.

FIRING RANGE
2264–2336°F (1240–1280°C)

PARTS DRY WEIGHT
Potash Feldspar	34
Quartz	23
Standard Borax Frit	14
China Clay	11
Whiting	11
Dolomite	5
Bentonite	2
+ B 100 Yellow Glaze Stain	5

Yellows and Oranges

OXIDIZED

DESCRIPTION
Satin yellow. Can be used on porcelain and stoneware bodies.

USES
Domestic and decorative.

FIRING RANGE
2264–2336°F (1240–1280°C)

PARTS DRY WEIGHT

Potash Feldspar	33
Talc	21
Quartz	16
China Clay	15
Whiting	12
Zinc Oxide	3
+ B 100 Yellow	
Glaze Stain	10
Titanium Dioxide	5

DESCRIPTION
Satin bright yellow. Can be used on porcelain and stoneware bodies.

USES
Domestic and decorative.

FIRING RANGE
2264–2336°F (1240–1280°C)

PARTS DRY WEIGHT

Potash Feldspar	33
Talc	21
Quartz	16
China Clay	15
Whiting	12
Zinc Oxide	3
+ B 100 Yellow	
Glaze Stain	10

DESCRIPTION
Glossy bright yellow. Can be used on porcelain and stoneware bodies.

USES
Domestic and decorative.

FIRING RANGE
2264–2336°F (1240–1280°C)

PARTS DRY WEIGHT

Potash Feldspar	34
Quartz	23
Standard Borax Frit	14
China Clay	11
Whiting	11
Dolomite	5
Bentonite	2
+ B 100 Yellow	
Glaze Stain	10

DESCRIPTION
Glossy orange yellow. Can be used on porcelain and stoneware bodies.

USES
Domestic and decorative.

FIRING RANGE
2264–2336°F (1240–1280°C)

PARTS DRY WEIGHT

Potash Feldspar	34
Quartz	23
Standard Borax Frit	14
China Clay	11
Whiting	11
Dolomite	5
Bentonite	2
+ B 186 Mandarin Yellow Glaze Stain	10

DESCRIPTION
Satin, smooth yellow opaque. Can be used on porcelain and stoneware bodies.

USES
Domestic and decorative.

FIRING RANGE
2264–2336°F (1240–1280°C)

PARTS DRY WEIGHT

Potash Feldspar	33
Quartz	16
Talc	21
China Clay	15
Whiting	12
Zinc Oxide	3
+ Titanium Dioxide	10
Nickel Oxide	3

DESCRIPTION
Gloss orange. Can be used on porcelain and stoneware bodies.

USES
Domestic and decorative.

FIRING RANGE
2264–2336°F (1240–1280°C)

PARTS DRY WEIGHT

Potash Feldspar	34
Quartz	23
Standard Borax Frit	14
China Clay	11
Whiting	11
Dolomite	5
Bentonite	2
+ B 122 Orange Glaze Stain	10

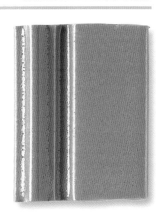

Yellows and Oranges
REDUCED

DESCRIPTION
Smooth satin/matte, white with yellow speckles where glaze is thinner.

USES
Domestic and decorative.

FIRING RANGE
2300–2336°F (1260–1280°C). Reduction from 2832°F (1000°C). Firing has a 12-hour cycle.

PARTS DRY WEIGHT
Potash Feldspar	46
Barium Carbonate	21
Zirconium Silicate	15
Talc	10
China Clay	5
Whiting	3
+ Iron Oxide Spangles	2
Red Iron Oxide	1

DESCRIPTION
Soft, semi-matte, cream/pale yellow.

USES
Domestic and decorative.

FIRING RANGE
2336–2372°F (1280–1300°C) with reduction starting at 1580°F (860°C).

PARTS DRY WEIGHT
Feldspar	50
China Clay	25
Dolomite	20
Whiting	4
Yellow Ocher	1

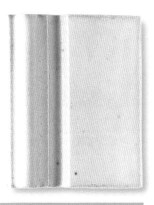

DESCRIPTION
Satin/matte pale yellow.

USES
Domestic and decorative.

FIRING RANGE
2300–2336°F (1260–1280°C). Reduction from 1832°F (1000°C). Firing has a 12-hour cycle.

PARTS DRY WEIGHT
Potash Feldspar	45
Barium Carbonate	20
Zirconium Silicate	15
Talc	10
China Clay	7
Whiting	3
+ Red Iron Oxide	3

DESCRIPTION
Glossy shino-type glaze, breaking to orange where thin.

USES
Decorative and domestic.

FIRING RANGE
2336–2372°F (1280–1300°C) with reduction starting at 1580°F (860°C).

PARTS DRY WEIGHT

Nepheline Syenite	46
Soda Feldspar	18
A. T. Ball Clay	17
Spodumene	15
Soda Ash	4

DESCRIPTION
Glossy shino-type glaze breaking to orange and orange speckle where thin.

USES
Decorative and domestic. Bisque firing half the ball clay helps to prevent crawling. Adding salt gives it more gloss.

FIRING RANGE
2336–2372°F (1280–1300°C) with reduction starting at 1580°F (860°C).

PARTS DRY WEIGHT

Nepheline Syenite	80
A. T. Ball Clay	10
A. T. Ball Clay (biscuited to 1832°F/1000°C)	10
+ Salt	3

DESCRIPTION
Shino type, breaking to rich orange where thin.

USES
Decorative and domestic.

FIRING RANGE
2336–2372°F (1280–1300°C) with reduction starting at 1580°F (860°C).

PARTS DRY WEIGHT

Nepheline Syenite	46
Soda Feldspar	18
A. T. Ball Clay	17
Petalite	15
Soda Ash	4

Yellows and Oranges
REDUCED

DESCRIPTION
Satin/matte. Very soft pale yellow, breaking to orange/rust where thin.

USES
Decorative and domestic.

FIRING RANGE
2336–2372°F (1280–1300°C) with reduction starting at 1580°F (860°C).

PARTS DRY WEIGHT

Feldspar	44
Barium Carbonate	18
Zircon Silicate	14
Talc	10
China Clay	8
Whiting	3
Iron Oxide	3

DESCRIPTION
Crystalline pale green, semi gloss. Slight speckle.

USES
Decorative.

FIRING RANGE
2336–2372°F (1280–1300°C) with reduction starting at 1580°F (860°C).

PARTS DRY WEIGHT

Feldspar	37
China Clay	18
Whiting	15
Quartz	10
Lithium Carbonate	9
Titanium Oxide	9
Copper Carbonate	1
Zinc Oxide	1

DESCRIPTION
Glossy speckled orange shino. Stronger on edges.

USES
Domestic and decorative.

FIRING RANGE
2300–2336°F (1260–1280°C). Reduction from 1832°F (1000°C). Firing has a 12-hour cycle.

PARTS DRY WEIGHT

Soda Feldspar	35
A. T. Ball Clay	35
Nepheline Syenite	30

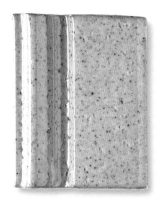

DESCRIPTION
Matte, stony mottled
yellow/orange.

USES
Decorative and sculptural.

FIRING RANGE
2300–2336°F
(1260–1280°C). Reduction
from 1832°F (1000°C). Firing
has a 12-hour cycle.

PARTS DRY WEIGHT

Red Earthenware Clay	34
Hvar Ball Clay	33
Whiting	33
+ Rutile	2

DESCRIPTION
Satin, orange to white shino
glaze. More orange where thin,
pooling to satin white where
thicker.

USES
Domestic, decorative and
sculptural.

FIRING RANGE
2336–2372°F (1280–1300°C)
with reduction starting at
1580°F (860°C).

PARTS DRY WEIGHT

Nepheline Syenite	43
China Clay	28
Spodumene	13
A. T. Ball Clay	12
Soda Ash	4

RICK MALMGREN I JAZZ ALIVE
Thrown and altered pot in white stoneware clay, reduction fired to
2192°F (1200°C) in a gas kiln. Layers of glaze were applied, and
then finished with sprayed swipes of two different glazes on top
the first a turquoise-red shade, the second a crawl glaze.
Height 13 in (32 cm).

Reds and Purples

OXIDIZED

DESCRIPTION
Satin opaque, white with pink mottling.

USES
Domestic.

FIRING RANGE
2354°F (1290°C)
Soak time—1 hour

PARTS DRY WEIGHT
Cornish Stone	28
Quartz	20
Dolomite	18
Whiting	16
China Clay	12
Bone Ash	4
Tin Oxide	2
+ Tin Oxide	7
Chrome Oxide	0.5

DESCRIPTION
Satin/matte, pink, breaking to white on rims and edges.

USES
Decorative and sculptural.

FIRING RANGE
2354°F (1290°C)
Soak time—1 hour

PARTS DRY WEIGHT
Potash Feldspar	45
Quartz	20
Whiting	20
China Clay	10
+ Manganese Dioxide	3

DESCRIPTION
Satin/gloss, pink, breaking to gray where thinner on edges and rims.

USES
Domestic and decorative.

FIRING RANGE
2354°F (1290°C)
Soak time—1 hour

PARTS DRY WEIGHT
Potash Feldspar	45
Quartz	20
Whiting	20
China Clay	10
Tin Oxide	5
+ Chrome Oxide	0.5

DESCRIPTION
Satin, gray, breaking to beige on rims and edges. Mauve/pink mottling where thicker.

USES
Domestic, decorative, and sculptural ware.

FIRING RANGE
2354°F (1290°C)
Soak time—1 hour

PARTS DRY WEIGHT
Cornish Stone	28
Quartz	20
Dolomite	18
Whiting	16
China Clay	12
Bone Ash	4
Tin Oxide	2
+ Tin Oxide	10
Chrome Oxide	0.5

DESCRIPTION
Satin/gloss, pale green with mottled pink where thicker, breaking to beige on rims and edges.

USES
Domestic and decorative.

FIRING RANGE
2354°F (1290°C)
Soak time—1 hour

PARTS DRY WEIGHT
Cornish Stone	28
Quartz	20
Dolomite	18
Whiting	16
China Clay	12
Bone Ash	4
Tin Oxide	2
+ Tin Oxide	5
Chrome Oxide	0.5

DESCRIPTION
Glossy orange, red with black speckle. Can be used on porcelain and stoneware bodies.

USES
Domestic and decorative.

FIRING RANGE
2264–2336°F (1240–1280°C)

PARTS DRY WEIGHT
Potash Feldspar	44
Quartz	14
Bone Ash	14
Talc	10
AK Ball Clay	8
HV Ball Clay	5
Lithium Carbonate	3
Bentonite	2
+ Red Iron Oxide	11

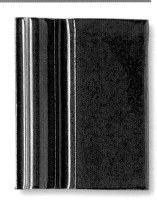

Reds and Purples
REDUCED

DESCRIPTION
Smooth matte, beige with dark speckle, breaking to white on edges.

USES
Domestic and decorative.

FIRING RANGE
2300–2336°F (1260–1280°C). Reduction from 1832°F (1000°C). Firing has a 12-hour cycle.

PARTS DRY WEIGHT

Potash Feldspar	50
Dolomite	20
China Clay	20
Bone Ash	10
+ Manganese Dioxide	3
Tin Oxide	3
Copper Oxide	1

DESCRIPTION
Satin/gloss, pale mauve. Good in combination with oxides for decoration.

USES
Domestic and decorative.

FIRING RANGE
2300–2336°F (1260–1280°C). Reduction from 1832°F (1000°C). Firing has a 12-hour cycle.

PARTS DRY WEIGHT

Cornish Stone	41
Quartz	27
China Clay	16
Whiting	11
Dolomite	5
+ Zinc Oxide	1.5
Copper Oxide	0.5

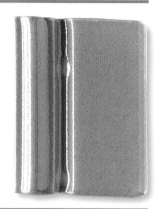

DESCRIPTION
Dry matte, light mauve, breaking to white on edges.

USES
Decorative or sculptural.

FIRING RANGE
2300–2336°F (1260–1280°C). Reduction from 1832°F (1000°C). Firing has a 12-hour cycle.

PARTS DRY WEIGHT

Nepheline Syenite	40
Potash Feldspar	38
Barium Carbonate	20
China Clay	2
+ Copper Carbonate	2

DESCRIPTION
Satin/matte, pale mauve,
breaking to white on edges.

USES
Domestic and decorative. Most
effective applied thinly.

FIRING RANGE
2300–2336°F (1260–1280°C).
Reduction from 1832°F
(1000°C). Firing has a 12-hour
cycle.

PARTS DRY WEIGHT
Nepheline Syenite	70
Dolomite	10
Flint	10
China Clay	7
Whiting	3
+ Zinc Oxide	2

DESCRIPTION
High gloss, semi-transparent
red/maroon with crazing over
surface.

USES
Decorative.

FIRING RANGE
2300–2336°F (1260–1280°C).
Reduction from 1832°F
(1000°C). Firing has a 12-hour
cycle.

PARTS DRY WEIGHT
Potash Feldspar	78
Whiting	13
Standard Borax Frit	9
+ Tin Oxide	4
Copper Oxide	1.5

DESCRIPTION
Satin/matte, maroon, breaking
to white on edges.

USES
Domestic and decorative.

FIRING RANGE
2300–2336°F
(1260–1280°C). Reduction
from 1832°F (1000°C). Firing
has a 12-hour cycle.

PARTS DRY WEIGHT
Soda Feldspar	60
Whiting	20
China Clay	20
+ Tin Oxide	3
Copper Carbonate	2

Reds and Purples
REDUCED

DESCRIPTION
Satin/matte, deep red with white edges breaking through where glaze is thinner.

USES
Domestic and decorative.

FIRING RANGE
2300–2336°F (1260–1280°C). Reduction from 1832°F (1000°C). Firing has a 12-hour cycle.

PARTS DRY WEIGHT

Nepheline Syenite	73
Dolomite	9
Quartz	9
China Clay	6
Whiting	3
+ Zinc Oxide	2
Copper Oxide	0.5

DESCRIPTION
Smooth satin/matte, red, breaking to white on edges.

USES
Domestic and decorative.

FIRING RANGE
2300–2336°F (1260–1280°C). Reduction from 2832°F (1000°C). Firing has a 12-hour cycle.

PARTS DRY WEIGHT

Potash Feldspar	58
Barium Carbonate	21
Flint	11
Dolomite	5
China Clay	5
+ Tin Oxide	2.5
Copper Carbonate	1.5

DESCRIPTION
Glossy semi-transparent, red, white on edges where thin.

USES
Domestic and decorative.

FIRING RANGE
2300–2336°F (1260–1280°C). Reduction from 1832°F (1000°C). Firing has a 12-hour cycle.

PARTS DRY WEIGHT

Potash Feldspar	43
Soda Feldspar	35
Whiting	12
Gerstley Borate	10
Copper Carbonate	0.5

DESCRIPTION
Glossy, red/pink, breaking to
white on edges.

USES
Domestic and decorative.

FIRING RANGE
2300–2336°F (1260–1280°C).
Reduction from 1832°F
(1000°C). Firing has a 12-hour
cycle.

PARTS DRY WEIGHT
Soda Feldspar	45
Flint	20
Standard Borax Frit	15
Whiting	15
China Clay	5
+ Tin Oxide	5
Copper Carbonate	0.75

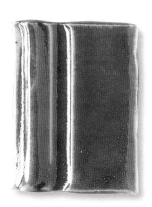

DESCRIPTION
Textured copper red. Bleeds out
to white on rims and edges.

USES
Decorative and domestic.

FIRING RANGE
2336–2372°F (1280–1300°C).
Reduction starts early, from
1382–1472°F (750–800°C).

PARTS DRY WEIGHT
Feldspar	40
Flint	24
Calcium Borate Frit	9
Dolomite	9
Whiting	7
Zinc Oxide	6
Tin Oxide	2.5
China Clay	2
Copper Carbonate	0.5

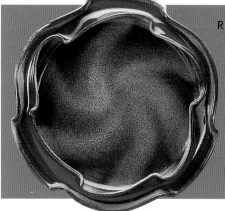

RICK MALMGREN I SWIRL PLATTER
Thrown, altered, and reduction fired to 2192°F
(1200°C) in a propane gas kiln. The piece was
glazed all over with the following bronze green
matte glaze: Whiting 24, Custer Feldspar 55,
Edgar Plastic Kaolin 14, Flint 7, + Zinc Oxide
10, Cobalt Oxide 0.5, Copper Carbonate 3,
Rutile 6. Then swipe lines of a copper-red glaze
and a crawl glaze were added.
Diameter 13 in (33 cm).

Reds and Purples
REDUCED

DESCRIPTION
Matte to broken gloss brown.
Slight textured surface.

USES
Domestic, decorative, and
sculptural.

FIRING RANGE
2300–2336°F (1260–1280°C).
Reduction from 1832°F
(1000°C). Firing has a 12-hour
cycle.

PARTS DRY WEIGHT
Nepheline Syenite	70
Dolomite	10
Flint	10
China Clay	7
Whiting	3
+ Red Iron Oxide	5
Titanium Dioxide	3
Zinc Oxide	2

DESCRIPTION
A glossy mid brown and
variegated, breaks to pale rust
color on edges.

USES
For use on either domestic
and/or decorative ware.

FIRING RANGE
2336–2372°F (1280–1300°C)
with reduction starting at
1580°F (860°C).

PARTS DRY WEIGHT
Nepheline Syenite	31
Flint	24
Iron Oxide	10
Whiting	8
Barium Carbonate	8
Calcium Borax Frit	8
China Clay	4
Rutile	4
Talc	3

DESCRIPTION
Glossy brick red/ brown, black
speckles.

USES
Domestic and decorative.

FIRING RANGE
2336–2372°F (1280–1300°C)
with reduction starting at
1580°F (860°C).

PARTS DRY WEIGHT
Feldspar	47
Bone Ash	14
Quartz	14
Iron Oxide	10
Talc	8
China Clay	7

DESCRIPTION
Orange/red gloss. Some darker speckling.

USES
Domestic and decorative.

FIRING RANGE
2300–2336°F (1260–1280°C). Reduction from 1832°F (1000°C). Firing has a 12-hour cycle.

PARTS DRY WEIGHT

Soda Feldspar	30
Potash Feldspar	30
Flint	15
China Clay	10
Bone Ash	10
Talc	5
+ Red Iron Oxide	8

DESCRIPTION
Deep copper red, bleeds out to white or green on edges and rims depending on clay used.

USES
Decorative and domestic. Can be brushed or trailed on as an effective overglaze.

FIRING RANGE
2336–2372°F (1280–1300°C) with reduction starting at 1580°F (860°C).

PARTS DRY WEIGHT

Feldspar	76
Whiting	13
Borax Frit	9
Tin Oxide	1.5
Copper Oxide	0.5

DESCRIPTION
Maroon satin/matte and variegated with hint of turquoise.

USES
Domestic, decorative, and sculptural. Gives a strong turquoise in oxidation atmosphere.

FIRING RANGE
2336–2372°F (1280–1300°C) with reduction starting at 1580°F (860°C).

PARTS DRY WEIGHT

Nepheline Syenite	56
Barium Carbonate	25
Flint	7
Ball Clay	6
Copper Carbonate	3
Lithium Carbonate	3

Reds and Purples
REDUCED

DESCRIPTION
High gloss, orange/red with black speckles.

USES
Domestic, decorative, and sculptural.

FIRING RANGE
2300–2336°F (1260–1280°C). Reduction from 1832°F (1000°C). Firing has a 12-hour cycle.

PARTS DRY WEIGHT
Cornish Stone	41
Flint	27
China Clay	16
Whiting	11
Dolomite	5
+ Red Iron Oxide	10
Rutile	2
Zinc Oxide	1.5

DESCRIPTION
Semi-gloss, dark brown/black and variegated, breaking to red rust on edges.

USES
Domestic and decorative.

FIRING RANGE
2336–2372°F (1280–1300°C) with reduction starting at 1580°F (860°C).

PARTS DRY WEIGHT
Feldspar	37
Red Clay	22
Flint	20
Whiting	6
A. T. Ball Clay	5
Iron Oxide	5
Ilmanite	5

DESCRIPTION
Glossy, deep purple/red, breaking to a pink/white on rims and edges.

USES
Domestic and decorative.

FIRING RANGE
2300–2336°F (1260–1280°C). Reduction from 1832°F (1000°C). Firing has a 12-hour cycle.

PARTS DRY WEIGHT
Nepheline Syenite	40
Flint	25
Calcium Borate Frit	15
Potash Feldspar	10
Whiting	8
China Clay	2
+ Tin Oxide	2
Copper Carbonate	0.75

DESCRIPTION
Deep gloss, red, breaking to white on edges where thin.

USES
Domestic and decorative.

FIRING RANGE
2300–2336°F (1260–1280°C). Reduction from 1832°F (1000°C). Firing has a 12-hour cycle.

PARTS DRY WEIGHT

Potash Feldspar	34
Quartz	19
Whiting	17
Cornish Stone	10
Borax Frit	10
China Clay	7
Colemanite	2
Bone Ash	1
+ Rutile	1
Red Iron Oxide	0.5
Copper Oxide	0.25

DESCRIPTION
Semi-matte, blue gray with purple mottling.

USES
Domestic and decorative.

FIRING RANGE
2300–2336°F (1260–1280°C). Reduction from 1832°F (1000°C). Firing has a 12-hour cycle.

PARTS DRY WEIGHT

Nepheline Syenite	70
Dolomite	10
Flint	10
China Clay	7
Whiting	3
+ Zinc Oxide	2
Rutile	2
Black Iron Oxide	1
Copper Oxide	1

DESCRIPTION
Satin/matte, dark orange/red. Patches of black where pooled.

USES
Domestic, decorative, and sculptural.

FIRING RANGE
2300–2336°F (1260–1280°C). Reduction from 1832°F (1000°C). Firing has a 12-hour cycle.

PARTS DRY WEIGHT

Hvar Ball Clay	29
Potash Feldspar	29
Quartz	29
Whiting	13
+ Red Iron Oxide	13

Blues
OXIDIZED

DESCRIPTION
High gloss, mottled white/blue, breaking to transparent on edges and rims.

USES
Domestic and decorative.

FIRING RANGE
2354°F (1290°C)
Soak time—1 hour

PARTS DRY WEIGHT
Potash Feldspar	60
Dolomite	20
Quartz	15
China Clay	5
+ Rutile	3
Cobalt Oxide	1

DESCRIPTION
High gloss, blue/white with brown speckle, breaking to brown where thin.

USES
Domestic and decorative.

FIRING RANGE
2354°F (1290°C)
Soak time—1 hour

PARTS DRY WEIGHT
Mix 50/50 Recipes A and B

Recipe A
Potash Feldspar	60
Dolomite	20
Quartz	15
China Clay	5

Recipe B
Quartz	41
Potash Feldspar	34
Whiting	16
China Clay	9

DESCRIPTION
Satin/gloss, pale blue with dark mottling, breaking to green on rims and edges.

USES
Decorative.

FIRING RANGE
2354°F (1290°C)
Soak time—1 hour

PARTS DRY WEIGHT
Potash Feldspar	65
Dolomite	15
Quartz	15
China Clay	5
+ Rutile Oxide	6
Cobalt Oxide	1

DESCRIPTION
Satin/matte, gray/mauve, breaking to gloss blue on edges and rims.

USES
Domestic and decorative.

FIRING RANGE
2354°F (1290°C)
Soak time—1 hour

PARTS DRY WEIGHT

Potash Feldspar	46
Dolomite	23
Quartz	15
Zircon	11
China Clay	5
+ Copper Carbonate	2
Cobalt Carbonate	2

DESCRIPTION
Satin/matte, blue/gray with dark blue speckle.

USES
Domestic and decorative.

FIRING RANGE
2354°F (1290°C)
Soak time—1 hour

PARTS DRY WEIGHT

Potash Feldspar	45
Dolomite	22
Quartz	16
Zirconium Silicate	11
China Clay	6
+ Cobalt Carbonate	2
Nickel Oxide	2

DESCRIPTION
Satin, mauve/gray, breaking to gloss blue on rims and edges.

USES
Domestic and decorative.

FIRING RANGE
2354°F (1290°C)
Soak time—1 hour

PARTS DRY WEIGHT

Potash Feldspar	45
Dolomite	22
Quartz	16
Zirconium Silicate	11
China Clay	6
+ Copper Carbonate	3
Cobalt Carbonate	1

Blues
OXIDIZED

DESCRIPTION
Satin, mauve, blue opaque.
Slight darker speckling.

USES
Domestic and decorative.

FIRING RANGE
2354°F (1290°C)
Soak time—1 hour

PARTS DRY WEIGHT
Potash Feldspar	45
Quartz	20
Whiting	20
China Clay	10
Tin Oxide	5
+ Cobalt Carbonate	1
Chrome Oxide	0.5

DESCRIPTION
Satin/matte, mauve/pink,
breaking to blue on edges and
rims. Slight brown speckle.

USES
Domestic, decorative, and
sculptural.

FIRING RANGE
2354°F (1290°C)
Soak time—1 hour

PARTS DRY WEIGHT
Potash Feldspar	45
Dolomite	22
Quartz	16
Zirconium Silicate	11
China Clay	6
+ Copper Carbonate	2
Cobalt Carbonate	2

DESCRIPTION
Satin/matte, mottled blue and
pink. Breaking to pale blue on
rims and edges.

USES
Domestic and decorative.

FIRING RANGE
2354°F (1290°C)
Soak time—1 hour

PARTS DRY WEIGHT
Potash Feldspar	46
Dolomite	23
Quartz	15
Zirconium Silicate	11
China Clay	5
+ Manganese Dioxide	2
Cobalt Carbonate	1
Red Iron Oxide	1

DESCRIPTION
Satin/matte, mauve, breaking
to blue where thinner.

USES
Domestic, decorative, and
sculptural.

FIRING RANGE
2354°F (1290°C)
Soak time—1 hour

PARTS DRY WEIGHT
Potash Feldspar	45
Dolomite	22
Quartz	16
Zirconium Silicate	11
China Clay	6
+ Cobalt Oxide	2

DESCRIPTION
Satin/matte, mottled blue and
pink.

USES
Domestic, decorative, and
sculptural.

FIRING RANGE
2354°F (1290°C)
Soak time—1 hour

PARTS DRY WEIGHT
Potash Feldspar	46
Dolomite	23
Quartz	15
Zirconium Silicate	11
China Clay	5
+ Copper Oxide	2
Cobalt Carbonate	1

DESCRIPTION
Satin/matte, mottled pink and
dark blue, breaking to blue on
rims and edges.

USES
Domestic, decorative, and
sculptural.

FIRING RANGE
2354°F (1290°C)
Soak time—1 hour

PARTS DRY WEIGHT
Potash Feldspar	46
Dolomite	23
Quartz	15
Zirconium Silicate	11
China Clay	5
+ Manganese Dioxide	2
Red Iron Oxide	2
Cobalt Carbonate	1

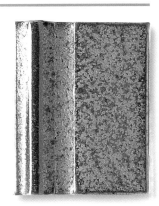

Blues
OXIDIZED

DESCRIPTION
Satin/gloss, blue with slight
dark blue mottling, breaking to
transparent on rims and edges.

USES
Domestic.

FIRING RANGE
2354°F (1290°C)
Soak time—1 hour

PARTS DRY WEIGHT

Cornish Stone	28
Quartz	20
Dolomite	18
Whiting	16
China Clay	12
Bone Ash	4
Tin Oxide	2
+ Tin Oxide	10
Cobalt Oxide	1

DESCRIPTION
Satin, mottled lavender blue,
breaking to white on rims and
edges.

USES
Domestic and decorative.

FIRING RANGE
2354°F (1290°C)
Soak time—1 hour

PARTS DRY WEIGHT

Cornish Stone	28
Quartz	20
Dolomite	18
Whiting	16
China Clay	12
Bone Ash	4
Tin Oxide	2
+ Tin Oxide	10
Copper Carbonate	2
Cobalt Carbonate	1

DESCRIPTION
High gloss, gray/blue with dark
blue speckle.

USES
Decorative.

FIRING RANGE
2354°F (1290°C)
Soak time—1 hour

PARTS DRY WEIGHT

Potash Feldspar	45
Quartz	20
Whiting	20
China Clay	10
Tin Oxide	5
+ Manganese Dioxide	3
Cobalt Carbonate	2

DESCRIPTION
Satin/matte, blue/gray, breaking
to green on rims and edges.

USES
Domestic, decorative, and
sculptural.

FIRING RANGE
2354°F (1290°C)
Soak time—1 hour

PARTS DRY WEIGHT
Potash Feldspar	60
Dolomite	20
Quartz	15
China Clay	5
+ Rutile Oxide	5
Cobalt Oxide	1

DESCRIPTION
Satin/matte, blue/green,
breaking to pale blue on rims
and edges.

USES
Domestic and decorative.

FIRING RANGE
2354°F (1290°C)
Soak time—1 hour

PARTS DRY WEIGHT
Cornish Stone	28
Quartz	20
Dolomite	18
Whiting	16
China Clay	12
Bone Ash	4
Tin Oxide	2
+ Tin Oxide	5
Cobalt Carbonate	1
Chrome Oxide	0.5

DESCRIPTION
Satin, opaque light blue with
dark speckle, breaking to pale
blue on edges.

USES
Domestic and decorative.

FIRING RANGE
2354°F (1290°C)
Soak time—1 hour

PARTS DRY WEIGHT
Cornish Stone	28
Quartz	20
Dolomite	18
Whiting	16
China Clay	12
Bone Ash	4
Tin Oxide	2
+ Tin Oxide	10
Cobalt Carbonate	1
Chrome Oxide	0.5

Blues
OXIDIZED

DESCRIPTION
High gloss, mottled blue and light blue, breaking to green on rims and edges.

USES
Domestic and decorative.

FIRING RANGE
2354°F (1290°C)
Soak time—1 hour

PARTS DRY WEIGHT

Potash Feldspar	60
Dolomite	20
Quartz	15
China Clay	5
+ Rutile Oxide	4
Cobalt Oxide	1

DESCRIPTION
High gloss, mid blue mottled dark blue, breaking to green on rims and edges.

USES
Domestic and decorative.

FIRING RANGE
2354°F (1290°C)
Soak time—1 hour

PARTS DRY WEIGHT

Potash Feldspar	60
Dolomite	20
Quartz	18
China Clay	3
+ Rutile Oxide	3
Cobalt Oxide	2

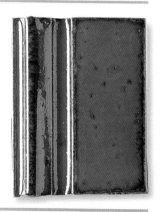

DESCRIPTION
Opaque gloss, light blue mottled with green, breaking to green on rims and edges.

USES
Decorative.

FIRING RANGE
2354°F (1290°C)
Soak time—1 hour.

PARTS DRY WEIGHT

Potash Feldspar	60
Dolomite	20
Quartz	18
China Clay	3
+ Rutile Oxide	4
Cobalt Oxide	2

DESCRIPTION
Satin/gloss, blue mottled with dark blue, breaking to light blue/white on rims and edges.

USES
Domestic and decorative.

FIRING RANGE
2354°F (1290°C)
Soak time—1 hour

PARTS DRY WEIGHT

Cornish Stone	28
Quartz	20
Dolomite	18
Whiting	16
China Clay	12
Bone Ash	4
Tin Oxide	2
+ Tin Oxide	5
Cobalt Oxide	2

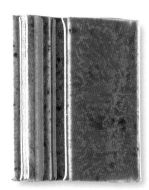

DESCRIPTION
Satin/matte, semi-transparent blue. Some dark blue mottling.

USES
Domestic and decorative.

FIRING RANGE
2354°F (1290°C)
Soak time—1 hour

PARTS DRY WEIGHT

Cornish Stone	28
Quartz	20
Dolomite	18
Whiting	16
China Clay	12
Bone Ash	4
Tin Oxide	2
+ Copper Carbonate	1

ASHLEY HOWARD I STONEWARE DISH

Thrown and altered dish form in a stoneware clay body. A copper-based slip was applied and covered with a barium-based glaze. A clear raku glaze was then added and the piece fired to 2228°F (1220°C) in an oxidizing atmosphere. The raku glaze has caused pools and channels of crazed areas, creating an exciting finish. Diameter 20 in (50 cm).

Blues
OXIDIZED

DESCRIPTION
High gloss, speckled dark blue.

USES
Domestic.

FIRING RANGE
2354°F (1290°C)
Soak time—1 hour

PARTS DRY WEIGHT
Potash Feldspar	45
Quartz	20
Whiting	20
China Clay	10
Tin Oxide	5
+ Manganese Dioxide	3
Cobalt Carbonate	1

DESCRIPTION
Gloss, dark blue, breaking to pale blue on rims and edges.

USES
Domestic and decorative.

FIRING RANGE
2354°F (1290°C)
Soak time—1 hour

PARTS DRY WEIGHT
Potash Feldspar	60
Dolomite	20
Quartz	15
China Clay	5
+ Rutile Oxide	3
Cobalt Oxide	1

DESCRIPTION
High gloss, dark blue, breaking to green on rims and edges.

USES
Domestic and decorative.

FIRING RANGE
Cone 9: 2354°F (1290°C)
Soak time—1 hour

PARTS DRY WEIGHT
Potash Feldspar	60
Dolomite	20
Quartz	18
China Clay	3
+ Rutile Oxide	3
Cobalt Oxide	1

DESCRIPTION
High gloss, deep blue, breaking
to semi-transparent on rims
and edges.

USES
Domestic and decorative.

FIRING RANGE
2354°F (1290°C)
Soak time—1 hour

PARTS DRY WEIGHT

Cornish Stone	28
Quartz	20
Dolomite	18
Whiting	16
China Clay	12
Bone Ash	4
Tin Oxide	2
+ Cobalt Oxide	2

DESCRIPTION
Satin/matte, dark blue/gray.
Lighter in tone on edges and
rims.

USES
Domestic and decorative.

FIRING RANGE
2354°F (1290°C)
Soak time—1 hour

PARTS DRY WEIGHT

Potash Feldspar	46
Dolomite	23
Quartz	15
Zircon	11
China Clay	5
+ Cobalt Oxide	1
Nickel Oxide	1

DESCRIPTION
Gloss opaque, deep blue,
breaking to white on edges
where thin.

USES
Domestic.

FIRING RANGE
2354°F (1290°C)
Soak time—1 hour

PARTS DRY WEIGHT

Potash Feldspar	45
Quartz	20
Whiting	20
China Clay	10
Tin Oxide	5
+ Cobalt Oxide	1
Copper Oxide	1

Blues
REDUCED

DESCRIPTION
Satin/gloss, pale blue. Breaks to white on edges. Apply thinly for "china" blue.

USES
Domestic, decorative, and sculptural.

FIRING RANGE
2300–2336°F (1260–1280°C). Reduction from 2832°F (1000°C). Firing has a 12-hour cycle.

PARTS DRY WEIGHT
Cornish Stone	41
Flint	27
China Clay	16
Whiting	11
Dolomite	5
+ Zinc Oxide	1.5
Cobalt Carbonate	1
Copper Carbonate	0.4

DESCRIPTION
Satin/gloss, blue with some crazing.

USES
Decorative.

FIRING RANGE
2300–2336°F (1260–1280°C). Reduction from 2832°F (1000°C). Firing has a 12-hour cycle.

PARTS DRY WEIGHT
Potash Feldspar	40
Quartz	30
Whiting	20
China Clay	10
+ Tin Oxide	2
Cobalt Oxide	0.15

DESCRIPTION
High gloss, semi-transparent blue with some crazing.

USES
Decorative.

FIRING RANGE
2300–2336°F (1260–1280°C). Reduction from 2832°F (1000°C). Firing has a 12-hour cycle.

PARTS DRY WEIGHT
Soda Feldspar	72
Flint	10
Gerstley Borate	10
Whiting	8
+ Tin Oxide	2
Cobalt Carbonate	0.25

DESCRIPTION
Variegated pale rutile blue, glossy, breaking to beige on rims and edges.

USES
Domestic and decorative.

FIRING RANGE
2336–2372°F (1280–1300°C) with reduction starting at 1580°F (860°C).

PARTS DRY WEIGHT
Feldspar	30
Flint	26
China Clay	17
Dolomite	16
Whiting	11
+ Rutile	8

DESCRIPTION
Satin/gloss, pale blue. Slight speckling, breaking to pale gray/white on edges.

USES
Domestic and decorative.

FIRING RANGE
2300–2336°F (1260–1280°C). Reduction from 1832°F (1000°C). Firing has a 12-hour cycle.

PARTS DRY WEIGHT
Potash Feldspar	40
Quartz	30
Whiting	20
China Clay	0
+ Red Iron Oxide	1
Cobalt Carbonate	0.25

DESCRIPTION
Stony matte, blue with darker speckles, breaking to beige on edges.

USES
Decorative and sculptural.

FIRING RANGE
2300–2336°F (1260–1280°C). Reduction from 1832°F (1000°C). Firing has a 12-hour cycle.

PARTS DRY WEIGHT
Soda Feldspar	60
Whiting	20
China Clay	20
+ Manganese Dioxide	2
Cobalt Carbonate	0.5

Blues
REDUCED

DESCRIPTION
Glossy deep blue. Effective when used in combination with white/pale glazes, brushed, poured, or splashed on.

USES
Domestic and decorative.

FIRING RANGE
2300–2336°F (1260–1280°C). Reduction from 1832°F (1000°C). Firing has a 12-hour cycle.

PARTS DRY WEIGHT

Cornish Stone	78
Whiting	11
China Clay	11
+ Zinc Oxide	10
Cobalt Carbonate	1

DESCRIPTION
Semi matte deep blue.

USES
Mainly decorative ware. Effective as an "overglaze" on whites etc.

FIRING RANGE
2300–2336°F (1260–1280°C). Reduction from 1832°F (1000°C). Firing has a 12-hour cycle.

PARTS DRY WEIGHT

Potash Feldspar	42
Whiting	30
Quartz	28
+ Tin Oxide	2
Cobalt Carbonate	1.5

DESCRIPTION
Satin/gloss, mid-blue. Very slight darker speckle.

USES
Domestic and decorative.

FIRING RANGE
2300–2336°F (1260–1280°C). Reduction from 1832°F (1000°C). Firing has a 12-hour cycle.

PARTS DRY WEIGHT

Cornish Stone	41
Flint	27
China Clay	16
Whiting	11
Dolomite	5
+ Zinc Oxide	1.5
Copper Carbonate	1
Cobalt Oxide	0.25

DESCRIPTION
Glossy, speckled pale blue, breaking to gray on edges.

USES
Domestic and decorative.

FIRING RANGE
2300–2336°F (1260–1280°C). Reduction from 1832°F (1000°C). Firing has a 12-hour cycle.

PARTS DRY WEIGHT

Potash Feldspar	40
Quartz	30
Whiting	20
China Clay	10
+ Cobalt Oxide	0.12
Black Iron Oxide	1

DESCRIPTION
Gloss, mid-blue, some variegation, breaking to beige where thin.

USES
Domestic and decorative.

FIRING RANGE
2336–2372°F (1280–1300°C) with reduction starting at 1580°F (860°C).

PARTS DRY WEIGHT
Mix 50/50 Recipes A and B

Recipe A		Recipe B	
Feldspar	30	Feldspar	40
Flint	26	Whiting	20
China Clay	17	Flint	15
Dolomite	16	Quartz	15
Whiting	11	China Clay	10
+ Rutile	8	+ Rutile	4
		Manganese Dioxide	1
		Manganese Carbonate	2
		Cobalt Oxide	1.5

JIM ROBISON I HAND-BUILT FORM
This stoneware blue vase was hand built and reduction fired in a gas kiln to 2300–2336°F (1260–1280°C). The glaze was sprayed onto the form in thin layers.
Height 30 in (75 cm).

Blues
REDUCED

DESCRIPTION
High gloss, slightly transparent blue, breaking to white on edges with some crazing.

USES
Decorative.

FIRING RANGE
2300–2336°F (1260–1280°C). Reduction from 1832°F (1000°C). Firing has a 12-hour cycle.

PARTS DRY WEIGHT

Potash Feldspar	43
Soda Feldspar	35
Whiting	12
Gerstley Borate	10
+ Tin Oxide	2
Cobalt Carbonate	0.5

DESCRIPTION
Smooth satin/matte blue. Deep blue where glaze is thicker.

USES
Domestic and decorative.

FIRING RANGE
2300–2336°F (1260–1280°C). Reduction from 1832°F (1000°C). Firing has a 12-hour cycle.

PARTS DRY WEIGHT

Cornish Stone	78
Whiting	11
China Clay	11
+ Zinc Oxide	10
Cobalt Carbonate	3

DESCRIPTION
Medium gloss, deep blue.

USES
Mainly decorative. Works well in combination (brushed and/or poured) over white glazes.

FIRING RANGE
2300–2336°F (1260–1280°C). Reduction from 1832°F (1000°C). Firing has a 12-hour cycle.

PARTS DRY WEIGHT

Potash Feldspar	42
Quartz	38
Whiting	20
+ Tin Oxide	2
Cobalt Oxide	2

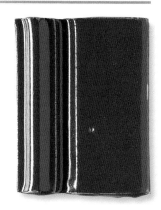

DESCRIPTION
Dark blue, gloss, and slightly variegated.

USES
Domestic and decorative.

FIRING RANGE
2336–2372°F (1280–1300°C) with reduction starting at 1580°F (860°C).

PARTS DRY WEIGHT

Feldspar	40
Whiting	20
Flint	15
Quartz	15
China Clay	10
+ Rutile	4
Manganese Carbonate	2
Cobalt Oxide	1.5
Manganese Dioxide	1

DESCRIPTION
Glossy blue/mauve, breaking to beige on rims and edges.

USES
Domestic and decorative.

FIRING RANGE
2336–2372°F (1280–1300°C) with reduction starting at 1580°F (860°C).

PARTS DRY WEIGHT

Feldspar	30	+ 10 parts of the following:	
Flint	26		
Dolomite	16	Feldspar	40
China Clay	7	Flint	24
Whiting	11	Calcium Borate Frit	9
		Dolomite	9
		Whiting	7
		Zinc Oxide	6
		Tin Oxide	2.5
		China Clay	2
		Copper Carbonate	0.5

DESCRIPTION
Shiny gloss, dark blue with edges breaking to gray/white where thinly applied.

USES
Domestic and decorative.

FIRING RANGE
2300–2336°F (1260–1280°C). Reduction from 1832°F (1000°C). Firing has a 12-hour cycle.

PARTS DRY WEIGHT

Potash Feldspar	40
Quartz	30
Whiting	20
China Clay	10
+ Rutile	3
Cobalt Oxide	0.25

Greens and Turquoises
OXIDIZED

DESCRIPTION
Smooth, satin, opaque yellow green (on stoneware clay). Can be used on porcelain and stoneware bodies.

USES
Domestic and decorative.

FIRING RANGE
2264–2336°F (1240–1280°C)

PARTS DRY WEIGHT
Potash Feldspar	33
Talc	21
Quartz	16
China Clay	15
Whiting	12
Zinc Oxide	3
+ Titanium Dioxide	5
Nickel Oxide	3

DESCRIPTION
High gloss, yellow/green, breaking to beige on edges and rims.

USES
Domestic and decorative.

FIRING RANGE
2354°F (1290°C)
Soak time—1 hour

PARTS DRY WEIGHT
Potash Feldspar	60
Dolomite	20
Quartz	15
China Clay	5
+ Rutile	5
Copper Carbonate	1

DESCRIPTION
Satin, light green with fine dark speckle.

USES
Domestic.

FIRING RANGE
2354°F (1290°C)
Soak time—1 hour

PARTS DRY WEIGHT
Potash Feldspar	60
Dolomite	20
Quartz	15
China Clay	5
+ Rutile Oxide	6
Copper Carbonate	1

DESCRIPTION
Satin, pale gray/green, breaking to gloss green on edges and rims.

USES
Domestic and decorative.

FIRING RANGE
2354°F (1290°C)
Soak time—1 hour

PARTS DRY WEIGHT

Potash Feldspar	45
Dolomite	22
Quartz	16
Zirconium Silicate	11
China Clay	6
+ Copper Carbonate	2

DESCRIPTION
Satin/gloss speckled gray/green. Can be used on porcelain and stoneware bodies.

USES
Domestic and decorative.

FIRING RANGE
2264–2336°F (1240–1280°C)

PARTS DRY WEIGHT

Potash Feldspar	33
Talc	21
Quartz	16
China Clay	15
Whiting	12
Zinc Oxide	3
+ Titanium Dioxide	7.5
Copper Oxide	2
Tin Oxide	1

PETER BEARD I STONEWARE FORM
Slab-built sculptural form fired to 2336°F (1280°C) in an electric kiln. Many layers of glaze were applied using wax as a resist between them.

Height 13 in (33 cm).

Greens and Turquoises
OXIDIZED

DESCRIPTION
Smooth satin green on porcelain clay. Can be used on porcelain and stoneware bodies.

USES
Domestic and decorative.

FIRING RANGE
2264–2336°F (1240–1280°C)

PARTS DRY WEIGHT

Potash Feldspar	33
Talc	21
Quartz	16
China Clay	15
Whiting	12
Zinc Oxide	3
+ Copper Oxide	4

DESCRIPTION
High gloss, semi-transparent green with blue specks and crazing.

USES
Decorative.

FIRING RANGE
2354°F (1290°C)
Soak time—1 hour

PARTS DRY WEIGHT

Potash Feldspar	60
Dolomite	20
Quartz	15
China Clay	5
+ Rutile	3
Copper Carbonate	1

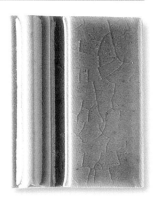

DESCRIPTION
Semi-transparent gloss, green, breaking to pale green on rims and edges. Speckled white. (To avoid "white specks" sieve materials through 120 sieve.)

USES
Domestic and decorative.

FIRING RANGE
2354°F (1290°C)
Soak time—1 hour

PARTS DRY WEIGHT

Quartz	41
China Clay	35
Whiting	24
+ Titanium Dioxide	4
Copper Carbonate	2

DESCRIPTION
Satin, light mottled green, breaking to pale green on rims and edges.

USES
Domestic and decorative.

FIRING RANGE
2354°F (1290°C)
Soak time—1 hour

PARTS DRY WEIGHT
Potash Feldspar	45
Dolomite	22
Quartz	16
Zirconium Silicate	11
China Clay	6
+ Copper Carbonate	2
Nickel Oxide	2

DESCRIPTION
Satin/gloss, green/turquoise with crazing breaking to transparent on rims and edges.

USES
Decorative.

FIRING RANGE
2354°F (1290°C)
Soak time—1 hour

PARTS DRY WEIGHT
Cornish Stone	28
Quartz	20
Dolomite	18
Whiting	16
China Clay	12
Bone Ash	4
Tin Oxide	2
+ Copper Carbonate	1

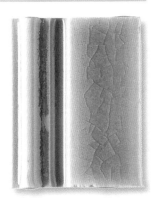

DESCRIPTION
Gloss, semi-transparent green/turquoise, breaking to pale green on rims and edges. Obvious crazing on surface.

USES
Decorative.

FIRING RANGE
2354°F (1290°C)
Soak time—1 hour

PARTS DRY WEIGHT
Potash Feldspar	45
Quartz	20
Whiting	20
China Clay	10
Tin Oxide	5
+ Zinc Oxide	2
Copper Carbonate	2
Lithium Carbonate	2

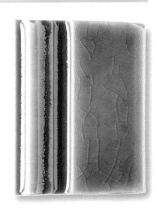

Greens and Turquoises
OXIDIZED

DESCRIPTION
Matte, mottled yellow/green,
breaking to beige on rims
and edges.

USES
Domestic and decorative.

FIRING RANGE
2354°F (1290°C)
Soak time—1 hour

PARTS DRY WEIGHT

Quartz	41
Potash Feldspar	34
Whiting	16
China Clay	9
+ Yellow Ocher	10
Copper Carbonate	2

DESCRIPTION
Satin texture, semi-opaque
green. Breaks to pale green on
edges and rims.

USES
Decorative and sculptural.

FIRING RANGE
2354°F (1290°C)
Soak time—1 hour

PARTS DRY WEIGHT

Potash Feldspar	45
Quartz	20
Whiting	20
China Clay	10
Tin Oxide	5
+ Zinc Oxide	4
Iron Oxide	2
Silicon Carbide	2

DESCRIPTION
High gloss, semi-transparent
green with mottled blue and
some crazing.

USES
Decorative.

FIRING RANGE
2354°F (1290°C)
Soak time—1 hour

PARTS DRY WEIGHT

Potash Feldspar	60
Dolomite	20
Quartz	15
China Clay	5
+ Rutile	4
Copper Carbonate	1

DESCRIPTION
High gloss, green and mottled blue where thicker. Some crazing over surface and breaking to transparent where thin on rims and edges.

USES
Decorative.

FIRING RANGE
2354°F (1290°C)
Soak time—1 hour

PARTS DRY WEIGHT

Potash Feldspar	60
Dolomite	20
Quartz	15
China Clay	5
+ Rutile	2
Copper Carbonate	1

DESCRIPTION
Shiny speckled pink/green. Can be used on porcelain and stoneware bodies.

USES
Domestic and decorative.

FIRING RANGE
2264–2336°F (1240–1280°C)

PARTS DRY WEIGHT

Potash Feldspar	33
Talc	21
Quartz	16
China Clay	15
Whiting	12
Zinc Oxide	3
+ Titanium Dioxide	7.5
Copper Oxide	4

DESCRIPTION
Satin/gloss, opaque and mottled gray/green, breaking to light brown on rims and edges.

USES
Domestic and decorative.

FIRING RANGE
2354°F (1290°C)
Soak time—1 hour

PARTS DRY WEIGHT

Potash Feldspar	60
Dolomite	20
Quartz	15
China Clay	5
+ Titanium Dioxide	3
Copper Carbonate	2
Nickel Oxide	1

Greens and Turquoises
OXIDIZED

DESCRIPTION
Gloss, vivid mottled blue/white with dark brown/black speckle, breaking to red/brown on rims and edges.

USES
Domestic and decorative.

FIRING RANGE
2354°F (1290°C)
Soak time—1 hour

PARTS DRY WEIGHT
Mix 50/50 Recipes A and B

Recipe A

Potash Feldspar	60
Dolomite	20
Quartz	15
China Clay	5

Recipe B

Quartz	41
Potash Feldspar	34
Whiting	16
China Clay	9

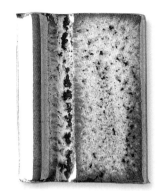

DESCRIPTION
High gloss, gray/green, breaking to light gray/white on rims and edges.

USES
Domestic and decorative.

FIRING RANGE
2354°F (1290°C)
Soak time—1 hour

PARTS DRY WEIGHT

Potash Feldspar	45
Quartz	20
Whiting	20
China Clay	10
Tin Oxide	5
+ Copper Carbonate	1

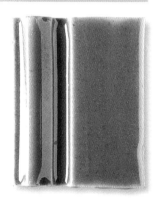

DESCRIPTION
High gloss, dark green with crazing, breaking to pale green on rims and edges.

USES
Decorative.

FIRING RANGE
2354°F (1290°C)
Soak time—1 hour

PARTS DRY WEIGHT

Cornish Stone	28
Quartz	20
Dolomite	18
Whiting	16
China Clay	12
Bone Ash	4
Tin Oxide	2
+ Copper Carbonate	2

DESCRIPTION
Satin, blue gray
with white speckle.

USES
Domestic.

FIRING RANGE
2354°F (1290°C)
Soak time—1 hour

PARTS DRY WEIGHT
Mix 50/50 Recipes A and B

Recipe A
Potash Feldspar 60
Dolomite 20
Quartz 15
China Clay 5

Recipe B
Potash Feldspar 45
Dolomite 22
Quartz 16

Zirconium
  Silicate 11
China Clay 6
+ Rutile 5
Copper
  Carbonate 2
Nickle Oxide 2
Cobalt Oxide 1

DESCRIPTION
Satin/matte, gray/green,
breaking to pale green on rims
and edges.

USES
Domestic and decorative.

FIRING RANGE
2354°F (1290°C)
Soak time—1 hour

PARTS DRY WEIGHT
Feldspar 46
Dolomite 23
Quartz 15
Zircon 11
China Clay 5
+ Copper Carbonate 2

DESCRIPTION
Satin, mottled mauve/green.
Breaking to light green/brown
on rims and edges.

USES
Domestic and decorative.

FIRING RANGE
2354°F (1290°C)
Soak time—1 hour

PARTS DRY WEIGHT
Feldspar 46
Dolomite 23
Quartz 15
Zircon 11
China Clay 5
+ Copper Carbonate 2
  Nickel Oxide 2

Greens and Turquoises
OXIDIZED

DESCRIPTION
Satin/matte, green/brown with dark speckle, breaking to pale green/brown on edges and rims.

USES
Decorative.

FIRING RANGE
2354°F (1290°C)
Soak time—1 hour

PARTS DRY WEIGHT
Cornish Stone	28
Quartz	20
Dolomite	18
Whiting	16
China Clay	12
Bone Ash	4
Tin Oxide	2
+ Chrome Oxide	1

DESCRIPTION
High gloss, dark brown/green, breaking to pale green on rims and edges.

USES
Domestic and decorative.

FIRING RANGE
2354°F (1290°C)
Soak time—1 hour

PARTS DRY WEIGHT
Potash Feldspar	45
Quartz	20
Whiting	20
China Clay	10
Tin Oxide	5
+ Copper Carbonate	2
Nickel Oxide	1

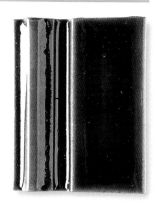

DESCRIPTION
Opaque, satin dark gray, breaking to pale green on rims and edges.

USES
Domestic and decorative.

FIRING RANGE
2354°F (1290°C)
Soak time—1 hour

PARTS DRY WEIGHT
Quartz	41
Potash Feldspar	34
Whiting	16
China Clay	9
+ Yellow Ocher	10
Copper Carbonate	3

DESCRIPTION
Satin, matte, blue/green with dark speckle, breaking to green on rims and edges.

USES
Domestic and decorative.

FIRING RANGE
2354°F (1290°C)
Soak time—1 hour

PARTS DRY WEIGHT

Potash Feldspar	50
Dolomite	30
Quartz	15
China Clay	5
+ Rutile Oxide	5
Cobalt Oxide	2

DESCRIPTION
Matte, dark blue/green, breaking to pale blue/green on rims and edges.

USES
Domestic and decorative.

FIRING RANGE
2354°F (1290°C)
Soak time—1 hour

PARTS DRY WEIGHT

Cornish Stone	28
Quartz	20
Dolomite	18
Whiting	16
China Clay	12
Bone Ash	4
Tin Oxide	2
+ Chrome Oxide	1
Cobalt Oxide	1

DESCRIPTION
Satin/gloss, green/black, breaking to matte blue/green on rims and edges.

USES
Domestic, decorative, and sculptural.

FIRING RANGE
2354°F (1290°C)
Soak time—1 hour

PARTS DRY WEIGHT

Quartz	41
China Clay	35
Whiting	24
+ Copper Carbonate	3
Titanium Dioxide	2
Cobalt Carbonate	2

Greens and Turquoises
REDUCED

DESCRIPTION
Satin/gloss, soft green. Slightly variegated with pale gray patches.

USES
Domestic and decorative.

FIRING RANGE
2300–2336°F (1260–1280°C). Reduction from 1832°F (1000°C). Firing has a 12-hour cycle.

PARTS DRY WEIGHT

Potash Feldspar	35
Flint	25
Whiting	18
Hvar Ball Clay	13
Talc	9
+ Red Iron Oxide	1.25

DESCRIPTION
Satin, pale gray/green with some dark speckling.

USES
Domestic and decorative.

FIRING RANGE
2300–2336°F (1260–1280°C). Reduction from 1832°F (1000°C). Firing has a 12-hour cycle.

PARTS DRY WEIGHT

Cornish Stone	41
Quartz	27
China Clay	16
Whiting	11
Dolomite	5
+ Zinc Oxide	1.5
Red Iron Oxide	1.0

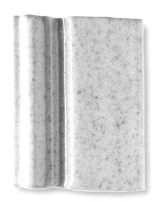

DESCRIPTION
Satin/gloss, pale gray with slight crazing.

USES
Decorative.

FIRING RANGE
2300–2336°F (1260–1280°C). Reduction from 1832°F (1000°C). Firing has a 12-hour cycle.

PARTS DRY WEIGHT

Potash Feldspar	40
Quartz	30
Whiting	20
China Clay	10
+ Red Iron Oxide	1

DESCRIPTION
Glossy "chun"-type glaze, pale green with crazing.

USES
Decorative.

FIRING RANGE
2300–2336°F (1260–1280°C). Reduction from 1832°F (1000°C). Firing has a 12-hour cycle.

PARTS DRY WEIGHT
Potash Feldspar	45
Quartz	25
Whiting	17
China Clay	9
Bone Ash	2
Dolomite	2
+ Red Iron Oxide	1

DESCRIPTION
Gloss, cream/gray with dark speckles.

USES
Domestic and decorative.

FIRING RANGE
2300–2336°F (1260–1280°C). Reduction from 1832°F (1000°C). Firing has a 12-hour cycle.

PARTS DRY WEIGHT
Cornish Stone	80
China Clay	10
Whiting	10
+ Black Iron Oxide	1

DESCRIPTION
Gloss, variegated gray/green. Slight crazing.

USES
Decorative.

FIRING RANGE
2300–2336°F (1260–1280°C). Reduction from 1832°F (1000°C). Firing has a 12-hour cycle.

PARTS DRY WEIGHT
Potash Feldspar	40
Quartz	30
Whiting	20
China Clay	10
+ Black Iron Oxide	8

Greens and Turquoises
REDUCED

DESCRIPTION
Glossy, pale green with some speckle.

USES
Decorative and domestic.

FIRING RANGE
2336–2372°F
(1280–1300°C). Reduction
starting at 1580°F (860°C).

PARTS DRY WEIGHT
Nepheline Syenite	35
Quartz	33
Dolomite	10
Whiting	8
Barium Carbonate	6
Rutile	4
China Clay	2
Copper Carbonate	2

DESCRIPTION
Satin/gloss, green with broken oatmeal speckle on rims and edges where thin.

USES
Domestic and decorative.

FIRING RANGE
2336–2372°F
(1280–1300°C). Reduction
starting at 1580°F (860°C).

PARTS DRY WEIGHT
Mixed Wood Ash	67
Feldspar	17
Red Clay	16

DESCRIPTION
Semi-gloss to matte, green and beige. Crazes over most clay bodies. The wood ash is unwashed and sieved dry through a 60-mesh sieve.

USES
Domestic and decorative.

FIRING RANGE
2336–2372°F
(1280–1300°C). Reduction
starting at 1580°F (860°C)

PARTS DRY WEIGHT
Wood Ash	38
Feldspar	30
China Clay	20
Flint	12

DESCRIPTION

Glossy, dark green. Burns out to orange where thin. Very fluid at top temperature—2372°F (1300°C). Do not apply thickly.

USES

Decorative and domestic.

FIRING RANGE

2336–2372°F (1280–1300°C). Reduction starting at 1580°F (860°C).

PARTS DRY WEIGHT

Feldspar	28
Wood Ash	18
Flint	16
China Clay	15
Whiting	10
Titanium Oxide	5
Talc	4
Copper Oxide	3
Bone Ash	1

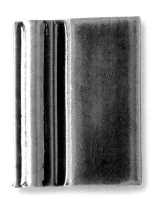

DESCRIPTION

Glossy, dark oily green, breaking to pale gray/green where thin on rims and edges.

USES

Domestic and decorative. Can be very fluid if thickly applied.

FIRING RANGE

2336–2372°F (1280–1300°C). Reduction starting at 1580°F (860°C).

PARTS DRY WEIGHT

Feldspar	28
Flint	24
Whiting	22
China Clay	12
Talc	8
Copper Oxide	5
Bone Ash	1

KATE SHAKESHAFT MURRAY I STRIPED JAR

This "triple green" striped jar was thrown and reduction fired to 2372°F (1300°C). Wax resist was used between the layers of glaze to create the striped effect. The following glazes were used. Soft Green: Custer Feldspar 35, Flint 35, Dolomite 15, Kaolin 9, Whiting 5, + Black Iron Oxide 2, Cobalt Carbonate 0.25, Chrome Oxide 0.5. McKenzie White: Custer Feldspar 41, Flint 21, Talc 14, Gerstley Borate 12, Dolomite 7, Ball Clay 5. Rutile Green: Custer Feldspar 30, Flint 26, Kaolin 17, Dolomite 16, Whiting 11, Rutile 8, + Copper Carbonate 5.

Greens and Turquoises
REDUCED

DESCRIPTION
Medium gloss, mid-green, even
coloration.

USES
Decorative.

FIRING RANGE
2300–2336°F
(1260–1280°C). Reduction
from 1832°F (1000°C). Firing
has a 12-hour cycle.

PARTS DRY WEIGHT
Cornish Stone	80
China Clay	10
Whiting	10
+ Chromium Oxide	0.25
Cobalt Carbonate	0.25

DESCRIPTION
Satin/gloss, dark green with
slight speckle.

USES
Domestic and decorative.

FIRING RANGE
2300–2336°F
(1260–1280°C). Reduction
from 1832°F (1000°C). Firing
has a 12-hour cycle.

PARTS DRY WEIGHT
Potash Feldspar	40
Quartz	30
Whiting	20
China Clay	10
Chromium Oxide	0.5
Cobalt Carbonate	0.25

DESCRIPTION
Satin/gloss, bottle-green.
All-over even color.

USES
Domestic and decorative.

FIRING RANGE
2300–2336°F
(1260–1280°C). Reduction
from 1832°F (1000°C). Firing
has a 12-hour cycle.

PARTS DRY WEIGHT
Cornish Stone	80
China Clay	10
Whiting	10
+ Chromium Oxide	1
Cobalt Oxide	0.25

DESCRIPTION

Semi-gloss, dark turquoise green.

USES

Decorative. Used mainly for brushing and trailing to form over-decoration on other glazes.

FIRING RANGE

2336–2372°F (1280–1300°C). Reduction starting at 1580°F (860°C).

PARTS DRY WEIGHT	
Alkaline Frit	43
Quartz	33
China Clay	18
Tin Oxide	4.5
Chrome Oxide	1
Cobalt Oxide	0.5

DESCRIPTION

Glossy, blue/green. Slightly darker speckled effect.

USES

Domestic and decorative.

FIRING RANGE

2300–2336°F (1260–1280°C). Reduction from 1832°F (1000°C). Firing has a 12-hour cycle.

PARTS DRY WEIGHT	
Potash Feldspar	63
Quartz	25
Whiting	7
China Clay	5
+ Cobalt Carbonate	0.5
Chromium Oxide	0.5

DESCRIPTION

Glossy, dark green/turquoise. Gives uniform effect if evenly applied.

USES

Domestic and decorative.

FIRING RANGE

2300–2336°F (1260–1280°C). Reduction from 1832°F (1000°C). Firing has a 12-hour cycle.

PARTS DRY WEIGHT	
Cornish Stone	80
China Clay	10
Whiting	10
+ Chromium Oxide	0.5
Cobalt Carbonate	0.5

Black, White, and Metallic
OXIDIZED

DESCRIPTION
Opaque gloss, white. Good all over cover.

USES
Mainly on domestic ware. Slight texture that can be removed by sieving through finer sieve, e.g. 120 mesh.

FIRING RANGE
2354°F (1290°C)
Soak time—1 hour

PARTS DRY WEIGHT
Potash Feldspar	60
Dolomite	20
Quartz	15
China Clay	5
+ Tin Oxide	10

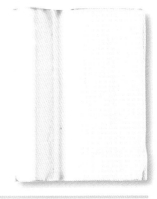

DESCRIPTION
Semi-opaque satin/gloss, white.

USES
Mainly on domestic ware. Very good when used in combination with oxide decoration.

FIRING RANGE
2354°F (1290°C)
Soak time—1 hour

PARTS DRY WEIGHT
Potash Feldspar	60
Dolomite	20
Quartz	15
China Clay	5
+ Tin Oxide	5

DESCRIPTION
Gloss, white, breaking to beige on edges.

USES
Mainly for domestic use and good in combination with oxide decoration, particularly cobalt.

FIRING RANGE
2354°F (1290°C)
Soak time—1 hour

PARTS DRY WEIGHT
Potash Feldspar	60
Dolomite	20
Quartz	15
China Clay	5
+ Zircon Silicate	5

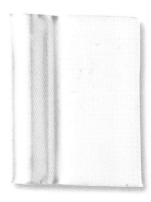

DESCRIPTION
Satin/gloss, white, breaking to beige on edges and rims.

USES
Mainly for domestic ware. Works very well in combination with oxide decoration, over or under glaze.

FIRING RANGE
2354°F (1290°C)
Soak time—1 hour

PARTS DRY WEIGHT
Potash Feldspar	60
Dolomite	20
Quartz	15
China Clay	5
+ Zircon Silicate	10

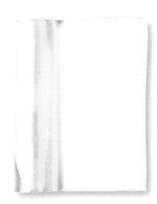

DESCRIPTION
Satin, white.

USES
Domestic and decorative. Very good with oxides as under- or overglaze decoration.

FIRING RANGE
2354°F (1290°C)
Soak time—1 hour

PARTS DRY WEIGHT
Feldspar	45
Dolomite	22
Quartz	16
Zirconium Silicate	11
China Clay	6

USCH SPETTIGUE I THROWN AND CUT VASE
Wheel-thrown and altered piece. It was raw glazed and fired to 2300°F (1260°C) in an oxidizing atmosphere. The white glaze consisted of: Feldspar 49.6, Dolomite 14, Ball Clay 12, China Clay 10.8, Whiting 10, Quartz 3.6, + Bentonite 10.
Height 13 in (33 cm).

Black, White, and Metallic
OXIDIZED

DESCRIPTION
Satin, black, mottled deep
green where glaze is thickly
applied.

USES
Domestic and decorative.

FIRING RANGE
2354°F (1290°C)
Soak time—1 hour

PARTS DRY WEIGHT
Quartz	41
Potash Feldspar	34
Whiting	16
China Clay	9
+ Yellow Ocher	10
Chrome Oxide	1
Nickel Oxide	1

DESCRIPTION
Satin/gloss, black, mottled with
brown.

USES
Domestic and decorative.

FIRING RANGE
2354°F (1290°C)
Soak time—1 hour.

PARTS DRY WEIGHT
Quartz	41
Potash Feldspar	34
Whiting	16
China Clay	9
+ Red Iron Oxide	5
Cobalt Oxide	2
Manganese Dioxide	2

DESCRIPTION
High gloss, shiny dark
brown/black.

USES
Domestic.

FIRING RANGE
2354°F (1290°C)
Soak time—1 hour.

PARTS DRY WEIGHT
Quartz	41
Potash Feldspar	34
Whiting	16
China Clay	9
+ Red Iron Oxide	10

DESCRIPTION
High gloss, black, breaking to
brown on edges.

USES
Domestic.

FIRING RANGE
2354°F (1290°C)
Soak time—1 hour

PARTS DRY WEIGHT

Quartz	41
Potash Feldspar	34
Whiting	16
China Clay	9
+ Black Iron Oxide	10

DESCRIPTION
High gloss, solid black,
breaking to blue on rims and
edges.

USES
Mainly for use on domestic
ware.

FIRING RANGE
2354°F (1290°C)
Soak time—1 hour

PARTS DRY WEIGHT

Potash Feldspar	45
Quartz	20
Whiting	20
China Clay	10
Tin Oxide	5
+ Manganese Dioxide	2
Iron Oxide	2
Cobalt Oxide	2

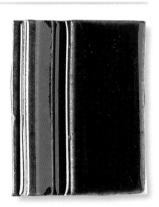

DESCRIPTION
Satin, black.

USES
Domestic and decorative.

FIRING RANGE
2354°F (1290°C)
Soak time—1 hour

PARTS DRY WEIGHT

Quartz	41
Potash Feldspar	34
Whiting	16
China Clay	9
+ Red Iron Oxide	12

Black, White, and Metallic
OXIDIZED

DESCRIPTION
Satin, matte "pewter" metallic glaze.

USES
Decorative and sculptural.

FIRING RANGE
2264–2300°F (1240–1260°C)

PARTS DRY WEIGHT
Manganese Dioxide	77
China Clay	23

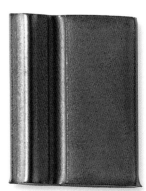

DESCRIPTION
Dry, matte and textured gold.

USES
Decorative and sculptural.

FIRING RANGE
2264–2300°F
(1240–1260°C)

PARTS DRY WEIGHT
China Clay	70
Manganese Dioxide	23
Copper Oxide	7

DESCRIPTION
Smooth, satin black/brown stoneware glaze.

USES
Decorative and sculptural.

FIRING RANGE
2264–2300°F (1240–1260°C)

PARTS DRY WEIGHT
Potash Feldspar	50
China Clay	20
Dolomite	10
Whiting	10
Quartz	10
+ Manganese Dioxide	3.0
Red Iron Oxide	3.0
Cobalt Oxide	1.0

DESCRIPTION
Textured, matte gold metallic glaze.

USES
Decorative and sculptural.

FIRING RANGE
2264–2300°F (1240–1260°C)

PARTS DRY WEIGHT
Manganese Dioxide	70
China Clay	23
Copper Oxide	7

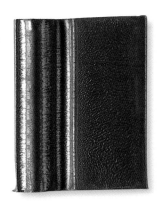

DESCRIPTION
Textured, matte gold metallic glaze.

USES
Decorative and sculptural.

FIRING RANGE
2264–2300°F (1240–1260°C)

PARTS DRY WEIGHT
Manganese Dioxide	65
China Clay	21
Copper Oxide	14

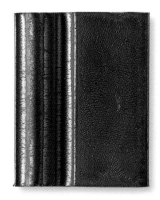

DESCRIPTION
Satin, matte gold metallic glaze.

USES
Decorative and sculptural.

FIRING RANGE
2264–2300°F (1240–1260°C)

PARTS DRY WEIGHT
Manganese Dioxide	61
China Clay	23
Copper Oxide	8
Cobalt Oxide	8

Black, White, and Metallic
REDUCED

DESCRIPTION
Hard, glossy shiny white.

USES
Decorative and domestic. This glaze works very well over cobalt oxide decoration.

FIRING RANGE
2336–2372°F (1280–1300°C) with reduction starting at 1580°F (860°C).

PARTS DRY WEIGHT
Feldspar	35
Flint	23
Whiting	23
Zircon Silicate	10
China Clay	9

DESCRIPTION
Satin/gloss, white. Effective used in combination with coloring oxides for decoration.

USES
Domestic and decorative.

FIRING RANGE
2300–2336°F (1260–1280°C). Reduction from 1832°F (1000°C). Firing has a 12-hour cycle.

PARTS DRY WEIGHT
Potash Feldspar	40
Quartz	16
Whiting	14
Hvar Ball Clay	10
China Clay	10
Zirconium Silicate	10

DESCRIPTION
Smooth satin/gloss, white. Works well with oxides under or over glaze decoration.

USES
Domestic and decorative.

FIRING RANGE
2300–2336°F (1260–1280°C). Reduction from 1832°F (1000°C). Firing has a 12-hour cycle.

PARTS DRY WEIGHT
Potash Feldspar	55
China Clay	15
Quartz	15
Whiting	10
Talc	5

DESCRIPTION
Glossy, soft shiny white.

USES
Decorative and domestic. Again works well over oxide decoration.

FIRING RANGE
2336–2372°F (1280–1300°C) with reduction starting at 1580°F (860°C).

PARTS DRY WEIGHT

China Clay	21
Feldspar	20
Flint	20
Whiting	11
Talc	11
Zircon Silicate	6
Ball Clay	6
Bone Ash	5

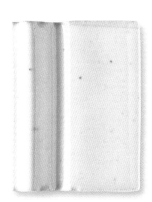

DESCRIPTION
Smooth matte, white with slight yellow speckling. Eggshell type glaze effective in combination with oxides.

USES
Domestic and decorative.

FIRING RANGE
2300–2336°F (1260–1280°C). Reduction from 1832°F (1000°C). Firing has a 12-hour cycle.

PARTS DRY WEIGHT

Potash Feldspar	46
Barium Carbonate	21
Zirconium Silicate	15
Talc	5
China Clay	5
Whiting	3
+ Red Iron Oxide	1.0

DESCRIPTION
Satin/matte, white with mottled and speckled gray areas.

USES
Decorative ware and could work on sculptural pieces.

FIRING RANGE
2300–2336°F (1260–1280°C). Reduction from 1832°F (1000°C). Firing has a 12-hour cycle.

PARTS DRY WEIGHT

Potash Feldspar	34
China Clay	30
Whiting	21
Flint	12
Talc	3
+ Titanium Dioxide	6

Black, White, and Metallic
REDUCED

DESCRIPTION
Stony matte, gray/blue. Pink glow, breaking to beige/white on edges where thin.

USES
Decorative and sculptural.

FIRING RANGE
2300–2336°F (1260–1280°C). Reduction from 1832°F (1000°C). Firing has a 12-hour cycle.

PARTS DRY WEIGHT

Potash Feldspar	50
Dolomite	20
China Clay	20
Bone Ash	10
+ Nickel Oxide	0.5
Cobalt Carbonate	0.5

DESCRIPTION
Matte, gray with dark speckled effect.

USES
Decorative and sculptural.

FIRING RANGE
2300–2336°F (1260–1280°C). Reduction from 1832°F (1000°C). Firing has a 12-hour cycle.

PARTS DRY WEIGHT

Barium Carbonate	50
Nepheline Syenite	50
+ Bentonite	3
Nickel Oxide	0.5

DESCRIPTION
Dry matte gray with mauve tint on edges.

USES
Decorative and sculptural.

FIRING RANGE
2300–2336°F (1260–1280°C). Reduction from 2832°F (1000°C). Firing has a 12-hour cycle.

PARTS DRY WEIGHT

Barium Carbonate	50
Nepheline Syenite	50
+ Bentonite	3
Copper Carbonate	1.5

DESCRIPTION
Satin/matte, gray/mauve.
Yellow on edges where glaze is
thinner.

USES
Domestic, decorative, and
sculptural.

FIRING RANGE
2300–2336°F (1260–1280°C).
Reduction from 1832°F (1000°C).
Firing has a 12-hour cycle.

PARTS DRY WEIGHT
Nepheline Syenite	70
Dolomite	10
Flint	10
China Clay	7
Whiting	2
+ Zinc Oxide	2
Titanium Dioxide	2
Red Iron Oxide	0.5

DESCRIPTION
Variegated matte to shiny
charcoal black.

USES
Mainly sculptural.

FIRING RANGE
2336–2372°F (1280–1300°C)
with reduction starting at
1580°F (860°C).

PARTS DRY WEIGHT
Manganese Dioxide	70
Rutile	20
Cobalt Carbonate	10

DESCRIPTION
Dry charcoal matte black.

USES
Mainly sculptural. This glaze
can also be used to good effect
as a blue decorative pigment.

FIRING RANGE
2336–2372°F (1280–1300°C)
with reduction starting at
1580°F (860°C).

PARTS DRY WEIGHT
Iron Oxide	30
China Clay	28
Cobalt Oxide	20
Feldspar	12
Flint	10

Black, White, and Metallic
REDUCED

DESCRIPTION
High gloss, "mirror" black, metallic in areas. Brown on edges.

USES
Domestic, decorative, and sculptural.

FIRING RANGE
2300–2336°F (1260–1280°C). Reduction from 1832°F (1000°C). Firing has a 12-hour cycle.

PARTS DRY WEIGHT

Ball Clay	26
Quartz	26
Feldspar	21
Whiting	16
Talc	5
+ Red Iron Oxide	12

DESCRIPTION
Satin/gloss, variegated black and green, breaking on edges and rims to a rust red/brown.

USES
Domestic and decorative.

FIRING RANGE
2300–2336°F (1260–1280°C). Reduction from 1832°F (1000°C). Firing has a 12-hour cycle.

PARTS DRY WEIGHT

Potash Feldspar	77
Hvar Ball Clay	10
Whiting	9
Quartz	3
+ Red Iron Oxide	8

DESCRIPTION
Semi-gloss, dark brown/khaki and variegated, breaking to red rust on edges.

USES
Excellent for domestic and decorative ware.

FIRING RANGE
2336–2372°F (1280°C–1300°C) with reduction starting at 1580°F (860°C).

PARTS DRY WEIGHT

Feldspar	37
Red Clay	22
Flint	20
Whiting	6
A.T. Ball Clay	5
Ilmanite	5
Iron Oxide	5

DESCRIPTION
Semi-matte, black, breaking slightly to reddish/brown.

USES
Domestic, decorative, and sculptural.

FIRING RANGE
2300–2336°F (1260–1280°C). Reduction from 1832°F (1000°C). Firing has a 12-hour cycle.

PARTS DRY WEIGHT

Cornish Stone	41
Flint	27
China Clay	16
Whiting	11
Dolomite	5
+ Red Iron Oxide	8
Manganese Dioxide	3
Zinc Oxide	1.5
Cobalt Oxide	1

DESCRIPTION
High gloss, solid black when applied thickly, breaking to rust red/brown on edges.

USES
Domestic and decorative.

FIRING RANGE
2300–2336°F (1260–1280°C). Reduction from 1832°F (1000°C). Firing has a 12-hour cycle.

PARTS DRY WEIGHT

Potash Feldspar	60
Quartz	20
Hvar Ball Clay	10
Whiting	10
+ Red Iron Oxide	8

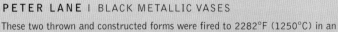

PETER LANE | BLACK METALLIC VASES
These two thrown and constructed forms were fired to 2282°F (1250°C) in an oxidizing atmosphere (electric kiln). The surfaces were evenly sprayed with the following metallic, black glaze: Potash Feldspar 65, China Clay 25, Manganese Dioxide 20, Flint 4, Whiting 3, Dolomite 2, Red Iron Oxide 1.
Height 16 in (39 cm).

SODA

Useful Information For Soda Firing

- The soda tiles were all fired in an 8 cu ft propane gas kiln to 2372°F (1300°C).

- 1½ lb (0.75kg) of soda crystals (sodium bicarbonate) was dissolved in 4 pt (2l) of hot water.

- The soda is introduced into the kiln at about 2228°F (1220°C). It volatilizes and combines with the silica in the clay to form sodium alumina silicate glaze.

- Soda glaze has a distinctive effect upon the surface of the ware, causing an "orange peel" finish.

- The way that the pots are packed in the kiln is a vital factor in creating a unique finish for each piece. Enough space must be left between the pots to allow the vapor to travel throughout the kiln. This placing of the pots in the kiln can therefore provide some control over how much vapor affects each piece.

- As with all the other firing methods, the "heatwork" of the kiln together with the skill of controlling the kiln atmosphere will greatly affect the outcome!

REBECCA HARVEY I LIDDED POTS
Soda-fired lidded jar and teapot. The soda is introduced to the kiln atmosphere and from around 2264–2336°F (1240–1280°C) it fuses with the silica in the clay body or slip/glaze to produce the characteristic orange-peel texture.

Firing Schedule

1922°F (1050°C)
Begin the reduction process.

2228°F (1220°C)
Introduce the soda solution into the kiln atmosphere every 10 minutes for an hour (oxidation atmosphere).

2354°F (1290°)
Soak for 10 minutes or until 2372°F (1300°C) is reached.

2372–1832°F (1300°C–1000°C)
"Crash cool" the kiln (open all bungs). Then close up the kiln until it is cool enough to unpack the ware.

CAUTION
Salt firing is a toxic process, producing hydrochloric acid fumes. Therefore many potters choose the less polluting option of soda firing. This is less corrosive of the kiln interior and produces softer and brighter colors.

DESCRIPTION
Smooth matte white, breaking to tan on edges.

USES
Domestic, decorative, and sculptural.

FIRING RANGE
2336–2372°F (1280–1300°C)
Soak time—10 minutes

PARTS DRY WEIGHT
China Clay   100

DESCRIPTION
Glossy gray, breaking to a warm tan yellow where thin.

USES
Domestic, decorative, and sculptural.

FIRING RANGE
2336–2372°F (1280–1300°C)
Soak time—10 minutes

PARTS DRY WEIGHT
Nepheline Syenite	34
Hymod A.T. Ball Clay	33
Potash Feldspar	33

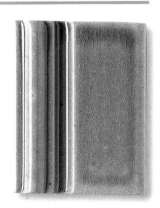

DESCRIPTION
Glossy, pale green, with transparent quality.

USES
Domestic, decorative, and sculptural.

FIRING RANGE
2336–2372°F (1280–1300°C)
Soak time—10 minutes

PARTS DRY WEIGHT
Wollastonite	28
Quartz	25
Potash Feldspar	24
China Clay	20
Talc	3
+ Black Iron Oxide	2

Soda
REDUCED

DESCRIPTION
Smooth satin tan/yellow.

USES
Domestic, decorative, and sculptural.

FIRING RANGE
2336–2372°F (1280–1300°C)
Soak time—10 minutes

PARTS DRY WEIGHT
Hyplas 71 Ball Clay	38
China Clay	38
Nepheline Syenite	24
+ Rutile Oxide	8

DESCRIPTION
Glossy, mottled tan yellow/gray/green.

USES
Domestic, decorative, and sculptural.

FIRING RANGE
2336–2372°F (1280–1300°C)
Soak time—10 minutes

PARTS DRY WEIGHT
Nepheline Syenite	34
Hymod A.T. Ball Clay	33
China Clay	33

DESCRIPTION
Smooth satin/gloss, orange/tan.

USES
Domestic, decorative, and sculptural.

FIRING RANGE
2336–2372°F (1280–1300°C)
Soak time—10 minutes

PARTS DRY WEIGHT
Hymod A.T. Ball Clay	60
Nepheline Syenite	40

DESCRIPTION
Satin/matte tan yellow/orange.

USES
Domestic, decorative, and sculptural.

FIRING RANGE
2336–2372°F (1280–1300°C)
Soak time—10 minutes

PARTS DRY WEIGHT

China Clay	52
Hymod A.T. Ball Clay	33
Potash Feldspar	8
Quartz	5
Bentonite	2

DESCRIPTION
Satin/matte, brown.

USES
Domestic, decorative, and sculptural.

FIRING RANGE
2336–2372°F (1280–1300°C)
Soak time—10 minutes

PARTS DRY WEIGHT

China Clay	70
Nepheline Syenite	30
+ Venadium Pentoxide	7
Chrome Oxide	2

MICHAEL CASSON | SALT-GLAZED JUG
Salt glazed stoneware jug fired to 2372°F (1300°C) in wood-fired kiln. This piece was made with an iron-bearing clay and coated with a slip of a 50/50 mix of nepheline syenite and ball clay. This, combined with the wood-fired salt glazing, has resulted in a wonderful, warm, and rich surface on this pot.
Height 14½ in (36 cm).

Soda
REDUCED

DESCRIPTION
Smooth satin/gloss metallic brown.

USES
Decorative, domestic, and sculptural.

FIRING RANGE
2336°F–2372°F
(1280°C–1300°C)
Soak time—10 minutes

PARTS DRY WEIGHT
Hyplas 71 Ball Clay	70
Nepheline Syenite	30
+ Rutile	8
Red Iron Oxide	5
Manganese Dioxide	1

DESCRIPTION
Glossy "orange peel" light blue.

USES
Domestic, decorative, and sculptural.

FIRING RANGE
2336°F–2372°F
(1280°C–1300°C)
Soak time—10 minutes

PARTS DRY WEIGHT
China Clay	60
Potash Feldspar	40
+ Cobalt Carbonate	1
Titanium Dioxide	1

DESCRIPTION
Glossy dark green/turquoise.

USES
Domestic, decorative, and sculptural.

FIRING RANGE
2336–2372°F (1280–1300°C)
Soak time—10 minutes

PARTS DRY WEIGHT
Ball Clay	75
Hyplas	71
Nepheline Syenite	25
+ Turquoise Glaze Stain	8

DESCRIPTION
Satin/gloss, dark
green/turquoise.

USES
Domestic, decorative, and
sculptural.

FIRING RANGE
2336°F-2372°F
(1280°C-1300°C)
Soak time—10 minutes

PARTS DRY WEIGHT
Nepheline Syenite	75
China Clay	25
+ Turquoise Glaze Stain	7
Green Glaze Stain	3

DESCRIPTION
Smooth matte dark
blue/turquoise.

USES
Domestic, decorative, and
sculptural.

FIRING RANGE
2336°F-2372°F
(1280°C-1300°C)
Soak time—10 minutes

PARTS DRY WEIGHT
China Clay	70
Nepheline Syenite	30
+ Cobalt Carbonate	0.5
Titanium Dioxide	5

DESCRIPTION
Glossy dark blue/metallic.

USES
Domestic, decorative, and
sculptural.

FIRING RANGE
2336–2372°F (1280–1300°C)
Soak time—10 minutes

PARTS DRY WEIGHT
China Clay	50
Nepheline Syenite	50
+ Red Iron Oxide	7
Cobalt Oxide	2
Chrome Oxide	1

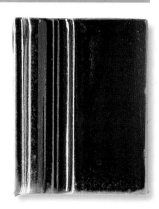

Porcelain

The tiles featured in this section were made with Valentines Clay Co. "Audrey Blackman" porcelain body. They were all biscuit fired to 1859°F (1015°C).

The name "porcelain" is said to be derived from the Italian "porcella" meaning "little pig," a Mediterranean sea snail whose shell is noted for its whiteness and translucency. This derivation demonstrates the nature of porcelain clays that are vitrified, white and translucent, i.e. they allow some light to pass through them.

Porcelain bodies usually have a china clay base to which feldspar is added to provide a flux. Flint and/or quartz are also added to aid stability, hardness, and a better "glaze fit."

Traditionally the firing range is higher than for stoneware: 2372–2642°F (1300–1450°C). However, porcelain bodies have recently been developed that show all the qualities of porcelain, and mature within the 2228–2336°F (1220–1280°C) temperature range. Potters have also experimented with various body recipes to produce a "throwable" porcelain body. The addition of even a small amount of ball clay tends to darken the body.

TOM COLEMAN
THROWN FORM
The pot was sprayed over with a crystal matte glaze after being coated with layers of colored slips. Dry wood ash was then sprinkled over the surface. Fired to 2372°F (1300°C) in a gas kiln.

David Leach has produced a well-known porcelain clay body. He overcame the problem of plasticity by introducing bentonite to the recipe:

"David Leach" Porcelain Body:

China Clay	55
Potash Feldspar	25
Quartz	15
White Bentonite	5

"David Leach" Porcelain Base Glaze:*

China Clay	25
Feldspar	25
Flint	25
Whiting	25

GARETH MASON I
COPPER RED JAR
This richly colored glaze is Derek Emms Red, (see page 239), poured and brushed on to bisque-fired porcelain.

*Can be modified and enhanced with the addition of various coloring oxides and commercial glaze stains.

ALAN FOXLEY I HAND-BUILT FORM The clay body is 80 percent porcelain and 20 percent "T" material, covered with a porcelain slip when leatherhard. A manganese oxide stain was rubbed into the surface. When the form was dry it was fired once to 2336°F (1280°C).

Porcelain is traditionally associated with the soft, subtle pale blues and greens of early Chinese celadons. As with stoneware, the higher firing range does inhibit the production of brighter, more vivid colors. However, the pure white burning clay bodies do promote some intense, deep, and brilliant colors. The potential for these has been significantly increased by the more recent development of commercial colors and stains that remain stable at higher temperatures.

Naturals and Browns
OXIDIZED

DESCRIPTION
Smooth matte. Cream/off-white.

USES
Domestic

FIRING RANGE
2336°F (1280°C)

PARTS DRY WEIGHT
Potash Feldspar	35
Quartz	20
China Clay	20
Dolomite	20
Whiting	5

DESCRIPTION
Smooth matte/satin. Light beige/cream.

USES
Domestic.

FIRING RANGE
2336°F (1280°C)

PARTS DRY WEIGHT
Potash Feldspar	36
China Clay	21
Whiting	17
Quartz	10
Talc	10
Ball Clay	6
+ Rutile	3

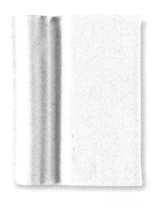

DESCRIPTION
Smooth matte/satin. Pale beige.

USES
Domestic.

FIRING RANGE
2336°F (1280°C)

PARTS DRY WEIGHT
Potash Feldspar	36
China Clay	21
Whiting	17
Quartz	10
Talc	10
Ball Clay	6
+ Rutile	8
Tin	8

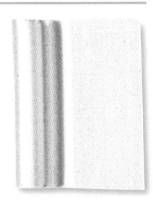

DESCRIPTION
Satin. Speckles if sieved
through 100 mesh, smooth
color if sieved through 200
mesh.

USES
Domestic.

FIRING RANGE
2336°F (1280°C)

PARTS DRY WEIGHT
Potash Feldspar	43
Quartz	30
Whiting	20
Talc	4
China Clay	2
Colemanite	1
+ Black Iron Oxide	5

DESCRIPTION
Satin/matte. Speckled cream.

USES
Domestic.

FIRING RANGE
2336°F (1280°C)

PARTS DRY WEIGHT
Potash Feldspar	35
Quartz	20
China Clay	20
Dolomite	20
Whiting	5
+ Red Iron Oxide	0.5

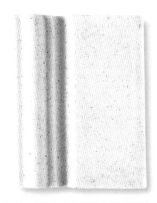

DESCRIPTION
Satin/matte. Speckled pale
beige/cream.

USES
Domestic.

FIRING RANGE
2336°F (1280°C)

PARTS DRY WEIGHT
Potash Feldspar	35
Quartz	20
China Clay	20
Dolomite	20
Whiting	5
+ Red Iron Oxide	1

Naturals and Browns
OXIDIZED

DESCRIPTION
Satin. Cream speckle if sieved through 100 mesh.

USES
Domestic.

FIRING RANGE
Electric 2336°F (1280°C)

PARTS DRY WEIGHT

Potash Feldspar	43
Quartz	30
Whiting	20
Talc	4
China Clay	2
Colemanite	1
+ Black Iron Oxide	1

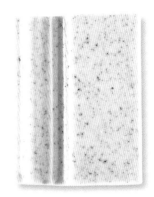

DESCRIPTION
Smooth matte. Speckled light brown.

USES
Domestic.

FIRING RANGE
2336°F (1280°C)

PARTS DRY WEIGHT

Potash Feldspar	35
Quartz	20
China Clay	20
Dolomite	20
Whiting	5
+ Red Iron Oxide	2

DESCRIPTION
Satin/gloss light ocher. Can be used on porcelain and stoneware bodies.

USES
Domestic and decorative.

FIRING RANGE
2264–2336°F (1240–1280°C)

PARTS DRY WEIGHT

Potash Feldspar	33
Talc	21
Quartz	16
China Clay	15
Whiting	12
Zinc Oxide	3
+ Titanium Dioxide	10
Vanadium Pentoxide	3

DESCRIPTION
Smooth matte. Speckled
brown.

USES
Domestic.

FIRING RANGE
2336°F (1280°C)

PARTS DRY WEIGHT
Potash Feldspar	35
Quartz	20
China Clay	20
Dolomite	20
Whiting	5
+ Red Iron Oxide	4

DESCRIPTION
Smooth, satin opaque light
yellow/ocher. Can be used on
porcelain and stoneware
bodies.

USES
Domestic and decorative.

FIRING RANGE
2264–2336°F (1240–1280°C)

PARTS DRY WEIGHT
Potash Feldspar	33
Talc	21
Quartz	16
China Clay	15
Whiting	12
Zinc Oxide	3
+ Titanium Dioxide	7.5
Tin Oxide	2.5
Chrome Oxide	1

GARETH MASON | THROWN PORCELAIN BOTTLE
Elegantly shaped thrown bottle in porcelain with a white matte glaze. The
glaze works well in both oxidation or reduction and should be fired in
the range 2300–2336°F (1260–1280°C). The glaze recipe is as
follows: Cornish Stone 60, China Clay 20, Dolomite 20.

Naturals and Browns
OXIDIZED

DESCRIPTION
Matte glaze in yellow and beige tones.

USES
Domestic.

FIRING RANGE
2336°F (1280°C)

PARTS DRY WEIGHT

Potash Feldspar	25
Whiting	21
China Clay	15
Molochite	13
Quartz	6
+ Red Iron Oxide	2

DESCRIPTION
Satin. Buff speckled if sieved through 100 mesh.

USES
Domestic.

FIRING RANGE
Electric 2336°F (1280°C)

PARTS DRY WEIGHT

Potash Feldspar	43
Quartz	30
Whiting	20
Talc	4
China Clay	2
Colemanite	1
+ Black Iron Oxide	2

DESCRIPTION
Satin/gloss yellow ocher. Can be used on porcelain and stoneware bodies.

USES
Domestic and decorative.

FIRING RANGE
2264–2336°F (1240–1280°C)

PARTS DRY WEIGHT

Potash Feldspar	33
Talc	21
Quartz	16
China Clay	15
Whiting	12
Zinc Oxide	3
+ Titanium Dioxide	10
Red Iron Oxide	4

DESCRIPTION
Satin, smooth mottled ocher.
Can be used on porcelain and
stoneware bodies.

USES
Domestic and decorative.

FIRING RANGE
2264–2336°F (1240–1280°C)

PARTS DRY WEIGHT
Potash Feldspar	33
Talc	21
Quartz	16
China Clay	15
Whiting	12
Zinc Oxide	3
+ Red Iron Oxide	4
Tin Oxide	2

DESCRIPTION
Satin/matte. Mottled
brown/yellow.

USES
Domestic.

FIRING RANGE
2336°F (1280°C)

PARTS DRY WEIGHT
Potash Feldspar	35
Quartz	20
China Clay	20
Dolomite	20
Whiting	5
+ Red Iron Oxide	6

DESCRIPTION
Satin/gloss. Tan/yellow with
mottled brown.

USES
Domestic.

FIRING RANGE
Electric 2336°F (1280°C)

PARTS DRY WEIGHT
Potash Feldspar	43
Quartz	30
Whiting	20
Talc	4
China Clay	2
Colemanite	1
+ Black Iron Oxide	3

Naturals and Browns
OXIDIZED

DESCRIPTION
Satin/matte, yellow finish with brown.

USES
Domestic.

FIRING RANGE
2336°F (1280°C)

PARTS DRY WEIGHT
Quartz	26
Potash Feldspar	25
Whiting	21
China Clay	15
Molochite	13
+ Red Iron Oxide	5

DESCRIPTION
Matte, muddy brown breaking to gold/beige.

USES
Domestic.

FIRING RANGE
2336°F (1280°C)

PARTS DRY WEIGHT
Potash Feldspar	35
Quartz	20
China Clay	20
Dolomite	20
Whiting	5
+ Red Iron Oxide	9

DESCRIPTION
Strong gloss, dark brown, breaking on edges.

USES
Domestic.

FIRING RANGE
2336°F (1280°C)

PARTS DRY WEIGHT
Potash Feldspar	43
Quartz	30
Whiting	20
Talc	4
China Clay	2
Colemanite	1
+ Black Iron Oxide	4

DESCRIPTION
Matte finish with a hint of satin in yellow and brown.

USES
Domestic.

FIRING RANGE
2336°F (1280°C)

PARTS DRY WEIGHT

Quartz	26
Potash Feldspar	25
Whiting	21
China Clay	15
Molochite	13
+ Red Iron Oxide	6

DESCRIPTION
Satin/gloss. Dark brown with a hint of green.

USES
Domestic.

FIRING RANGE
2336°F (1280°C)

PARTS DRY WEIGHT

Potash Feldspar	35
Quartz	20
China Clay	20
Dolomite	20
Whiting	5
+ Red Iron Oxide	20

DESCRIPTION
Dark brown with a satin finish.

USES
Domestic.

FIRING RANGE
2336°F (1280°C)

PARTS DRY WEIGHT

Quartz	26
Potash Feldspar	25
Whiting	21
China Clay	15
Molochite	13
+ Red Iron Oxide	8

Naturals and Browns
REDUCED

DESCRIPTION
Satin. Smooth off-white with a
hint of tan/yellow.

USES
Domestic.

FIRING RANGE
2372°F (1300°C)
Soak time—30 minutes

PARTS DRY WEIGHT
Quartz	26
Potash Feldspar	25
Whiting	21
China Clay	15
Molochite	13
+ B 186 Mandarin Yellow	
Glaze Stain	2

DESCRIPTION
Satin/matte. Very stable
gray/green to cream.

USES
Domestic.

FIRING RANGE
2372°F (1300°C)
Soak time—30 minutes

PARTS DRY WEIGHT
Potash Feldspar	36
China Clay	21
Whiting	17
Quartz	10
Talc	10
Ball Clay	6
+ Rutile	8
Tin	7

DESCRIPTION
Satin/matte. Breaking darker
where thicker.

USES
Domestic.

FIRING RANGE
2372°F (1300°C).
Soak time—30 minutes

PARTS DRY WEIGHT
Potash Feldspar	36
China Clay	21
Whiting	17
Quartz	10
Talc	10
Ball Clay	6
+ Rutile	6
Tin	5

DESCRIPTION
Satin/matte with crystals of blue/gray.

USES
Domestic.

FIRING RANGE
2372°F (1300°C)
Soak time—30 minutes

PARTS DRY WEIGHT

Potash Feldspar	36
China Clay	21
Whiting	17
Quartz	10
Talc	10
Ball Clay	6
+ Rutile	2

DESCRIPTION
Satin/matte with good crystals of gray/green.

USES
Domestic.

FIRING RANGE
2372°F (1300°C)
Soak time—30 minutes

PARTS DRY WEIGHT

Potash Feldspar	36
China Clay	21
Whiting	17
Quartz	10
Talc	10
Ball Clay	6
+ Tin	3
Rutile	3

DESCRIPTION
Satin/matte. Good crystals where thicker.

USES
Domestic.

FIRING RANGE
2372°F (1300°C)
Soak time—30 minutes

PARTS DRY WEIGHT

Potash Feldspar	36
China Clay	21
Whiting	17
Quartz	10
Talc	10
Ball Clay	6
+ Tin	5
Rutile	5

Naturals and Browns
REDUCED

DESCRIPTION
Gloss dark brown, breaking to tan/yellow on edges.

USES
Domestic.

FIRING RANGE
2372°F (1300°C)
Soak time—30 minutes

PARTS DRY WEIGHT
Potash Feldspar	35
Quartz	20
Dolomite	20
China Clay	20
Whiting	5
+ Red Iron Oxide	6

DESCRIPTION
Satin/matte olive, breaking to brown on edges.

USES
Domestic and decorative.

FIRING RANGE
2372°F (1300°C)
Soak time—30 minutes

PARTS DRY WEIGHT
Quartz	26
Potash Feldspar	25
Whiting	21
China Clay	15
Molochite	13
+ Red Iron Oxide	4

DESCRIPTION
Smooth matte. Deep brown/green. Breaks well.

USES
Domestic and decorative.

FIRING RANGE
2372°F (1300°C)
Soak time—30 minutes

PARTS DRY WEIGHT
Quartz	26
Potash Feldspar	25
Whiting	21
China Clay	15
Molochite	13
+ Red Iron Oxide	6

DESCRIPTION
Gloss dark brown, breaking to tan on edges.

USES
Domestic.

FIRING RANGE
Soak time—30 minutes

PARTS DRY WEIGHT

Potash Feldspar	35
Quartz	20
Dolomite	20
China Clay	20
Whiting	5
+ Red Iron Oxide	10

DESCRIPTION
Gloss brown on edges with yellow/brown crystals.

USES
Domestic.

FIRING RANGE
2372°F (1300°C)
Soak time—30 minutes

PARTS DRY WEIGHT

Potash Feldspar	43
Quartz	30
Whiting	20
Talc	4
China Clay	2
Colemanite	1
+ Red Iron Oxide	8

MARK BELL | PORCELAIN VASE
Wheel thrown and altered in porcelain clay and fired to 2336–2372°F (1280–1300°C) in a reducing atmosphere (gas kiln). The piece has been coated with layers of sprayed glaze of various thickness. Mark Bell says, "Quite often in my process the build-up becomes quite thick, but I keep the glaze thinner at the bottom so it does not run off the piece. During the firing the glazes mix and flow in unusual and often interesting ways."

Naturals and Browns
REDUCED

DESCRIPTION
Gloss. Speckled, dark
brown/green.

USES
Domestic.

FIRING RANGE
2372°F (1300°C)
Soak time—30 minutes

PARTS DRY WEIGHT

Potash Feldspar	35
Quartz	20
Dolomite	20
China Clay	20
Whiting	5
+ Red Iron Oxide	9

DESCRIPTION
Gloss. Dark brown/black,
breaking to tan on edges.

USES
Domestic.

FIRING RANGE
2372°F (1300°C)
Soak time—30 minutes

PARTS DRY WEIGHT

Potash Feldspar	35
Quartz	20
Dolomite	20
China Clay	20
Whiting	5
+ Red Iron Oxide	7

DESCRIPTION
Smooth matte. Breaks well on
edges.

USES
Domestic and decorative.

FIRING RANGE
2372°F (1300°C)
Soak time—30 minutes

PARTS DRY WEIGHT

Quartz	26
Potash Feldspar	25
Whiting	21
China Clay	15
Holochite	13
+ Red Iron Oxide	5

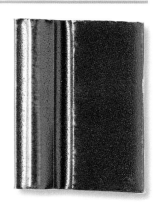

DESCRIPTION
Smooth satin/matte mottled
dark brown/green.

USES
Domestic.

FIRING RANGE
2372°F (1300°C)
Soak time—30 minutes

PARTS DRY WEIGHT

Cornish Stone	66
Whiting	14
China Clay	12
Ball Clay	8
+ Magnesium Carbonate	4
Iron Oxide	4
Cobalt Carbonate	2
Manganese Dioxide	1

DESCRIPTION
Smooth satin/matte, breaking
to rust/red brown on edges.

USES
Domestic.

FIRING RANGE
2372°F (1300°C)
Soak time—30 minutes

PARTS DRY WEIGHT

Cornish Stone	66
Whiting	14
China Clay	12
Ball Clay	8
+ Magnesium Carbonate	4
Red Iron Oxide	4
Cobalt Carbonate	2
Manganese Dioxide	2

DESCRIPTION
Satin/gloss. Dark brown with
rust red/brown speckle.

USES
Domestic.

FIRING RANGE
2372°F (1300°C)
Soak time—30 minutes

PARTS DRY WEIGHT

Potash Feldspar	43
Quartz	30
Whiting	20
Talc	4
China Clay	2
Colemanite	1
+ Red Iron Oxide	6

Yellows and Oranges
OXIDIZED

DESCRIPTION
Smooth matte. Off-white with yellow "blush."

USES
Decorative.

FIRING RANGE
2300°F (1260°C)

PARTS DRY WEIGHT
Potash Feldspar	35
Barium Carbonate	25
Zirconium Silicate	15
Dolomite	11
Ball Clay	8
Quartz	6
+ Red Iron Oxide	3

DESCRIPTION
Smooth satin. Pale yellow with a slight crackle.

USES
Domestic.

FIRING RANGE
1260°C (2300°F)

PARTS DRY WEIGHT
Nepheline Syenite	73
Flint	10
Bentonite	5
Dolomite	5
Whiting	4
Zinc Oxide	3
+ Uranium Oxide	1

DESCRIPTION
Satin. Light yellow, darker in grooves.

USES
Domestic.

FIRING RANGE
1260°C (2300°F)

PARTS DRY WEIGHT
Nepheline Syenite	73
Flint	10
Bentonite	5
Dolomite	5
Whiting	4
Zinc Oxide	3
+ Uranium Oxide	1.5

DESCRIPTION
Satin/matte. Cream with yellow tint.

USES
Decorative.

FIRING RANGE
1260°C (2300°F)

PARTS DRY WEIGHT

Quartz	26
Potash Feldspar	25
Whiting	21
China Clay	15
Molochite	13
+ B 186 Mandarin Yellow Glaze Stain	2

DESCRIPTION
Satin/matte. Smooth light yellow, darker in grooves.

USES
Decorative.

FIRING RANGE
1260°C (2300°F)

PARTS DRY WEIGHT

Potash Feldspar	35
Barium Carbonate	25
Zirconium Silicate	15
Dolomite	11
Ball Clay	8
Quartz	6
+ Red Iron Oxide	4

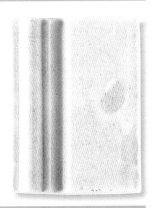

DESCRIPTION
Smooth matte. Light yellow.

USES
Decorative.

FIRING RANGE
1260°C (2300°F)

PARTS DRY WEIGHT

Potash Feldspar	35
Barium Carbonate	25
Zirconium Silicate	15
Dolomite	11
Ball Clay	8
Quartz	6
+ Red Iron Oxide	5

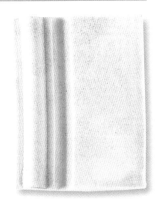

Yellows and Oranges

OXIDIZED

DESCRIPTION
Satin. Smooth light yellow.

USES
Domestic.

FIRING RANGE
1260°C (2300°F)

PARTS DRY WEIGHT

Nepheline Syenite	73
Flint	10
Bentonite	5
Dolomite	5
Whiting	4
Zinc Oxide	3
+ Uranium Oxide	2

DESCRIPTION
Smooth matte. Light yellow, darker in grooves.

USES
Decorative.

FIRING RANGE
2300°F (1260°C)

PARTS DRY WEIGHT

Quartz	26
Potash Feldspar	25
Whiting	21
China Clay	15
Molochite	13
+ Yellow Glaze Stain	
Potclays 4592	5

DESCRIPTION
Satin/gloss. Yellow.

USES
Domestic.

FIRING RANGE
2300°F (1260°C)

PARTS DRY WEIGHT

Nepheline Syenite	73
Flint	10
Bentonite	5
Dolomite	5
Whiting	4
Zinc Oxide	3
+ Uranium Oxide	2.5

DESCRIPTION
Smooth matte. Light yellow breaking to white on edges.

USES
Decorative.

FIRING RANGE
2300°F (1260°C)

PARTS DRY WEIGHT
Quartz	26
Potash Feldspar	25
Whiting	21
China Clay	15
Molochite	13
+ B 186 Mandarin Yellow Glaze Stain	5

DESCRIPTION
Smooth matte. Pale yellow.

USES
Decorative.

FIRING RANGE
2300°F (1260°C)

PARTS DRY WEIGHT
Potash Feldspar	35
Barium Carbonate	25
Zirconium Silicate	15
Dolomite	11
Ball Clay	8
Quartz	6
+ Red Iron Oxide	6

BRIDGET DRAKEFORD I BOWL
This porcelain bowl was fired to 2300°F (1260°C) in an oxidizing atmosphere. It was glazed with the following yellow glaze: Feldspar 64, Dolomite 13, Whiting 13, China Clay 10, + Yellow Stain 5. The rim was finished with a band of manganese dioxide that has run into the glaze most effectively.

Yellows and Oranges
OXIDIZED

DESCRIPTION
Matte. Smooth cream/yellow.

USES
Decorative.

FIRING RANGE
1260°C (2300°F).

PARTS DRY WEIGHT
Potash Feldspar	35
Barium Carbonate	25
Zirconium Silicate	15
Dolomite	11
Ball Clay	8
Quartz	6
+ Red Iron Oxide	7

DESCRIPTION
Satin. Deep cream speckle if sieved through 100 mesh.

USES
Domestic.

FIRING RANGE
2336°F (1280°C)

PARTS DRY WEIGHT
Potash Feldspar	43
Quartz	30
Whiting	20
Talc	4
China Clay	2
Colemanite	1
+ Black Iron Oxide	1.5

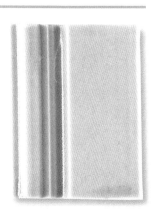

DESCRIPTION
Satin. Smooth yellow, darker in grooves.

USES
Decorative.

FIRING RANGE
1260°C (2300°F)

PARTS DRY WEIGHT
Nepheline Syenite	73
Flint	10
Bentonite	5
Dolomite	5
Whiting	4
Zinc Oxide	3
+ Uranium Oxide	3

DESCRIPTION
Smooth matte. Light yellow, darker in grooves.

USES
Decorative.

FIRING RANGE
1260°C (2300°F)

PARTS DRY WEIGHT

Quartz	26
Potash Feldspar	25
Whiting	21
China Clay	15
Molochite	13
+ B 186 Mandarin Yellow Glaze Stain	8

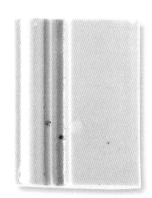

DESCRIPTION
Satin. Smooth yellow with a hint of green.

USES
Decorative.

FIRING RANGE
1260°C (2300°F)

PARTS DRY WEIGHT

Nepheline Syenite	73
Flint	10
Bentonite	5
Dolomite	5
Whiting	4
Zinc Oxide	3
+ Uranium Oxide	4

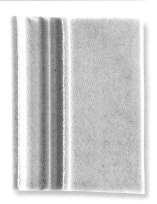

DESCRIPTION
Smooth matte/satin. Yellow with a hint of green.

USES
Decorative.

FIRING RANGE
1260°C (2300°F)

PARTS DRY WEIGHT

Potash Feldspar	35
Barium Carbonate	25
Zirconium Silicate	15
Dolomite	11
Ball Clay	8
Quartz	6
+ Red Iron Oxide	8

Yellows and Oranges
REDUCED

DESCRIPTION
Satin. Off-white/cream, gray with green tint.

USES
Decorative.

FIRING RANGE
2372°F (1300°C)
Soak time—30 minutes

PARTS DRY WEIGHT
Potash Feldspar	35
Barium Carbonate	25
Zirconium Silicate	15
Dolomite	11
Ball Clay	8
Quartz	6
+ Red Iron Oxide	1.5

DESCRIPTION
Satin. Smooth cream/ivory with yellow tint.

USES
Decorative.

FIRING RANGE
2372°F (1300°C)
Soak time—30 minutes

PARTS DRY WEIGHT
Potash Feldspar	35
Barium Carbonate	25
Zirconium Silicate	15
Dolomite	11
Ball Clay	8
Quartz	6
+ Red Iron Oxide	3

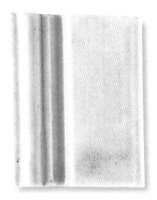

DESCRIPTION
Satin. Smooth pale yellow with a hint of brown.

USES
Domestic.

FIRING RANGE
2372°F (1300°C)
Soak time—30 minutes

PARTS DRY WEIGHT
Quartz	26
Potash Feldspar	25
Whiting	21
China Clay	15
Molochite	13
+ B 186 Mandarin Yellow Glaze Stain	5

DESCRIPTION
Satin. Light yellow with a hint of green.

USES
Domestic.

FIRING RANGE
2372°F (1300°C)
Soak time—30 minutes

PARTS DRY WEIGHT

Quartz	26
Potash Feldspar	25
Whiting	21
China Clay	15
Molochite	13
+ Yellow Glaze Stain	
Potclays 4592	5

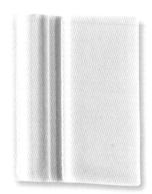

DESCRIPTION
Satin. Smooth very pale yellow.

USES
Decorative.

FIRING RANGE
2372°F (1300°C)
Soak time—30 minutes

PARTS DRY WEIGHT

Potash Feldspar	35
Barium Carbonate	25
Zirconium Silicate	15
Dolomite	11
Ball Clay	8
Quartz	6
+ Red Iron Oxide	4

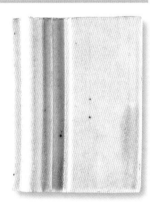

DESCRIPTION
Satin. Color varies with green/yellow-brown on edges.

USES
Decorative.

FIRING RANGE
2372°F (1300°C)
Soak time—30 minutes

PARTS DRY WEIGHT

Potash Feldspar	35
Barium Carbonate	25
Zirconium Silicate	15
Dolomite	11
Ball Clay	8
Quartz	6
+ Red Iron Oxide	5

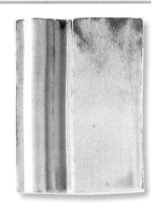

Yellows and Oranges
REDUCED

DESCRIPTION
Smooth satin. Pale yellow/orange, darker in grooves.

USES
Domestic.

FIRING RANGE
2372°F (1300°C)
Soak time—30 minutes

PARTS DRY WEIGHT
Quartz	26
Potash Feldspar	25
Whiting	21
China Clay	15
Molochite	13
+ B 186 Mandarin Yellow Glaze Stain	8

DESCRIPTION
Satin finish. Yellow, breaking to brown on edges.

USES
Decorative.

FIRING RANGE
2372°F (1300°C)
Soak time—30 minutes

PARTS DRY WEIGHT
Potash Feldspar	35
Barium Carbonate	25
Zirconium Silicate	15
Dolomite	11
Ball Clay	8
Quartz	6
+ Red Iron Oxide	6

DESCRIPTION
Satin. Brown/yellow broken surface luster.

USES
Decorative.

FIRING RANGE
2372°F (1300°C)
Soak time—30 minutes

PARTS DRY WEIGHT
Potash Feldspar	35
Barium Carbonate	25
Zirconium Silicate	15
Dolomite	11
Ball Clay	8
Quartz	6
+ Red Iron Oxide	7

DESCRIPTION
Satin. Yellow/brown varying color.

USES
Decorative.

FIRING RANGE
2372°F (1300°C)
Soak time—30 minutes

PARTS DRY WEIGHT
Potash Feldspar	35
Barium Carbonate	25
Zirconium Silicate	15
Dolomite	11
Ball Clay	8
Quartz	6
+ Red Iron Oxide	8

DESCRIPTION
Satin/gloss. Orange/brown, breaking to tan on edges.

USES
Domestic.

FIRING RANGE
2372°F (1300°C)
Soak time—30 minutes

PARTS DRY WEIGHT
Potash Feldspar	35
Quartz	20
Dolomite	20
China Clay	20
Whiting	5
+ Red Iron Oxide	15

DESCRIPTION
Satin/gloss. Dark orange/brown, breaking to tan on edges.

USES
Domestic.

FIRING RANGE
2372°F (1300°C)
Soak time—30 minutes

PARTS DRY WEIGHT
Potash Feldspar	35
Quartz	20
Dolomite	20
China Clay	20
Whiting	5
+ Red Iron Oxide	20

Reds and Purples
OXIDIZED

DESCRIPTION
Matte/satin. Pale soft pink.

USES
Domestic.

FIRING RANGE
Electric 2336°F (1280°C)

PARTS DRY WEIGHT

Potash Feldspar	36
China Clay	21
Whiting	17
Quartz	10
Talc	10
Barium Carbonate	6
+ Rutile	8
Tin	7

DESCRIPTION
Smooth matte. Pink/mauve, darker in grooves.

USES
Decorative.

FIRING RANGE
1260°C (2300°F)

PARTS DRY WEIGHT

Quartz	26
Potash Feldspar	25
Whiting	21
China Clay	15
Molochite	13
+ B 187 Rosso Red	
Glaze Stain	2

DESCRIPTION
Smooth matte. Pink, white on edges.

USES
Decorative.

FIRING RANGE
1260°C (2300°F)

PARTS DRY WEIGHT

Quartz	26
Potash Feldspar	25
Whiting	21
China Clay	15
Molochite	13
+ B 185 Coral	
Glaze Stain	2

DESCRIPTION
Smooth matte. Light red, breaking to white on edges. Hint of purple.

USES
Decorative.

FIRING RANGE
1260°C (2300°F)

PARTS DRY WEIGHT

Quartz	26
Potash Feldspar	25
Whiting	21
China Clay	15
Molochite	13
+ Blythe Strong Red Glaze Stain	5

DESCRIPTION
Smooth matte. Pale pink/red, white on edges.

USES
Decorative.

FIRING RANGE
1260°C (2300°F)

PARTS DRY WEIGHT

Quartz	26
Potash Feldspar	25
Whiting	21
China Clay	15
Molochite	13
+ B 187 Rosso Red Glaze Stain	5

RICHARD BAXTER | BOTTLE FORM
Porcelain bottle fired in an electric kiln to 2264°F (1240°C). The pot was thrown and then glazed using the following recipe: Barium Carbonate 39, Potash Feldspar 33, Zinc Oxide 16, Quartz 6, China Clay 5, + Green Nickel Oxide 0.5. Over the glaze was brushed a spiral with a 50/50 mixture of zinc and china clay, which gives a blue. Height 5½in (14 cm).

Reds and Purples
OXIDIZED

DESCRIPTION
Glossy light red/pink. Can be used on porcelain and stoneware bodies.

USES
Domestic and decorative.

FIRING RANGE
2264–2336°F (1240–1280°C)

PARTS DRY WEIGHT
Nepheline Syenite	47
Quartz	28
Dolomite	13
Whiting	7
Lithium Carbonate	3
China Clay	2
+ Blythe Strong	
Red Glaze Stain	10

DESCRIPTION
Smooth matte. Red, darker in grooves.

USES
Decorative.

FIRING RANGE
1260°C (2300°F)

PARTS DRY WEIGHT
Quartz	26
Potash Feldspar	25
Whiting	21
China Clay	15
Molochite	13
+ Blythe Strong	
Red Glaze Stain	8

DESCRIPTION
Glossy red/pink. Can be used on porcelain and stoneware bodies.

USES
Domestic and decorative.

FIRING RANGE
2264–2336°F (1240–1280°C)

PARTS DRY WEIGHT
Nepheline Syenite	47
Quartz	28
Dolomite	13
Whiting	7
Lithium Carbonate	3
China Clay	2
+ Rosso Red	
Glaze Stain	10

DESCRIPTION
Smooth matte. Red, even color over surface.

USES
Decorative.

FIRING RANGE
2300°F (1260°C)

PARTS DRY WEIGHT

Quartz	26
Potash Feldspar	25
Whiting	21
China Clay	15
Molochite	13
+ B 187 Rosso Red	
Glaze Stain	8

DESCRIPTION
Smooth matte. Red, darker in grooves, hint of mauve.

USES
Decorative.

FIRING RANGE
2300°F (1260°C)

PARTS DRY WEIGHT

Quartz	26
Potash Feldspar	25
Whiting	21
China Clay	15
Molochite	13
+ B 185 Coral	
Glaze Stain	5

DESCRIPTION
Satin/matte. Pink/red with slight white speckling over surface.

USES
Decorative.

FIRING RANGE
2300°F[a] (1260°C)

PARTS DRY WEIGHT

Quartz	26
Potash Feldspar	25
Whiting	21
China Clay	15
Molochite	13
+ B 185 Coral	
Glaze Stain	8

Reds and Purples
OXIDIZED

DESCRIPTION
Glossy pink. Can be used on porcelain and stoneware bodies.

USES
Domestic and decorative.

FIRING RANGE
2264–2336°F (1240–1280°C)

PARTS DRY WEIGHT
Potash Feldspar	34
Quartz	23
Standard Borax Frit	14
China Clay	11
Whiting	11
Dolomite	5
Bentonite	2
+ B 187 Rosso	
Red Glaze Stain	10

DESCRIPTION
Glossy pink/red. Can be used on porcelain and stoneware bodies.

USES
Domestic and decorative.

FIRING RANGE
2264–2336°F (1240–1280°C)

PARTS DRY WEIGHT
Potash Feldspar	34
Quartz	23
Standard Borax Frit	14
China Clay	11
Whiting	11
Dolomite	5
Bentonite	2
+ B 185 Coral	
Glaze Stain	10

DESCRIPTION
Glossy coral red. Can be used on porcelain and stoneware bodies.

USES
Domestic and decorative.

FIRING RANGE
2264–2336°F (1240–1280°C)

PARTS DRY WEIGHT
Nepheline Syenite	47
Quartz	28
Dolomite	13
Whiting	7
Lithium Carbonate	3
China Clay	2
+ B 185 Coral	
Glaze Stain	10

DESCRIPTION
Satin/matte. Smooth purple
breaking to white on edges.

USES
Decorative.

FIRING RANGE
2300°F (1260°C)

PARTS DRY WEIGHT
Barium Carbonate	40
Potash Feldspar	35
Zinc Oxide	15
China Clay	5
Quartz	5
+ Nickel Oxide	0.3

DESCRIPTION
Satin/matte. Smooth purple,
darker in grooves.

USES
Decorative.

FIRING RANGE
2300°F (1260°C)

PARTS DRY WEIGHT
Barium Carbonate	40
Potash Feldspar	35
Zinc Oxide	15
China Clay	5
Quartz	5
+ Nickel Oxide	0.5

DESCRIPTION
Satin/matte. Smooth purple,
darker in grooves.

USES
Decorative.

FIRING RANGE
2300°F (1260°C)

PARTS DRY WEIGHT
Barium Carbonate	40
Potash Feldspar	35
Zinc Oxide	15
China Clay	5
Quartz	5
+ Nickel Oxide	1

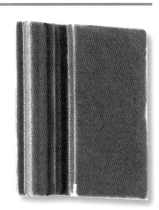

Reds and Purples
OXIDIZED

DESCRIPTION
Smooth matte/satin.
Pink/purple, darker in grooves.

USES
Decorative.

FIRING RANGE
2300°F (1260°C)

PARTS DRY WEIGHT
Barium Carbonate	40
Potash Feldspar	35
Zinc Oxide	15
China Clay	5
Quartz	5
+ Nickel Oxide	1.5

DESCRIPTION
Smooth matte/satin. Purple,
pink on edges.

USES
Decorative.

FIRING RANGE
2300°F (1260°C)

PARTS DRY WEIGHT
Barium Carbonate	40
Potash Feldspar	35
Zinc Oxide	15
China Clay	5
Quartz	5
+ Nickel Oxide	2.5

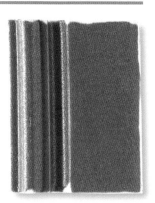

DESCRIPTION
Matte/satin. Smooth
mauve/red, darker in grooves.

USES
Decorative.

FIRING RANGE
2300°F (1260°C)

PARTS DRY WEIGHT
Barium Carbonate	40
Potash Feldspar	35
Zinc Oxide	15
China Clay	5
Quartz	5
+ Nickel Oxide	3

DESCRIPTION
Matte/satin. Smooth dark
purple/red.

USES
Decorative.

FIRING RANGE
2300°F (1260°C)

PARTS DRY WEIGHT

Barium Carbonate	40
Potash Feldspar	35
Zinc Oxide	15
China Clay	5
Quartz	5
+ Nickel Oxide	3
Red Iron Oxide	2

DESCRIPTION
Smooth matte/satin. Dark
"plum" purple, even color over
surface.

USES
Decorative.

FIRING RANGE
2300°F (1260°C)

PARTS DRY WEIGHT

Barium Carbonate	40
Potash Feldspar	35
Zinc Oxide	15
China Clay	5
Quartz	5
+ Nickel Oxide	3
Red Iron Oxide	2
Cobalt Carbonate	0.5

DESCRIPTION
Matte/satin. Dark purple
breaking through to white clay
body on edges.

USES
Decorative.

FIRING RANGE
2300°F (1260°C)

PARTS DRY WEIGHT

Barium Carbonate	40
Potash Feldspar	35
Zinc Oxide	15
China Clay	5
Quartz	5
+ Nickel Oxide	3
Red Iron Oxide	2
Cobalt Carbonate	0.5
Manganese Dioxide	0.5

Reds and Purples
REDUCED

DESCRIPTION
Satin. Smooth off-white with pink glow.

USES
Decorative.

FIRING RANGE
2372°F (1300°C)
Soak time—30 minutes

PARTS DRY WEIGHT

Quartz	26
Potash Feldspar	25
Whiting	21
China Clay	15
Molochite	13
+ Blythe Strong Red Glaze Stain	??

DESCRIPTION
Satin. Smooth off-white with pink tint.

USES
Domestic.

FIRING RANGE
2372°F (1300°C)
Soak time—30 minutes

PARTS DRY WEIGHT

Quartz	26
Potash Feldspar	25
Whiting	21
China Clay	15
Molochite	13
+ B 185 Coral Glaze Stain	2

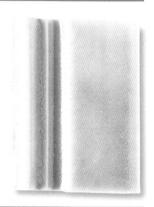

DESCRIPTION
Satin/gloss. Pale pink "blush."

USES
Domestic.

FIRING RANGE
2372°F (1300°C)
Soak time—30 minutes

PARTS DRY WEIGHT

Quartz	26
Potash Feldspar	25
Whiting	21
China Clay	15
Molochite	13
+ B 187 Rosso Red Glaze Stain	5

DESCRIPTION
Satin/gloss. Pink/red, even color over surface.

USES
Decorative.

FIRING RANGE
2372°F (1300°C)
Soak time—30 minutes

PARTS DRY WEIGHT

Quartz	26
Potash Feldspar	25
Whiting	21
China Clay	15
Molochite	13
+ Blythe Strong Red Glaze Stain	8

DESCRIPTION
Gloss red/pink. Varies with amount of reduction in kiln.

USES
Domestic.

FIRING RANGE
2372°F (1300°C)
Soak time—30 minutes

PARTS DRY WEIGHT

Soda Feldspar	45
Quartz	17
Borax Frit	15
Whiting	13
China Clay	5
Tin	5
+ Copper Carbonate	0.5

DESCRIPTION
Pink Blush. A reliable, pale, fine speckle copper pink.

USES

FIRING RANGE
2300–2372°F (1260–1300°C)

PARTS DRY WEIGHT

Cornish Stone	50
Whiting	20
Flint	15
China Clay	15
+ High Alkaline Frit	5
Copper Carbonate	2

Reds and Purples
REDUCED

DESCRIPTION
Satin/gloss. Light pink/red.

USES
Domestic.

FIRING RANGE
2372°F (1300°C)
Soak time—30 minutes

PARTS DRY WEIGHT
Quartz	26
Potash Feldspar	25
Whiting	21
China Clay	15
Molochite	13
+ B 185 Coral Glaze Stain	5

DESCRIPTION
Satin/gloss. Red/pink, darker in grooves.

USES
Domestic.

FIRING RANGE
2372°F (1300°C)
Soak time—30 minutes

PARTS DRY WEIGHT
Quartz	26
Potash Feldspar	25
Whiting	21
China Clay	15
Molochite	13
+ B 187 Rosso Red Glaze Stain	8

DESCRIPTION
Satin/gloss. Red, even color over surface.

USES
Domestic.

FIRING RANGE
2372°F (1300°C)
Soak time—30 minutes

PARTS DRY WEIGHT
Quartz	26
Potash Feldspar	25
Whiting	21
China Clay	15
Molochite	13
+ B 185 Coral Glaze Stain	8

DESCRIPTION
Gloss. Red where more heavily reduced, green where oxidized.

USES
Domestic and decorative.

FIRING RANGE
2372°F (1300°C)
Soak time—30 minutes

PARTS DRY WEIGHT
Soda Feldspar	45
Quartz	17
Borax Frit	15
Whiting	13
China Clay	5
Tin	5
+ Copper Carbonate	1.5

DESCRIPTION
Satin/gloss. Red with areas of mottled white.

USES
Domestic and decorative.

FIRING RANGE
2372°F (1300°C)
Soak time—30 minutes

PARTS DRY WEIGHT
Soda Feldspar	45
Quartz	17
Borax Frit	15
Whiting	13
China Clay	5
Tin	5
+ Copper Carbonate	1

DESCRIPTION
Gloss. In reduction more red, green in oxidation.

USES
Domestic and decorative.

FIRING RANGE
2372°F (1300°C)
Soak time—30 minutes

PARTS DRY WEIGHT
Soda Feldspar	45
Quartz	17
Borax Frit	15
Whiting	13
China Clay	5
Tin	5
+ Copper Carbonate	2.5

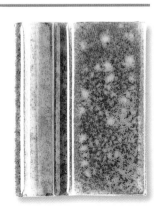

Reds and Purples
REDUCED

DESCRIPTION
Gloss. Sang de boeuf red.
Mottled light and dark
green/gray, breaking to red
on edges.

USES
Domestic.

FIRING RANGE
2372°F (1300°C).
Soak time—30 minutes

PARTS DRY WEIGHT
Soda Feldspar	45
Quartz	17
Borax Frit	15
Whiting	13
China Clay	5
Tin	5
+ Copper Carbonate	1.5

DESCRIPTION
Fluid pink blush. Dolomite
White over Derek Emms Red.

USES
Domestic and decorative.

FIRING RANGE
2300–2372°F (1260–1300°C)

PARTS DRY WEIGHT
Dolomite White
Cornish Stone	60
China Clay	20
Dolomite	20

Derek Emms Red
Soda Feldspar	42
Flint	19
Whiting	14
High Alkaline Frit	14
China Clay	5
Tin Oxide	5
Copper Carbonate	1

DESCRIPTION
Manganese copper red. Rustier,
aged variation on the Derek
Emms original (page 239, top).
Fluid. Watch kiln shelves.

USES
Domestic and decorative.

FIRING RANGE
2300–2372°F (1260–1300°C)

PARTS DRY WEIGHT
Soda (or Potash) Feldspar	42
Flint	19
Whiting	14
High Alkaline Frit	14
China Clay	5
Tin Oxide	5
Copper Carbonate	1
+ Manganese Dioxide	5

DESCRIPTION
Derek Emms Red. Apply
medium to thick for the fullest
cherry red, but beautiful
serendipitous pink blushes can
be achieved where applied
thinly. Fluid where thick.

USES
Domestic and decorative.

FIRING RANGE
2300–2372°F (1260–1300°C)

PARTS DRY WEIGHT

Soda Feldspar	42
Flint	19
Whiting	14
High Alkaline Frit	14
China Clay	5
Tin Oxide	5
Copper Carbonate	1

DESCRIPTION
Satin White layered
over Derek Emms
Red.

USES
Domestic and
decorative.

FIRING RANGE
2300–2372°F
(1260–1300°C)

PARTS DRY WEIGHT

Satin White		Derek Emms Red	
Potash Feldspar	50	Soda Feldspar	42
China Clay	23	Flint	19
Dolomite	20	Whiting	14
Quartz	4	High Alkaline Frit	14
Bone Ash	3	China Clay	5
		Tin Oxide	5
		Copper Carbonate	1

SONIA LEWIS | PORCELAIN VESSELS
Three copper-red porcelain pieces, all fired to 2336°F (1280°C) in a reduction
atmosphere. All the pots were thrown, then glazed with the following recipe: Soda
Feldspar 45, Flint 20, Borax Frit 15, Whiting 15, China Clay 5, + Tin 5, + Copper
Carbonate 0.5.
Height (tallest) 5½ in (14
cm).

Reds and Purples

REDUCED

DESCRIPTION
Gloss. Dark sang de boeuf red,
inclined to run on vertical
surfaces.

USES
Domestic.

FIRING RANGE
2372°F (1300°C)
Soak time—30 minutes

PARTS DRY WEIGHT
Soda Feldspar	45
Quartz	17
Borax Frit	15
Whiting	13
China Clay	5
Tin	5
+ Copper Carbonate	4

DESCRIPTION
Gloss. Sang de boeuf red, some
speckling green where oxidized.
Inclined to run on vertical
surfaces.

USES
Domestic.

FIRING RANGE
2372°F (1300°C)
Soak time—30 minutes

PARTS DRY WEIGHT
Soda Feldspar	45
Quartz	17
Borax Frit	15
Whiting	13
China Clay	5
Tin	5
+ Copper Carbonate	3.5

DESCRIPTION
Smooth matte. Some
crystallization showing where
thick.

USES
Domestic and decorative.

FIRING RANGE
2372°F (1300°C)
Soak time—30 minutes

PARTS DRY WEIGHT
Quartz	26
Potash Feldspar	25
Whiting	21
China Clay	15
Molochite	13
Red Iron Oxide	9

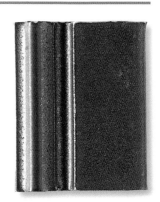

DESCRIPTION
Satin matte. Crystallization
showing where thick.

USES
Domestic and decorative.

FIRING RANGE
2372°F (1300°C)
Soak time—30 minutes

PARTS DRY WEIGHT

Quartz	26
Potash Feldspar	25
Whiting	21
China Clay	15
Molochite	13
+ Red Iron Oxide	10

DESCRIPTION
Satin breaking to gloss. Rust
crystallizing black against
brown.

USES
Domestic.

FIRING RANGE
2372°F (1300°C)
Soak time—30 minutes

PARTS DRY WEIGHT

Quartz	26
Potash Feldspar	25
Whiting	21
China Clay	15
Molochite	13
+ Red Iron Oxide	15

DESCRIPTION
Satin/gloss. Deep, rich, and
smooth.

USES
Domestic.

FIRING RANGE
2372°F (1300°C)
Soak time—30 minutes

PARTS DRY WEIGHT

Quartz	26
Potash Feldspar	25
Whiting	21
China Clay	15
Molochite	13
+ Red Iron Oxide	20

Blues
OXIDIZED

DESCRIPTION
Satin. Smooth off-white with
mottled and speckled blue.

USES
Domestic.

FIRING RANGE
2336°F (1280°C)

PARTS DRY WEIGHT
Cornish Stone	66
Whiting	14
China Clay	12
Ball Clay	8
+ Magnesium Carbonate	4
Cobalt Carbonate	1

DESCRIPTION
Satin, mid-blue with darker
speckles.

USES
Domestic.

FIRING RANGE
2336°F (1280°C)

PARTS DRY WEIGHT
Cornish Stone	66
Whiting	14
China Clay	12
Ball Clay	8
+ Magnesium Carbonate	4
Cobalt Carbonate	3

DESCRIPTION
Satin/gloss. Blue with darker
speckle evenly spread over
surface.

USES
Domestic.

FIRING RANGE
2336°F (1280°C)

PARTS DRY WEIGHT
Cornish Stone	66
Whiting	14
China Clay	12
Ball Clay	8
+ Cobalt Carbonate	5
Magnesium Carbonate	4

DESCRIPTION
Satin. Smooth blue with mottled areas of light blue/cream.

USES
Domestic.

FIRING RANGE
2336°F (1280°C)

PARTS DRY WEIGHT

Cornish Stone	66
Whiting	14
China Clay	12
Ball Clay	8
+ Magnesium Carbonate	4
Cobalt Carbonate	7

DESCRIPTION
Satin White over Mirror Blue. Layered glaze. Shiny blue where thick, predominantly a satin lilac hue.

USES
Domestic and decorative.

FIRING RANGE
2300–2372°F (1260–1300°C)

PARTS DRY WEIGHT
Satin White

Potash Feldspar	50
China Clay	23
Dolomite	20
Quartz	4
Bone Ash	3

Mirror Blue

Cornish Stone	70
China Clay	10
Whiting	10
Zinc Oxide	10
+ Cobalt Oxide	2

DESCRIPTION
Dolomite White over Mirror Blue. Layered glaze. Paler matted blue with white flecking.

USES
Domestic and decorative.

FIRING RANGE
2300–2372°F (1260–1300°C)

PARTS DRY WEIGHT
Dolomite White

Cornish Stone	60
China Clay	20
Dolomite	20

Mirror Blue

Cornish Stone	70
China Clay	10
Whiting	10
Zinc Oxide	10
+ Cobalt Oxide	2

Blues
OXIDIZED

DESCRIPTION
Gloss. Blue with darker patches, particularly in grooves.

USES
Domestic.

FIRING RANGE
2300°F (1260°C)

PARTS DRY WEIGHT
Nepheline Syenite	73
Flint	10
Bentonite	5
Dolomite	5
Whiting	4
Zinc Oxide	3
+ Cobalt Carbonate	0.5
Red Iron Oxide	0.5

DESCRIPTION
Gloss. Could run on a vertical surface.

USES
Domestic.

FIRING RANGE
1260°C (2300°F)

PARTS DRY WEIGHT
Nepheline Syenite	73
Flint	10
Bentonite	5
Dolomite	5
Whiting	4
Zinc Oxide	3
+ Cobalt Carbonate	1
Red Iron Oxide	1

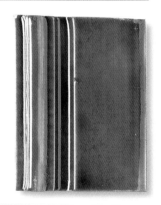

DESCRIPTION
Satin. Smooth medium blue, even color over surface.

USES
Domestic.

FIRING RANGE
2336°F (1280°C)

PARTS DRY WEIGHT
Cornish Stone	66
Whiting	14
China Clay	12
Ball Clay	8
+ Magnesium Carbonate	4
Cobalt Carbonate	1

DESCRIPTION
Satin. Smooth, strong, even blue. Darker in grooves.

USES
Domestic.

FIRING RANGE
2336°F (1280°C)

PARTS DRY WEIGHT

Cornish Stone	66
Whiting	14
China Clay	12
Ball Clay	8
+ Magnesium Carbonate	4
Cobalt Carbonate	1.3

DESCRIPTION
Satin/gloss. Dark blue, even color over surface.

USES
Domestic.

FIRING RANGE
2336°F (1280°C)

PARTS DRY WEIGHT

Cornish Stone	66
Whiting	14
China Clay	12
Barium Carbonate	8
Magnesium Carbonate	4
Cobalt Carbonate	2
Red Iron Oxide	2

DELAN COOKSON I PORCELAIN BOTTLE

This piece was thrown in a porcelain clay, then fired to 2264°F (1240°C) in an oxidizing atmosphere (electric kiln). The brilliant blue glaze used is barium-based and has been applied quite thickly. The smooth satin/matte surface is just "on the edge" of melting and therefore 2264°F (1240°C) is the optimum temperature as any higher would make the glaze run on to kiln shelves with those associated problems!

Height 6½ in (16 cm).

Blues

OXIDIZED

DESCRIPTION
Glossy pure blue named Mirror
Blue (also see page 243).
Sieve finely to ensure even
distribution of the cobalt. It
can shrink a little as it dries
where thick.

USES
Domestic and decorative.

FIRING RANGE
2300–2372°F (1260–1300°C)

PARTS DRY WEIGHT
Cornish Stone	70
China Clay	10
Whiting	10
Zinc Oxide	10
+ Cobalt Oxide	2

DESCRIPTION
Gloss. Could run on a vertical
surface.

USES
Domestic.

FIRING RANGE
1260°C (2300°F)

PARTS DRY WEIGHT
Nepheline Syenite	73
Flint	10
Bentonite	5
Dolomite	5
Whiting	4
Zinc Oxide	3
+ Cobalt Carbonate	1.5
Red Iron Oxide	1

DESCRIPTION
Gloss. Could run on a vertical
surface.

USES
Domestic.

FIRING RANGE
2300°F (1260°C)

PARTS DRY WEIGHT
Nepheline Syenite	73
Flint	10
Bentonite	5
Dolomite	5
Whiting	4
Zinc Oxide	3
+ Cobalt Carbonate	1.5
Red Iron Oxide	1.5

DESCRIPTION
Gloss. Could run on a vertical
surface.

USES
Domestic.

FIRING RANGE
2300°F (1260°C)

PARTS DRY WEIGHT
Nepheline Syenite	73
Flint	10
Bentonite	5
Dolomite	5
Whiting	4
Zinc Oxide	3
+ Cobalt Carbonate	2
Red Iron Oxide	2

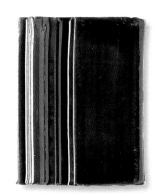

DESCRIPTION
Satin finish. Midnight blue with
"dust."

USES
Domestic.

FIRING RANGE
2336°F (1280°C)

PARTS DRY WEIGHT
Cornish Stone	60
Whiting	14
China Clay	12
Barium Carbonate	8
Red Iron Oxide	5
Magnesium Carbonate	4
Cobalt Carbonate	2

DESCRIPTION
Smooth satin. Very dark blue,
even color over surface.

USES
Domestic.

FIRING RANGE
2336°F (1280°C)

PARTS DRY WEIGHT
Cornish Stone	66
Whiting	14
China Clay	12
Ball Clay	8
+ Magnesium Carbonate	4
Cobalt Carbonate	2
Red Iron Oxide	1

Blues
REDUCED

DESCRIPTION
Gloss with a slight crackle.
Cobalt specks if sieved through
100 mesh.

USES
Domestic.

FIRING RANGE
2372°F (1300°C)
Soak time—30 minutes

PARTS DRY WEIGHT

Soda Feldspar	45
Quartz	17
Borax Frit	15
Whiting	13
China Clay	5
Tin	5
+ Cobalt Carbonate	0.1
Chrome Oxide	0.1

DESCRIPTION
Gloss. Cobalt specks if sieved
through 100 mesh.

USES
Domestic.

FIRING RANGE
2372°F (1300°C)
Soak time—30 minutes

PARTS DRY WEIGHT

Soda Feldspar	45
Quartz	17
Borax Frit	15
Whiting	13
China Clay	5
Tin	5
+ Cobalt Carbonate	0.2
Chrome Oxide	0.2

DESCRIPTION
Satin/gloss. Blue pooling to
darker areas, especially in
grooves.

USES
Domestic.

FIRING RANGE
2372°F (1300°C)
Soak time—30 minutes

PARTS DRY WEIGHT

Cornish Stone	66
Whiting	14
China Clay	12
Ball Clay	8
+ Magnesium Carbonate	4
Cobalt Carbonate	1

DESCRIPTION
Satin/gloss. Dark blue, fairly
even color over surface.

USES
Domestic.

FIRING RANGE
2372°F (1300°C)
Soak time—30 minutes

PARTS DRY WEIGHT
Cornish Stone	66
Whiting	14
China Clay	12
Ball Clay	8
+ Magnesium Carbonate	4
Cobalt Carbonate	2

DESCRIPTION
Satin/gloss. Very dark blue.

USES
Domestic.

FIRING RANGE
2372°F (1300°C).
Soak time—30 minutes

PARTS DRY WEIGHT
Cornish Stone	66
Whiting	14
China Clay	12
Ball Clay	8
+ Magnesium Carbonate	4
Cobalt Carbonate	2
Red Iron Oxide	0.5

DESCRIPTION
Satin. Subtle blend of the iron
and cobalt makes this a
pleasing color.

USES
Domestic.

FIRING RANGE
2372°F (1300°C)
Soak time—30 minutes

PARTS DRY WEIGHT
Cornish Stone	66
Whiting	14
China Clay	12
Ball Clay	8
+ Magnesium Carbonate	4
Cobalt Carbonate	2
Red Iron Oxide	1

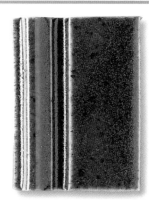

Greens and Turquoises
OXIDIZED

DESCRIPTION
Copper Green. Needs to be applied medium thickness. Pale green, excellent fit. Slight craze/opacity if too thick.

USES
Domestic and decorative.

FIRING RANGE
2300–2372°F (1260–1300°C)

PARTS DRY WEIGHT
Cornish Stone	50
Whiting	20
Flint	15
China Clay	15
+ High Alkaline Frit	5
Copper Carbonate	2

DESCRIPTION
Lithium copper green. Subtly darker and more fluid than copper green (above).

USES
Domestic and decorative.

FIRING RANGE
2300–2372°F (1260–1300°C)

PARTS DRY WEIGHT
Cornish Stone	50
Whiting	20
Flint	15
China Clay	15
+ Lithium Carbonate	5
Copper Carbonate	2

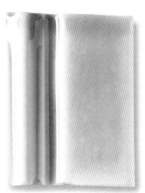

DESCRIPTION
Satin White layered over Derek Emms Red. In reduction, layering intensifies the red development and patterning. In oxidation there is a turquoise/green mix.

USES
Domestic and decorative.

FIRING RANGE
2300–2372°F (1260–1300°C)

PARTS DRY WEIGHT

Satin White		Derek Emms Red	
Potash Feldspar	50	Soda Feldspar	42
China Clay	23	Flint	19
Dolomite	20	Whiting	14
Quartz	4	High Alkaline Frit	14
Bone Ash	3	China Clay	5
		Tin Oxide	5
		Copper Carbonate	1

DESCRIPTION
Smooth satin. Turquoise/green
with white edges where thinner.

USES
Domestic.

FIRING RANGE
2336°F (1280°C)

PARTS DRY WEIGHT
Soda Feldspar	45
Quartz	17
Borax Frit	15
Whiting	13
China Clay	5
Tin Oxide	5
+ Copper Carbonate	0.1

DESCRIPTION
Smooth satin. Pale turquoise
revealing white edges.

USES
Domestic.

FIRING RANGE
2336°F (1280°C)

PARTS DRY WEIGHT
Soda Feldspar	45
Quartz	17
Borax Frit	15
Whiting	13
China Clay	5
Tin Oxide	5
+ Copper Carbonate	0.5

DESCRIPTION
Derek Emms Red. Soft
turquoise in oxidation. See
page 239 for color in
reduction.

USES
Domestic and decorative.

FIRING RANGE
2300–2372°F (1260–1300°C)

PARTS DRY WEIGHT
Soda Feldspar	42
Flint	19
Whiting	14
High Alkaline Frit	14
China Clay	5
Tin Oxide	5
Copper Carbonate	1

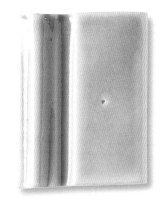

Greens and Turquoises
OXIDIZED

DESCRIPTION
Satin. Light turquoise/green,
darker in pooled areas.

USES
Domestic.

FIRING RANGE
2336°F (1280°C)

PARTS DRY WEIGHT
Soda Feldspar	45
Quartz	17
Borax Frit	15
Whiting	13
China Clay	5
Tin Oxide	5
+ Copper Carbonate	1.5

DESCRIPTION
Satin/gloss. Light
turquoise/green with effective
pooling in grooves.

USES
Domestic.

FIRING RANGE
2336°F (1280°C)

PARTS DRY WEIGHT
Soda Feldspar	45
Quartz	17
Borax Frit	15
Whiting	13
China Clay	5
Tin Oxide	5
+ Copper Carbonate	2

DESCRIPTION
Satin/gloss. Mid-
green/turquoise. Pooling to
darker areas in grooves.

USES
Domestic.

FIRING RANGE
2336°F (1280°C)

PARTS DRY WEIGHT
Soda Feldspar	45
Quartz	17
Borax Frit	15
Whiting	13
China Clay	5
Tin Oxide	5
+ Copper Carbonate	2.5

DESCRIPTION
Smooth satin, light green. Can be used on porcelain and stoneware bodies.

USES
Domestic and decorative.

FIRING RANGE
2264–2336°F (1240–1280°C)

PARTS DRY WEIGHT

Potash Feldspar	33
Talc	21
Quartz	16
China Clay	15
Whiting	12
Zinc Oxide	3
+ Copper Oxide	2
Tin Oxide	2

DESCRIPTION
Smooth satin, opaque gray/green. Can be used on porcelain and stoneware bodies.

USES
Domestic and decorative.

FIRING RANGE
2264–2336°F (1240–1280°C)

PARTS DRY WEIGHT

Potash Feldspar	33
Talc	21
Quartz	16
China Clay	15
Whiting	12
Zinc Oxide	3
+ Copper Oxide	4
Tin Oxide	2.5

BRIDGET DRAKEFORD | PORCELAIN
Wheel-thrown jug fired to 2300°F (1260°C) in an oxidizing atmosphere. The piece was glazed with a "copper crackle" glaze. Bridget achieves the distinctive, elegantly shaped spouts on her pots with sensitive cutting and carving. Height 12 in (30 cm).

Greens and Turquoises
OXIDIZED

DESCRIPTION
Gloss. Dark green, pooling to darker areas, particularly in grooves.

USES
Domestic.

FIRING RANGE
2336°F (1280°C)

PARTS DRY WEIGHT
Soda Feldspar	45
Quartz	17
Borax Frit	15
Whiting	13
China Clay	5
Tin Oxide	5
+ Copper Carbonate	3

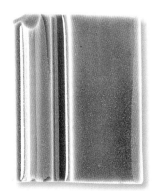

DESCRIPTION
Shiny green, breaking to white on edges and rims. Can be used on porcelain and stoneware bodies.

USES
Domestic and decorative.

FIRING RANGE
2264–2336°F (1240–1280°C)

PARTS DRY WEIGHT
Potash Feldspar	32
Quartz	24
Barium Carbonate	16
China Clay	14
Standard Borax Frit	10
Whiting	4
+ Copper Carbonate	4

DESCRIPTION
Gloss. Dark olive green, darker pooling in grooves.

USES
Domestic.

FIRING RANGE
2336°F (1280°C)

PARTS DRY WEIGHT
Soda Feldspar	45
Quartz	17
Borax Frit	15
Whiting	13
China Clay	5
Tin Oxide	5
+ Copper Carbonate	3.5

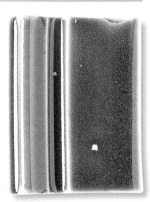

DESCRIPTION
Gloss. Rick dark green,
revealing white edges where
thin.

USES
Domestic.

FIRING RANGE
2336°F (1280°C)

PARTS DRY WEIGHT
Soda Feldspar	45
Quartz	17
Borax Frit	15
Whiting	13
China Clay	5
Tin Oxide	5
+ Copper Carbonate	4

DESCRIPTION
Very dark gloss, bottle green.

USES
Domestic.

FIRING RANGE
2336°F (1280°C)

PARTS DRY WEIGHT
Soda Feldspar	45
Quartz	17
Borax Frit	15
Whiting	13
China Clay	5
Tin Oxide	5
+ Copper Carbonate	5

DESCRIPTION
Very dark green/black, pooling
well in grooves.

USES
Domestic.

FIRING RANGE
2336°F (1280°C)

PARTS DRY WEIGHT
Soda Feldspar	45
Quartz	17
Borax Frit	15
Whiting	13
China Clay	5
Tin Oxide	5
+ Copper Carbonate	6

Greens and Turquoises
OXIDIZED

DESCRIPTION
Satin/gloss. Cream with cobalt blue/green speckling unless sieved through 200 mesh.

USES
Domestic.

FIRING RANGE
2336°F (1280°C)

PARTS DRY WEIGHT
Soda Feldspar	45
Quartz	17
Borax Frit	15
Whiting	13
China Clay	5
Tin Oxide	5
+ Cobalt Carbonate	0.1
Chrome Oxide	0.2

DESCRIPTION
Satin/gloss. Pale blue/green with fine cobalt speckling.

USES
Domestic.

FIRING RANGE
2336°F (1280°C)

PARTS DRY WEIGHT
Soda Feldspar	45
Quartz	17
Borax Frit	15
Whiting	13
China Clay	5
Tin Oxide	5
+ Cobalt Carbonate	0.2
Chrome Oxide	0.2

DESCRIPTION
Satin/gloss. Light blue/green with cobalt speckle. (If speckle not required, sieve through 200 mesh.)

USES
Domestic.

FIRING RANGE
2336°F (1280°C)

PARTS DRY WEIGHT
Soda Feldspar	45
Quartz	17
Borax Frit	15
Whiting	13
China Clay	5
Tin Oxide	5
+ Cobalt Carbonate	0.2
Chrome Oxide	0.3

DESCRIPTION
Satin/gloss. Mid-blue/green with
darker cobalt speckling.

USES
Domestic.

FIRING RANGE
2336°F (1280°C)

PARTS DRY WEIGHT
Soda Feldspar	45
Quartz	17
Borax Frit	15
Whiting	13
China Clay	5
Tin Oxide	5
+ Cobalt Carbonate	0.3
Chrome Oxide	0.4

DESCRIPTION
Satin/gloss. Cobalt blue/green
with evenly spread darker
speckle.

USES
Domestic.

FIRING RANGE
2336°F (1280°C)

PARTS DRY WEIGHT
Soda Feldspar	45
Quartz	17
Borax Frit	15
Whiting	13
China Clay	5
Tin Oxide	5
+ Cobalt Carbonate	0.5
Chrome Oxide	0.5

DESCRIPTION
Gloss. Dark blue/green with
slight cobalt speckling.

USES
Domestic.

FIRING RANGE
2336°F (1280°C)

PARTS DRY WEIGHT
Soda Feldspar	45
Quartz	17
Borax Frit	15
Whiting	13
China Clay	5
Tin Oxide	5
+ Cobalt Carbonate	1
Chrome Oxide	1

Greens and Turquoises
OXIDIZED

DESCRIPTION
Satin matte turquoise. Can be used on porcelain and stoneware bodies.

USES
Domestic and decorative.

FIRING RANGE
2264–2336°F (1240–1280°C)

PARTS DRY WEIGHT
Potash Feldspar	49
Barium Carbonate	27
Whiting	14
HP71 Ball Clay	9
Bentonite	1
+ Copper Carbonate	2.5

DESCRIPTION
Satin/gloss. Dark blue with even cobalt speckling.

USES
Domestic.

FIRING RANGE
2336°F (1280°C)

PARTS DRY WEIGHT
Soda Feldspar	45
Quartz	17
Borax Frit	15
Whiting	13
China Clay	5
Tin Oxide	5
+ Cobalt Carbonate	0.4
Chrome Oxide	0.4

DESCRIPTION
Gloss. Dark cobalt blue with darker speckle.

USES
Domestic.

FIRING RANGE
2336°F (1280°C)

PARTS DRY WEIGHT
Soda Feldspar	45
Quartz	17
Borax Frit	15
Whiting	13
China Clay	5
Tin Oxide	5
+ Chrome Oxide	1
Cobalt Carbonate	0.5

DESCRIPTION
Gloss. Dark blue/green with evenly spread cobalt speckle.

USES
Domestic.

FIRING RANGE
2336°F (1280°C)

PARTS DRY WEIGHT

Soda Feldspar	45
Quartz	17
Borax Frit	15
Whiting	13
China Clay	5
Tin Oxide	5
+ Chrome Oxide	1.5
Cobalt Carbonate	1

DESCRIPTION
Gloss. dark cobalt blue/green with slight hint of cobalt speckling.

USES
Domestic.

FIRING RANGE
2336°F (1280°C)

PARTS DRY WEIGHT

Soda Feldspar	45
Quartz	17
Borax Frit	15
Whiting	13
China Clay	5
Tin Oxide	5
+ Cobalt Carbonate	1.5
Chrome Oxide	1.5

DESCRIPTION
Satin/gloss green speckled with black. Can be used on porcelain and stoneware bodies.

USES
Domestic and decorative.

FIRING RANGE
2264–2336°F (1240–1280°C)

PARTS DRY WEIGHT

Quartz	39
Whiting	20
Standard Borax Frit	10
Nepheline Syenite	10
Hvar Ball Clay	10
Potash Feldspar	10
Bentonite	1
+ Zirconium Silicate	10
Copper Carbonate	8

Greens and Turquoises
REDUCED

DESCRIPTION
Dolomite White over Frank Hamer Transparent. Slight sheen.

USES
Domestic and decorative.

FIRING RANGE
2300–2372°F (1260–1300°C)

PARTS DRY WEIGHT
Dolomite White

Cornish Stone	60
China Clay	20
Dolomite	20

Frank Hamer Transparent

Cornish Stone	50
Whiting	20
Flint	15
China Clay	15

DESCRIPTION
Satin—celadon type. Pools well and is useful for resist decorative effect e.g. fluting/shellac.

USES
Domestic and decorative.

FIRING RANGE
2372°F (1300°C)
Soak time—30 minutes

PARTS DRY WEIGHT

Quartz	26
Potash Feldspar	25
Whiting	21
China Clay	15
Holochite	13
+ Red Iron Oxide	0.5

DESCRIPTION
Satin—celadon type. Pools well, enhancing edges.

USES
Domestic and decorative.

FIRING RANGE
2372°F (1300°C)
Soak time—30 minutes

PARTS DRY WEIGHT

Quartz	26
Potash Feldspar	25
Whiting	21
China Clay	15
Holochite	13
+ Red Iron Oxide	1

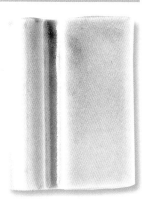

DESCRIPTION
Blue/Green Celadon. A crazed, glassy, pale blue green.

USES
Domestic and decorative.

FIRING RANGE
2300–2372°F (1260–1300°C) Less fluid when fired at 2300°F (1260°C). Tends to bubble if soaked at 2372°F (1300°C)

PARTS DRY WEIGHT

Cornish Stone	27
Whiting	27
China Clay	23
Flint	23
+ Red Iron Oxide	0.75

DESCRIPTION
Dolomite White over Blue/Green Celadon. Allow each layer to dry thoroughly. Matte or shiny. Bluer than the Blue/Green Celadon alone.

USES
Domestic and decorative.

FIRING RANGE
2300–2372°F (1260–1300°C)

PARTS DRY WEIGHT
Dolomite White

Cornish Stone	60
China Clay	20
Dolomite	20

Blue Green Celadon

Cornish Stone	27
Whiting	27
China Clay	23
Flint	23
+ Red Iron Oxide	0.75

SONIA LEWIS I PORCELAIN BOWL
Pale turquoise bowl, reduction fired in a gas kiln to 2372°F (1300°C). This piece was thrown and altered, then glazed using the following recipe: Quartz 26, Potash Feldspar 25, Whiting 21, China Clay 15, Molochite 13, + Red Iron Oxide 0.5. Diameter 12 in (30 cm).

Greens and Turquoises
REDUCED

DESCRIPTION
Gloss crackle. Pale turquoise with slight iron speckling.

USES
Domestic.

FIRING RANGE
2372°F (1300°C)
Soak time—30 minutes

PARTS DRY WEIGHT
Potash Feldspar	43
Quartz	30
Whiting	20
Talc	4
China Clay	2
Colemanite	1
+ Black Iron Oxide	0.5

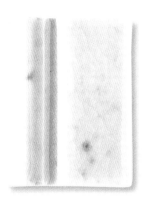

DESCRIPTION
Gloss. Pale green with slight crackle and darker speckle.

USES
Domestic.

FIRING RANGE
2372°F (1300°C)
Soak time— 30 minutes

PARTS DRY WEIGHT
Potash Feldspar	35
Quartz	20
Dolomite	20
China Clay	20
Whiting	5
+ Red Iron Oxide	1

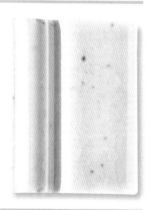

DESCRIPTION
Gloss. Cobalt specks if sieved through 100 mesh.

USES
Domestic.

FIRING RANGE
2372°F (1300°C)
Soak time—30 minutes

PARTS DRY WEIGHT
Soda Feldspar	45
Quartz	17
Borax Frit	15
Whiting	13
China Clay	5
Tin 5	
+ Cobalt Carbonate	0.1
Chrome Oxide	0.2

DESCRIPTION
Gloss. Pale turquoise/green
with iron speckling in evidence.
Slight crackle.

USES
Domestic.

FIRING RANGE
Soak time—30 minutes

PARTS DRY WEIGHT

Potash Feldspar	43
Quartz	30
Whiting	20
Talc	4
China Clay	2
Colemanite	1
+ Black Iron Oxide	1.5

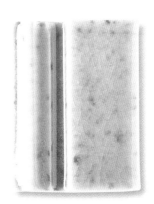

DESCRIPTION
Gloss crackle. Pale
turquoise/blue with strong iron
speckling.

USES
Domestic.

FIRING RANGE
2372°F (1300°C).
Soak time—30 minutes

PARTS DRY WEIGHT

Potash Feldspar	43
Quartz	30
Whiting	20
Talc	4
China Clay	2
Colemanite	1
+ Black Iron Oxide	2

DESCRIPTION
Blue/Green Celadon over
Hamada Celadon. Layered
glaze. A pleasant glassy pale
green, darker in pooled areas.

USES
Domestic and decorative.

FIRING RANGE
2300–2372°F (1260–1300°C)

PARTS DRY WEIGHT
Blue/Green Celadon

Cornish Stone	27
Whiting	27
China Clay	23
Flint	23

Hamada Celadon

Potash Feldspar	75
Whiting	15
China Clay	5
Flint	5
+ Red Iron Oxide	5

Greens and Turquoises
REDUCED

DESCRIPTION
Gloss, slight crackle. Pale green/gray with blue speckling if sieved through 100 mesh.

USES
Domestic.

FIRING RANGE
2372°F (1300°C)
Soak time—30 minutes

PARTS DRY WEIGHT
Soda Feldspar	45
Quartz	17
Borax Frit	15
Whiting	13
China Clay	5
Tin	5
+ Cobalt Carbonate	0.2
Chrome Oxide	0.3

DESCRIPTION
Gloss. Green/gray with blue speckling if sieved through 100 mesh.

USES
Domestic.

FIRING RANGE
2372°F (1300°C)
Soak time—30 minutes

PARTS DRY WEIGHT
Soda Feldspar	45
Quartz	17
Borax Frit	15
Whiting	13
China Clay	5
Tin	5
+ Cobalt Carbonate	0.3
Chrome Oxide	0.4

DESCRIPTION
Gloss. Dark green/gray with blue speckling if sieved through 100 mesh.

USES
Domestic.

FIRING RANGE
2372°F (1300°C)
Soak time—30 minutes

PARTS DRY WEIGHT
Soda Feldspar	45
Quartz	17
Borax Frit	15
Whiting	13
China Clay	5
Tin	5
+ Cobalt Carbonate	0.4
Chrome Oxide	0.4

DESCRIPTION
Gloss. Some blue specks if
sieved through 100 mesh.

USES
Domestic.

FIRING RANGE
2372°F (1300°C)
Soak time—30 minutes

PARTS DRY WEIGHT
Soda Feldspar	45
Quartz	17
Borax Frit	15
Whiting	13
China Clay	5
Tin	5
+ Cobalt Carbonate	0.5
Chrome Oxide	0.5

DESCRIPTION
Gloss. Dark green/blue with
light cobalt speckling.

USES
Domestic.

FIRING RANGE
2372°F (1300°C)
Soak time—30 minutes

PARTS DRY WEIGHT
Soda Feldspar	45
Quartz	17
Borax Frit	15
Whiting	13
China Clay	5
Tin	5
+ Cobalt Carbonate	1
Chrome Oxide	1

DESCRIPTION
Gloss. Dark green/turquoise
with slight cobalt speckling.

USES
Domestic.

FIRING RANGE
2372°F (1300°C)
Soak time—30 minutes

PARTS DRY WEIGHT
Soda Feldspar	45
Quartz	17
Borax Frit	15
Whiting	13
China Clay	5
Tin	5
+ Chrome Oxide	1.5
Cobalt Carbonate	1

Greens and Turquoises
REDUCED

DESCRIPTION
Satin—celadon type. Pools
well, enhancing edges.

USES
Domestic and decorative.

FIRING RANGE
2372°F (1300°C)
Soak time—30 minutes

PARTS DRY WEIGHT
Quartz	26
Potash Feldspar	25
Whiting	21
China Clay	15
Holochite	13
+ Red Iron Oxide	2

DESCRIPTION
Satin. Gives sharp definition to
edges.

USES
Domestic and decorative.

FIRING RANGE
2372°F (1300°C)
Soak time—30 minutes

PARTS DRY WEIGHT
Quartz	26
Potash Feldspar	25
Whiting	21
China Clay	15
Holochite	13
+ Red Iron Oxide	3

DESCRIPTION
Derek Emms Red
over Hamada
Celadon. Red tends
to be more evident
in the pooling.

USES
Domestic and
decorative.

FIRING RANGE
2300–2372°F
(1260–1300°C)

PARTS DRY WEIGHT

Derek Emms Red		Hamada Celadon	
Soda Feldspar	42	Potash Feldspar	75
Flint	19	Whiting	15
Whiting	14	China Clay	5
High Alkaline		Flint	5
Frit	14	+ Red Iron Oxide	5
China Clay	5		
Tin Oxide	5		
Copper Carbonate	1		

DESCRIPTION
Gloss. Olive green with slight pooling to darker areas.

USES
Domestic.

FIRING RANGE
2372°F (1300°C)
Soak time—30 minutes

PARTS DRY WEIGHT

Potash Feldspar	35
Quartz	20
Dolomite	20
China Clay	20
Whiting	5
+ Red Iron Oxide	3

DESCRIPTION
Gloss. Green/tan with heavy iron speckle.

USES
Domestic.

FIRING RANGE
2372°F (1300°C)
Soak time—30 minutes

PARTS DRY WEIGHT

Potash Feldspar	35
Quartz	20
Dolomite	20
China Clay	20
Whiting	5
+ Red Iron Oxide	4

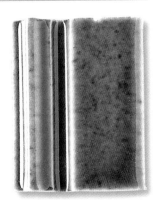

DESCRIPTION
Hamada Celadon. Bottle green but uninteresting brown where thin. Best applied thick, but this is where it is most fluid. Lower the temperature to counter this.

USES
Domestic and decorative.

FIRING RANGE
2300–2372°F (1260–1300°C)

PARTS DRY WEIGHT

Potash Feldspar	75
Whiting	15
China Clay	5
Flint	5
+ Red Iron Oxide	5

Black, White, and Metallic
OXIDIZED

DESCRIPTION
Satin/matte white, very good
for oxide under- or on-glaze
painting.

USES
Domestic.

FIRING RANGE
2336°F (1280°C)

PARTS DRY WEIGHT
Cornish Stone	66
Whiting	14
China Clay	12
Ball Clay	8
+ Magnesium Carbonate	4

DESCRIPTION
Smooth satin. Pure white. Very
even surface.

USES
Domestic.

FIRING RANGE
2336°F (1280°C)

PARTS DRY WEIGHT
Soda Feldspar	45
Quartz	17
Borax Frit	15
Whiting	13
China Clay	5
Tin Oxide	5

DESCRIPTION
Satin. Smooth, off-white/
cream. Very even surface.

USES
Domestic.

FIRING RANGE
2336°F (1280°C)

PARTS DRY WEIGHT
Cornish Stone	66
Whiting	14
China Clay	12
Barium Carbonate	8
Magnesium Carbonate	4
Cobalt Carbonate	2
Red Iron Oxide	2

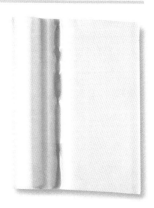

DESCRIPTION
Frank Hamer Transparent.
Shiny. Reflects porcelain body
color in oxidation and
reduction. Crazes slightly where
thick.

USES
Domestic and decorative.

FIRING RANGE
2300–2372°F (1260–1300°C)

PARTS DRY WEIGHT

Cornish Stone	50
Whiting	20
Flint	15
China Clay	15

DESCRIPTION
Glossy light celadon. White
with hint of green. Can be used
on porcelain and stoneware
bodies.

USES
Domestic and decorative.

FIRING RANGE
2264–2336°F (1240–1280°C)

PARTS DRY WEIGHT

Potash Feldspar	33
Quartz	16
Talc	21
China Clay	15
Whiting	12
Zinc Oxide	3
+ Copper Oxide	3
Tin Oxide	5

CLAUDE FRERE-SMITH I PORCELAIN VASE
Porcelain vase fired in an electric kiln to 2300°F (1260°C). After biscuit
firing, a thick layer of the following glaze was applied: Feldspar 83, Whiting
9, Flint 8, which gives an excellent crackled surface. While the pot was still
warm from the kiln, black Indian ink was painted into the surface to
emphasize and enhance the crackled effect.

Black, White, and Metallic
OXIDIZED

DESCRIPTION
Smooth matte. Pure white;
works well with oxide painting.

USES
Decorative.

FIRING RANGE
2300°F (1260°C)
Soak time—30 minutes

PARTS DRY WEIGHT
Potash Feldspar	35
Barium Carbonate	25
Zirconium Silicate	15
Dolomite	11
Ball Clay	8
Quartz	6

DESCRIPTION
Transparent. If applied too
thickly this glaze tends to pull
away from edges and joins as it
dries, so take heed in
application. A perfect fit to
every porcelain. Takes oxides
and stains well.

USES
Domestic and decorative.

FIRING RANGE
2300–2372°F (1260–1300°C)

PARTS DRY WEIGHT
Cornish Stone	70
China Clay	10
Whiting	10
Zinc Oxide	10

DESCRIPTION
Satin/matte. Smooth, off-white.
Good, even surface.

USES
Decorative.

FIRING RANGE
2300°F (1260°C)

PARTS DRY WEIGHT
Potash Feldspar	35
Barium Carbonate	25
Zirconium Silicate	15
Dolomite	11
Ball Clay	8
Quartz	6
+ Red Iron Oxide	1

DESCRIPTION
Smooth matte. Off-white/cream, darker pooling in grooves.

USES
Domestic

FIRING RANGE
2336°F (1280°C)

PARTS DRY WEIGHT

Cornish Stone	66
Whiting	14
China Clay	12
Ball Clay	8

DESCRIPTION
Dolomite White. Matte buttery off-white in oxidation and matte marble white in reduction.

USES
Domestic and decorative.

FIRING RANGE
2300–2372°F (1260–1300°C)

PARTS DRY WEIGHT

Cornish Stone	60
China Clay	20
Dolomite	20

DESCRIPTION
Satin. Smooth, strong, pure white. Good base for on-glaze decoration.

USES
Domestic.

FIRING RANGE
2300°F (1260°C)

PARTS DRY WEIGHT

Nepheline Syenite	73
Flint	10
Bentonite	5
Dolomite	5
Whiting	4
Zinc Oxide	3

Black, White, and Metallic
OXIDIZED

DESCRIPTION
Satin. Smooth dark gray/black with a hint of blue.

USES
Domestic.

FIRING RANGE
2336°F (1280°C)

PARTS DRY WEIGHT

Potash Feldspar	43
Quartz	30
Whiting	20
Talc	4
China Clay	2
Colmenite	1

DESCRIPTION
Satin/matte. Black with blue tint from cobalt.

USES
Domestic.

FIRING RANGE
2336°F (1280°C)

PARTS DRY WEIGHT

Cornish Stone	66
Whiting	14
China Clay	12
Ball Clay	8
+ Magnesium Carbonate	4
Red Iron Oxide	4
Cobalt Carbonate	2

DESCRIPTION
Satin/matte. Breaks satin to matte, varying according to thickness.

USES
Domestic.

FIRING RANGE
2336°F (1280°C)

PARTS DRY WEIGHT

Cornish Stone	66
Whiting	14
China Clay	12
Ball Clay	8
Magnesium Carbonate	4
Red Iron Oxide	4
Cobalt Carbonate	2
Manganese Dioxide	1

DESCRIPTION
Satin/matte. Breaks satin to matte where thick to thin.

USES
Domestic.

FIRING RANGE
2336°F (1280°C)

PARTS DRY WEIGHT
Cornish Stone	66
Whiting	14
China Clay	12
Barium Carbonate	8
Magnesium Carbonate	4
Red Iron Oxide	4
Cobalt Carbonate	2
Manganese Dioxide	1

DESCRIPTION
Dark brown with a satin finish.

USES
Can be used for all types of ware, but especially suitable for domestic ware.

FIRING RANGE
2336°F (1280°C)

PARTS DRY WEIGHT
Quartz	26
Potash Feldspar	25
Whiting	21
China Clay	15
Molochite	13
+ Red Iron Oxide	9

DESCRIPTION
Very dark brown with a satin finish.

USES
Domestic.

FIRING RANGE
2336°F (1280°C)

PARTS DRY WEIGHT
Quartz	26
Potash Feldspar	25
Whiting	21
China Clay	15
Molochite	13
+ Red Iron Oxide	10

Black, White, and Metallic
REDUCED

DESCRIPTION
Satin—celadon type. Best
if used thick to enhance
"buttery" quality.

USES
Domestic and decorative.

FIRING RANGE
2372°F (1300°C)
Soak time—30 minutes

PARTS DRY WEIGHT
Quartz	26
Potash Feldspar	25
Whiting	21
China Clay	15
Molochite	13

DESCRIPTION
Slight crackle satin/gloss. Pale
celadon type—works well over
carved surface.

USES
Domestic.

FIRING RANGE
2372°F (1300°C)
Soak time—30 minutes

PARTS DRY WEIGHT
Potash Feldspar	35
Quartz	20
Dolomite	20
China Clay	20
Whiting	5

DESCRIPTION
Gloss crackle. Off-white/cream
with very slight speckle.

USES
Domestic.

FIRING RANGE
2372°F (1300°C)
Soak time—30 minutes

PARTS DRY WEIGHT
Potash Feldspar	43
Quartz	30
Whiting	20
Talc	4
China Clay	2
Colemanite	1

DESCRIPTION
Dolomite White. Matte buttery off-white in oxidation and matte marble white in reduction.

USES
Domestic and decorative.

FIRING RANGE
2300–2372°F (1260–1300°C)

PARTS DRY WEIGHT
Cornish Stone	60
China Clay	20
Dolomite	20

DESCRIPTION
Gloss slight crackle.

USES
Domestic.

FIRING RANGE
2372°F (1300°C)
Soak time—30 minutes

PARTS DRY WEIGHT
Soda Feldspar	45
Quartz	17
Borax Frit	15
Whiting	13
China Clay	5
Tin	5

JOYCE DAVISON | WHITE CRACKLE GLAZE VASE

This thrown piece was biscuit fired then glazed using a white crackle glaze consisting of Potash Feldspar 45, China Clay 18, Quartz 15, Whiting 14, Talc 6, Bentonite 2. A mixture of copper and manganese oxides (equal parts) was applied to the top section of the pot. Indian ink stain was rubbed into the glaze to enhance the crackle effect. It was reduction fired in a gas kiln to 2336°F (1280°C), reduction taking place from 1652°F (900°C), with up to a one-hour soak.
Height 7½ in (19 cm).

Black, White, and Metallic
REDUCED

DESCRIPTION
Satin. Green/white speckling
from ball clay.

USES
Domestic.

FIRING RANGE
2372°F (1300°C)
Soak time—30 minutes

PARTS DRY WEIGHT

Cornish Stone	66
Whiting	14
China Clay	12
Ball Clay	8

DESCRIPTION
Satin. Smooth vellum white
with very slight iron speckle.

USES
Decorative.

FIRING RANGE
2372°F (1300°C)
Soak time—30 minutes

PARTS DRY WEIGHT

Potash Feldspar	35
Barium Carbonate	25
Zirconium Silicate	15
Dolomite	11
Ball Clay	8
Quartz	6
+ Red Iron Oxide	1

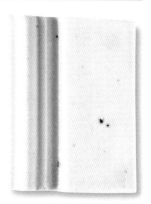

DESCRIPTION
Gloss with a fine crackle.

USES
Domestic.

FIRING RANGE
2372°F (1300°C)
Soak time—30 minutes

PARTS DRY WEIGHT

Nepheline Syenite	73
Flint	10
Bentonite	5
Dolomite	5
Whiting	4
Zinc Oxide	3
+ Uranium Oxide	0.5

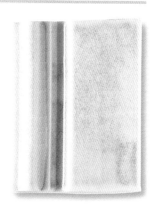

DESCRIPTION
Gloss with a fine crackle.

USES
Domestic.

FIRING RANGE
2372°F (1300°C)
Soak time—30 minutes

PARTS DRY WEIGHT
Nepheline Syenite	73
Flint	10
Bentonite	5
Dolomite	5
Whiting	4
Zinc Oxide	3

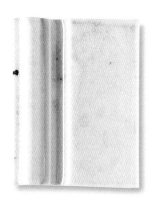

DESCRIPTION
Satin. Warm creamy white.

USES
Domestic.

FIRING RANGE
2372°F (1300°C)
Soak time—30 minutes

PARTS DRY WEIGHT
Potash Feldspar	36
China Clay	21
Whiting	17
Quartz	10
Talc	10
Ball Clay	6

DESCRIPTION
Smooth satin. Off-white/gray
with very slight warm pink
glow.

USES
Decorative.

FIRING RANGE
2372°F (1300°C)
Soak time—30 minutes

PARTS DRY WEIGHT
Quartz	26
Potash Feldspar	25
Whiting	21
China Clay	15
Molochite	13
+ Blythe Strong	
Red Glaze Stain	2

Black, White, and Metallic
REDUCED

DESCRIPTION
Smooth satin. Off-white/cream
with hint of pink.

USES
Domestic.

FIRING RANGE
2372°F (1300°C)
Soak time—30 minutes

PARTS DRY WEIGHT

Quartz	26
Potash Feldspar	25
Whiting	21
China Clay	15
Molochite	13
+ B 187 Rosso Red	
Glaze Stain	2

DESCRIPTION
Satin White. Paler than
Dolomite White in oxidation,
attractive ocher blush in
reduction.

USES
Domestic and decorative.

FIRING RANGE
2300–2372°F (1260–1300°C)

PARTS DRY WEIGHT

Potash Feldspar	50
China Clay	23
Dolomite	20
Quartz	4
Bone Ash	3

DESCRIPTION
Satin/gloss, fine crackle.
Breaks nicely with iridescence.

USES
Domestic.

FIRING RANGE
2372°F (1300°C)
Soak time—30 minutes

PARTS DRY WEIGHT

Nepheline Syenite	73
Flint	10
Bentonite	5
Dolomite	5
Whiting	4
Zinc Oxide	3
+ Uranium Oxide	1

DESCRIPTION
Satin/gloss. Mottled
cream/gray. Evenly textured
surface.

USES
Domestic.

FIRING RANGE
2372°F (1300°C)
Soak time—30 minutes

PARTS DRY WEIGHT
Nepheline Syenite	73
Flint	10
Bentonite	5
Dolomite	5
Whiting	4
Zinc Oxide	3
+ Uranium Oxide	1.5

DESCRIPTION
Satin/gloss. Dark gray/black,
white on edges.

USES
Domestic.

FIRING RANGE
2372°F (1300°C)
Soak time—30 minutes

PARTS DRY WEIGHT
Nepheline Syenite	73
Flint	10
Bentonite	5
Dolomite	5
Whiting	4
Zinc Oxide	3
+ Uranium Oxide	2

DESCRIPTION
Satin/gloss. "Cloudy" dark to
light gray mottled surface.

USES
Domestic.

FIRING RANGE
2372°F (1300°C)
Soak time—30 minutes

PARTS DRY WEIGHT
Nepheline Syenite	73
Flint	10
Bentonite	5
Dolomite	5
Whiting	4
Zinc Oxide	3
+ Uranium Oxide	2.5

Black, White, and Metallic
REDUCED

DESCRIPTION
Satin/gloss. Dark gray/black with yellow tint.

USES
Decorative.

FIRING RANGE
2372°F (1300°C)
Soak time—30 minutes

PARTS DRY WEIGHT

Nepheline Syenite	73
Flint	10
Bentonite	5
Dolomite	5
Whiting	4
Zinc Oxide	3
+ Uranium Oxide	4

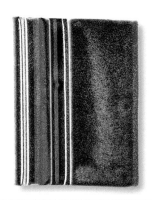

DESCRIPTION
Gloss/satin. Dark gray/black with slight yellow tint on "cloudy" effect.

USES
Decorative.

FIRING RANGE
2372°F (1300°C)
Soak time—30 minutes

PARTS DRY WEIGHT

Nepheline Syenite	73
Flint	10
Bentonite	5
Dolomite	5
Whiting	4
Zinc Oxide	3
+ Uranium Oxide	3

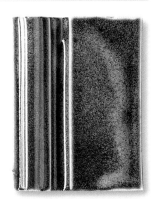

DESCRIPTION
Satin/gloss.

USES
Domestic.

FIRING RANGE
2372°F (1300°C)
Soak time—30 minutes

PARTS DRY WEIGHT

Cornish Stone	66
Whiting	14
China Clay	12
Ball Clay	8
+ Magnesium Carbonate	4
Red Iron Oxide	4
Cobalt Carbonate	2

DESCRIPTION
Gloss. Pools well, defines edges.

USES
Domestic.

FIRING RANGE
2372°F (1300°C)
Soak time—30 minutes

PARTS DRY WEIGHT
Potash Feldspar	43
Quartz	30
Whiting	20
Talc	4
China Clay	2
Colemanite	1
+ Red Iron Oxide	4

DESCRIPTION
Gloss crackle.

USES
Domestic.

FIRING RANGE
2372°F (1300°C)
Soak time—30 minutes

PARTS DRY WEIGHT
Potash Feldspar	43
Quartz	30
Whiting	20
Talc	4
China Clay	2
Colemanite	1

TOM COLEMAN I PORCELAIN VASE
Thrown and altered porcelain vase fired to 2372°F (1300°C) in a
reduction atmosphere in a gas kiln. An ash glaze has been sprayed
over a black slip to create a metallic and mottled surface.
Height 16 in (40 cm).

Chemical Formulas and Cone Tables

TABLE OF FORMULAS

Name	Chemical formula	Name	Chemical formula
Alumina	Al_2O_3	Lead Sesquisilicate	$2PbO.3SiO_2$
Antimony Oxide	Sb_2O_3	Lepidolite	$Li_2F_2.Al_2O_3.3SiO_2$
Barium Carbonate	$BaCO_3$	Lithium Oxide	Li_2O
Bentonite	$Al_2O_3.4SiO_2.H_2O$	Lithium Carbonate	Li_2CO_3
Bismuth Oxide	Bi_2O_3	Magnesium Oxide (Periclase)	MgO
Bone Ash	$Ca_3(PO_4)_2$	Magnesium Carbonate (Magnesite)	$MgCO_3$
Borax	$Na_2B_4O_7.10H_2O$	Magnesium Carbonate light	$3MgCO_3.Mg(OH)_2.3H_2O$
Calcium Borate	$Ca(BO_2)_2$		
Calcium Carbonate	$CaCO_3$	Manganese Carbonate	$MnCO_3$
China Clay	$Al_2O_3.2SiO_2.2H_2O$	Manganese Dioxide (Pyrolusite)	MnO_2
Chromium Oxide	Cr_2O_3	Nephiline Syenite	$K_2O.3Na_2O.4Al_2O_3.8SiO_2$
Cobalt Carbonate	$CoCO_3$	Nickel Oxide	NiO
Cobalt Carbonate basic	$CoCO_3.Co(OH)_2$	Petalite (Lithium Feldspathoid)	$Li_2O.Al_2O_3.8SiO_2$
Cobalt Oxide	CoO		
Cobalt Oxide	Co_3O_4	Quartz	SiO_2
Comemanite	$2CaO.3B_2O_3.5H_2O$	Rutile	TiO_2
Copper Carbonate	$CuCO_3$	Silica	SiO_2
Copper Carbonate basic	$CuCO_3.Cu(OH)_2$	Silicon Carbide	SiC
Copper Oxide black	CuO	Sodalite (Sodium Feldspathoid)	$3NaAlSiO_4.NaCl$
Copper Oxide red	Cu_2O	Sodium carbonate (Soda Ash)	Na_2CO_3
Crocus Martis	$FeSO_4$	Spodumene (Lithium Feldspathoid)	$Li_2O.Al_2O_3.4SiO_2$
Cryolite	Na_3AlF_6		
Dolomite	$CaMg(CO_3)_2$	Talc	$3MgO.4SiO_2.H_2O$
Feldspar Potassium (Orthoclase)	$K_2O.Al_2O_3.6SiO_2$	Tin Oxide White	SnO_2
		Tatanium Oxide	TiO_2
Feldspar Sodium (Albite)	$Na_2O.Al_2O_3.6SiO_2$	Uranium Oxide	U_3O_8
Flint	SiO_2	Vanadium Oxide	V_2O_5
Ilmenite	$FeTiO_3$	Whiting	$CaCO_3$
Iron Oxide black	FeO	Wollastonite	$CaSiO_3$
Iron Oxide red	Fe_2O_3	Yellow Ocher	$2Fe_2O_3.3H_2O$
Iron Pyrites	FeS_2	Zinc Oxide (Zincite)	ZnO
Iron Spangles	Fe_3O_4	Zirconium Oxide	ZrO_2
Lead Bisilicate	$PbO.2SiO_2$	Zirconium Silicate (Zircon)	$ZrSiO_4$

ORTON PYROMETRIC CONES

(The Edward Orton Jr Ceramic Foundation, Westerville, Ohio, USA)

Large cones; squatting temperatures when heated at:

Cone No.	108°F/hr	60°C/hr	270°F/hr	150°C/hr
022	1069	576	1086	586
021	1116	602	1137	614
020	1157	625	1175	635
019	1234	668	1261	683
018	1285	696	1323	717
017	1341	727	1377	747
016	1407	764	1458	792
015	1454	790	1479	804
014	1533	834	1540	838
013	1537	836	1582	861
012	1573	836	1582	861
011	1602	872	1621	883
010	1616	880	1634	890
09	1679	915	1693	923
08	1733	945	1751	955
07	1783	973	1803	984
06	1816	991	1915	999
05	1888	1031	1915	1046
04	1922	1050	1940	1060
03	1987	1086	2014	1101
02	2014	1101	2048	1120
01	2043	1117	2079	1137
1	2077	1136	2109	1154
2	2088	1142	2124	1162
3	2106	1152	2134	1168
4	2134	1168	2167	1186
5	2151	1177	2185	1196
6	2194	1201	2232	1222
7	2219	1215	2264	1240
8	2257	1236	2305	1263
9	2300	1260	2336	1280
10	2345	1285	2381	1305
11	2361	1294	2399	1315
12	2383	1306	2419	1326
13	2410	1321	2455	1346
14	2530	1388	2491	1366

*These temperatures are approximate. They were not determined at the National Bureau of Standards

SEGER PYROMETRIC CONES

(Staatliche Porzellan-Manufaktur Berlin distributed by H. Welte Ing GmbH & Co, Hürth-Hermülheim, Germany)

Large cones; squatting temperatures when heated at 270°F/hr (150°C/hr)

Cone No.	°F	°C
022	1103	595
021	1184	640
020	1220	660
019	1265	685
018	1301	705
017	1346	730
016	1391	755
015a	1436	780
014a	1481	805
013a	1535	835
012a	1580	860
011a	1652	900
010a	1688	920
09a	1715	935
08a	1751	955
07a	1778	970
06a	1814	990
05a	1832	1000
04a	1877	1025
03a	1931	1055
02a	1985	1085
01a	2021	1105
1a	2057	1125
2a	2102	1150
3a	2138	1170
4a	2183	1195
5a	2219	1215
6a	2264	1240
7	2300	1260
8	2336	1280
9	2372	1300
10	2408	1320
11	2444	1340
12	2480	1360
13	2516	1380
14	2552	1400

How We Made This Book

Stephen Murfitt

When this project was first being discussed, it was clear that we would need contributions from a variety of specialists to make it viable. Several potters were invited, and those illustrated agreed to take part.

THE CONTRIBUTORS

Potters contributed recipes and glazed tiles generated by experimentation through their own specialist practices. Most potters using glazes work from a few tried and tested base recipes. Existing glazes were fully utilized and several untried recipes were explored using new combinations to create a wide range of colors.

Will Illsley

Most contributors agreed that they had discovered some exciting results through taking part in the project.

As this book demonstrates, achieving a particular color is not only about using a certain recipe. Many variables are involved: types of clay, slips, methods of application, kilns, and firing process all play an important part. Potters have been typically generous in providing details of individual approaches to glazing and firing ceramics.

Susan Bruce

Sonia Lewis

Sally Reilly

Mark Judson

Rebecca Harvey

Rob Bibby

To achieve the illustrated results, each potter fired several batches of tiles. Many were discarded by an instinctive quality control system.

Rebecca Harvey's skill in controlling her kiln atmosphere was required for producing her soda tiles. To achieve the desired effect the tiles had to be propped up in a specific area of the kiln. This enabled them to catch enough soda to create the special "orange peel" texture, unique to that process.

Rob Bibby's sensitive brushstrokes are well documented in this book, and as his description of majolica painting demonstrates, a brushstroke can carry many possibilities!

The knowledge of Mike Bailey is much in evidence. As well as producing the tiles, he provided some recipes and glazed tiles for the luster, earthenware, and stoneware sections.

I am very grateful to all the potters featured (and some who are not). Without them this book would not have been possible.

Tony Pugh

Gareth Mason

Mike Bailey

Suppliers

All glaze stains used in the recipes with a code number preceded by B, were supplied by Bath Potters Supplies.

UNITED KINGDOM

BATH POTTERS
SUPPLIES*
2 Dorset Close
Bath
BA2 3RF
Tel: 01225 337046
www.bathpotters.demon.co.uk
*Clays, glazes, colours,
raw materials, tools and
equipment.*

CERAMIC SUPPLY CO.
8 Percy Avenue
Kingsgate
Broadstairs
Kent CT10 3LB
Tel: 01843 864 198
*Clays, glazes, colours,
tools and equipment.*

HERAEUS
Unit A Cinderhill Industrial
Estate
Weston Coyney Rd
Longton
Stoke on Trent ST3 5LB
Tel: 01782 599423
Mfr. of lustres.

POTCLAYS LTD
Brickkiln Lane
Etruria
Stoke-on-Trent ST4 7BP
Tel: 01782 219816
*Clays, glazes, colours,
raw materials, tools and
equipment.*

POTTERYCRAFTS
Campbell Road
Stoke on Trent ST4 4ET
Tel: 01782 745000
www.potterycrafts.co.uk
*Clays, glazes, colours,
raw materials, tools and
equipment.*

SCAVA POTTERY
SUPPLIES
Unit 20
Scava Rd Ind. Est.
Banbridge
N. Ireland BT32 3QD
Tel: (028) 406 69700
Clays, glazes, equipment.

STANTON POTTERY
SUPPLIES
Foley Goods Yard
King St
Fenton Staffs ST4 3DE
Tel: 01782 312316
Kilns and accessories.

UNITED STATES

AARDVARK CLAY AND
SUPPLIES
1400 East Pomona St
Santa Ana CA 92705
Tel: (714) 541 4157
*Ceramic materials and
equipment.*

ALPHA CERAMIC
SUPPLIES
10170 Croydon Way
Sacramento CA 95827
Tel: (916) 361 3611
Kilns, tools, cones, clays.

BIG CERAMIC STORE
463 Miwok Crt.
Femont CA 94539
www.bigceramicstore.com
*Online supplier of clays,
glazes, tools and equipment.*

CLAY ART CENTER ONLINE
www.clayartcenteronline.com
*Clays, glazes, colors,
raw materials, tools, and
equipment.*

HAMILL & GILLESPIE INC.
154 South Livingston Avenue
PO Box 104
Livingston NJ 07039
Tel: (800) 454 8846
*Raw materials: clays,
feldspars, silicas, etc.*

MASON COLOR WORKS
INC.
250E. 2nd St
PO Box 76, East Liverpool
Ohio 43902-5076
Tel: (330) 385 4400
Ceramic stains and colors.

OLD HICKORY CLAY CO.
PO Box 66
Hickory KY 42051-0066
Tel: (270) 247 3042
Clay producer.

POURAWAY
PO Box 205
St Johns AZ 85936
www.pouraway.com
Glazes, tools, equipment.

STANDARD CERAMIC
SUPPLY
PO Box 4435
Pittsburgh PA 15205
Tel: (412) 276 6333
*Clays, glazes, colors,
raw materials, tools and
equipment.*

CANADA

CERAMICS ART & CRAFT
SUPPLY LTD
3103 Mainway Drive
Burlington
Ontario
Tel: 905 335 1515
*Clays, glazes, tools and
equipment.*

PLAINSMAN CLAYS LTD
Box 1266
702 Wood St
Medicine Hat
Alberta T1A 7M9
Tel: 403 527 8535
Clay suppliers.

TERRA NOVA CERAMIC &
CRAFT SUPPLIES
4 Sala Drive
Richmond Hill
Ontario L4C 8C2
Tel: 905 771 7532

AUSTRALIA

CERAMIC SOLUTIONS
Unit 1
12 Vernon Avenue
West Heidelberg
Melbourne 3081
Tel: +6 3 9459 7284
*Mfr. of glazes, underglazes,
crackle colour, and
specialty products.*

DIANA CERAMICS
354 Brighton Road, Hove
South Australia 5048
Tel: 08 8296 2802
Clays and glazes.

GEEPERS CERAMICS
SOLUTIONS
1/3 Judd Crt.
Slacks Creek
Queensland 4127
Tel 07 3290 3700

NSW POTTERY SUPPLIES
50 Holker St,
Silverwater, NSW 2128
Tel: (02) 9648 5567

THE PUG MILL
17a Rose Street
Mile End
South Australia 5031
Tel: 61 88443 4544
Clays, slips, glazes, tools.

WALKER CERAMICS
55 Lusher Road
Croydon
Victoria 3136
Tel: +613 9725 7255

NEW ZEALAND

SMITH & SMITH LTD
213 Tuam Street
Christchurch
Box 22-496
Tel: 64 649
Materials and equipment.

TALISMAN POTTERS
SUPPLIES
171 Archers Road
TaKapuna
Auckland
Tel: 480 735
*Clays, raw materials,
colours and equipment.*

WESTERN POTTERS
SUPPLIES
Unit 4
Winwood Park
43a Linwood Avenue
Mt Albert, Auckland
Tel: 0061-9-815-1513
*Clays, glazes, colours,
raw materials, tools and
equipment.*

Credits

Quarto and the author would like to thank the following for supplying pictures reproduced in this book. All photographs by the artists unless a photographer's name appears in brackets.

Key: b = Bottom, t = Top, c = Center, l = Left, r = Right

6: Art Archive/Musée du Louvre, Paris/Jaqueline Hyde; 7t: Art Archive/Archaeolgical Museum Istanbul/Dagli Orti; 7b: Art Archive/Staffordshire University School of Art/Michael Cardew; 8tl: Art Directors/M.Barlow; 8tr:Victor Knibbs; 8b:Tony Pugh 10t: Stephen Murfitt (Terry Beard); 10b: Jo Connell; 15t: Gareth Mason; 15b: Kate Malone: 20l Rob Bibby; 20r Sutton Taylor/Hart Gallery; 24t: Susan Bruce (Iain Bruce); 24b: Kate Malone; 25t: Stephen Murfitt; 25b: Kate Malone; 29: Bryan Trueman; 35: Kate Malone; 41: Lindsay Toop; 49: Richard Slade; 53: Roger Mulley; 61: Wynne Wilbur; 67, 73: Fenella Mallalieu; 79: David Jones (Rod Dorling); 82: Wynne Wilbur; 91 Rob Bibby; 97: Posey Bacopoules; 102: Stephen Murfitt; 105: Stephen Murfitt; 109: David Jones; 113 Stephen Murfitt; 114: Susan Tutton; 117: Tony Laverick; 120t: Tom Coleman; 120b: Emily Myers (Mark Somerville) 122t: Ashley Howard (Stephen Brayne); 121b: Mark Judson (James Austin); 125: Emily Myers (Mark Somerville);139, 145: Rick Malmgren;157: Ashley Howard (Stephen Brayne); 163: Jim Robison; 167: Peter Beard; 179: Kate Shakeshaft Murray; 183: Usch Spettigue (Mike Kwasniak); 193: Peter Lane; 194t Rebecca Harvey (Graham Murrell); 194b Deborah Baynes; 197: Michael Casson (Peter Harper); 200: Tom Coleman; 201t: Gareth Mason; 201b: Alan Foxley; 205: Gareth Mason; 213: Mark Bell (Ken Woisard); 219: Bridget Drakeford (Lyn Medwell); 227: Richard Baxter; 239: Sonia Lewis; 245: Delan Cookson;253: Bridget Drakeford (Lyn Medwell);261 Sonia Lewis; 269: Claude Frere-Smith; 275: Joyce Davison; 281: Tom Coleman.

All other photographs and illustrations are the copyright of Quarto. While every effort has been made to credit contributors, we apologize should there have been any omissions or errors.

The author would like to thank the potters who contributed recipes and glazed tiles:
Rob Bibby, Sue Bruce, Rebecca Harvey, Mark Judson, Will Illsley, Sonia Lewis, Gareth Mason, Anthony Pugh, and Sally Reilly.
A special thanks to **Mike Bailey** and **Bath Potters Supplies** who provided help, advice, materials, and the tiles used in the production of the book. Tel: +44 1225 337046.
Web site: www.bathpotters.demon.co.uk
And finally, thanks to **Potterycrafts Ltd.**, who also provided some of the materials for use in the glaze recipes. Web site: www.potterycrafts.co.uk

SELECTED BIBLIOGRAPHY

Glazes for the Craft Potter **Harry Fraser**	Pitman
Clay and Glazes for the Potter **Daniel Rhodes**	Chilton
The Potter's Dictionary of Materials and Techniques **Frank & Janet Hamer**	A&C Black
The Potter's Book of Glaze Recipes **Emmanuel Cooper**	Batsford
The Potter's Palette **Christine Constant & Steve Ogden**	Apple
The Encyclopaedia of Pottery Techniques **Peter Cosentino**	Headline
Practical Solutions for Potters **Gill Bliss**	Sterling/Silver
Two Books in One Ceramics: **Steve Mattison**	Sterling/Silver
A Potters Book **Bernard Leach**	Faber
Raku **Tim Andrews**	Black/Chilton
Raku **Christopher Tyler & Richard Hirsch**	Pitman